Rough South, Rural South

Rough South, Rural South

Region and Class in Recent Southern Literature

Edited by Jean W. Cash and Keith Perry

University Press of Mississippi   Jackson

www.upress.state.ms.us

The University Press of Mississippi is a member
of the Association of American University Presses.

First printing 2016
∞

Library of Congress Cataloging-in-Publication Data

Rough South, rural South : region and class in recent southern literature / edited by Jean W. Cash,
Keith Perry.
    pages cm
    Includes bibliographical references and index.
    ISBN 978-1-4968-0233-0 (hardback) — ISBN 978-1-4968-0496-9 (ebook) 1. American litera-
ture—Southern States—History and criticism. 2. Authors, American—Southern States—History. 3.
Southern States—In literature. 4. Working class in literature. 5. Southern States—Intellectual life. 6.
Literature and society—United States—History. 7. American literature—20th century—History and
criticism. 8. American literature—21st century—History and criticism. I. Cash, Jean W., 1938– editor,
II. Perry, Keith Ronald, 1967– editor. III. Title: Region and class in recent southern literature.
    PS261.R58 2016
    810.9′975—dc23
                              2015020367
British Library Cataloging-in-Publication Data available

It is easy to make up characters who live in double-wide mobile homes, wear beehive hairdos and feed caps, never put a "g" on the end of a participle, have sex with their cousins, voted for George Wallace, who squint and spit whenever an out-of-towner uses a polysyllabic word; who aspire only to own a bass boat, scare a Yankee, have sex with their cousins again, burn a cross, eat something fried, speak in tongues, do anything butt nekkid, be a guest on a daytime talk show, and make the next payment on a satellite dish that points toward Venus and picks up 456 separate channels on a clear day. What is difficult is to take the poor, the uneducated, the superstitious, the backward, the redneck, the "trailer-trash," and make them real human beings, with hopes and dreams and aspirations as real and valid, and as worthy of our fair consideration, as any Cheeverian Westchester County housewife.

—Tony Earley, "Letter from Sister: What We Learned at the P.O."

CONTENTS

INTRODUCTION

Rough South, Rural South

Jean W. Cash

Setting out to collect and edit essays on contemporary writers of the Rough South, Keith Perry and I began with the work of Gary Hawkins and Erik Bledsoe. Hawkins, a documentary filmmaker, was the first to apply the term "Rough South" to a distinctive group of southern writers whose careers began in the last third of the twentieth century. Discovering the work of Harry Crews, Tim McLaurin, and Larry Brown, Hawkins interviewed and filmed feature-length documentaries about each. Bledsoe wrote the seminal essay "The Rise of Southern Redneck and White Trash Writers" (published in *Southern Cultures* in 2000), delineating in greater detail the differences between late-century working-class writers who followed in the footsteps of Crews—McLaurin, Brown, and Dorothy Allison in particular—and their predecessors.

The first authors Perry and I considered including were Crews, McLaurin, Brown, Allison, and two more recent writers, William Gay and Tom Franklin. I soon realized, however, that many of the other late twentieth- and early twenty-first-century writers we'd been reading didn't quite qualify as authentic descendants of Harry Crews—and that even Crews, McLaurin, Allison, and Franklin had earned college degrees, giving themselves a way out of the Rough South. Brian Carpenter faced a similar difficulty when choosing authors to excerpt in *Grit Lit: A Rough South Reader* (2012). He writes that he and his co-editor, Franklin himself, realized that "by restricting ourselves only to those who had 'walked the walk,' so to speak, we would be neglecting the work of a good many others who had just as much to say on the subject" of the hard-core rural South (xv).

Like Carpenter, then, I had come to realize that several other writers— writers from distinctly southern backgrounds but not of the working class— have biographies that read, broadly speaking, less like that of Crews than that of Cormac McCarthy. Like McCarthy, who was born into the middle class but wrote several early works about down-and-out inhabitants of the hardscrabble South, these writers emerged from a relatively stable socioeconomic background or worked their way into one via higher education. Some of them hold rather dichotomized attitudes about who they are and what they write. Tim Gautreaux, for example, has said, "[You] begin to feel that your plainer beginnings are something you should leave behind. And I think that's sad. You begin to lose all sense of history and all sense of the past, and then you lose the sense of the importance of present things" ("An Interview with Tim Gautreaux" 114). Gautreaux believes that a writer must not ignore "his own territory[;] he does so to his own peril, because unless he is a born researcher, what he discovers will never be as authentic as his impressions of his family and culture witnessed in childhood. What you discover will never be as good as your own background" ("A Conversation with Tim Gautreaux" 157). Franklin jokes, "[W]hile some of us second-or-third generation Grit Litters did earn M.F.A.s, we feel vaguely guilty about it and know we're a level less pure than our older, grittier counterparts" (viii).

Throughout the 1980s and '90s and into the twenty-first century, then, white southern writers have fallen into these two rather distinct categories. One group consists of writers born into the working class who decided to become writers and did so through their own concentrated efforts, without benefit of higher education: Brown, Gay, and most recently Barb Johnson. The others came from lower- or middle-class backgrounds and became writers by combining effort *and* education: McLaurin, Allison, Franklin, Gautreaux, Clyde Edgerton, Kaye Gibbons, Silas House, Jill McCorkle, Chris Offutt, Ron Rash, Lee Smith, Brad Watson, Daniel Woodrell, and Steve Yarbrough. Their twenty-first-century colleagues are John Brandon, Wiley Cash, Peter Farris, Skip Horack, Michael Farris Smith, and Joe Samuel Starnes.

Most members of the second group were born into the middle class or lower classes and, often encouraged by their parents, saw education as a way to move up. Many came to realize that what they knew best was the rural life that they had tried to leave behind, a legacy they often went on to praise in their writing. They share some of the same reverence for the rural South that the Nashville Agrarians exemplified in *I'll Take My Stand* (1925), but their approach is more personal than political or philosophical. These writers of the Rough South and other, at least slightly more genteel (see the Hawkins essay below) Souths care deeply about the poor—whether they came from an impoverished background themselves, as Brown, Gay, and Johnson did, or were a generation removed from one, like Edgerton, McCorkle, Offutt, Lee Smith, and Michael Farris Smith.

Bledsoe, in his seminal article, excerpted below, distinguishes Rough South writers from writers like William Faulkner and Erskine Caldwell, asserting that earlier writers, looking on from the outside, generally created working-class characters to occupy three roles: villains, victims, or comic relief. He asserts that the younger writers who followed Crews and "were born in and write about the Rough South . . . more commonly referred to as the world of the redneck or white trash" (68), force readers "to reexamine long-held stereotypes and beliefs while challenging the literary role traditionally assigned poor whites" (68). I would add that the other writers mentioned above accomplish also as much.

After a short essay by Hawkins on the origin of the Rough South designation and an excerpt from Bledsoe's essay, the essays that follow begin with Crews and McCarthy, the original influences on subsequent generations. Other essays address members of both groups—the hard-core self-educated and the college-educated—whose work has achieved strong recognition. The essential quality both groups share is a clear understanding of the value of working-class southerners and their culture—which, in almost every case addressed here, happen to be white. When Perry and I started planning the collection, race never once entered our discussions about which authors to include. We began with Rough South writers, all of whom—as Bledsoe, Carpenter, and Franklin illustrate—are white, and when we expanded our focus to include writers from more broadly rural backgrounds, we decided to include only one African American. Writers of both races have set works in the hardscrabble South, of course, but because so many recent African American writers from the region—Alice Walker and Randall Kenan, for example—address race more than class, we include only one here. Jesmyn Ward's 2011 National Book Award–winning *Salvage the Bones* may tell a tale of African American characters, but it's a novel less about race than humanity, about such timeless universals as family and landscape, loss and our attempts to recover from it. Class, not race, is the more salient issue in *Salvage the Bones*, just as it is in all the works examined here. All of these writers, both late-twentieth-century and more recent, both white and African American, share a clear reverence for the South's landscape and its inhabitants that gives rise to realistic depictions of landscape and of working-class characters who transcend dated stereotypes and, ultimately, achieve universal meaning.

Works Cited

Bledsoe, Erik. "The Rise of Southern Redneck and White Trash Writers." *Southern Cultures* 6.1 (2000): 68–90. Print.

Carpenter, Brian. "Introduction: Blood and Bone." *Grit Lit: A Rough South Reader*. Ed. Carpenter and Tom Franklin. Columbia: U of South Carolina P, 2012. xiii–xxxii. Print.

Franklin, Tom. "Preface: What's Grit Lit?" *Grit Lit: A Rough South Reader*. Ed. Brian Carpenter and Franklin. Columbia: U of South Carolina P, 2012. vii–viii. Print.

Gautreaux, Tim. "A Conversation with Tim Gautreaux." Interview by Dayne Sherman. *Conversations with Tim Gautreaux*. Ed. L. Lamar Nisly. Jackson: UP of Mississippi, 2012. 152–63.

———. "An Interview with Tim Gautreaux." Interview by Maria Hebert-Leiter. *Conversations with Tim Gautreaux*. Ed. L. Lamar Nisly. Jackson: UP of Mississippi, 2012. 110–19. Print.

Rough South, Rural South

"Rough South": Beginnings

Gary Hawkins

Meeting Larry Brown was the closest I came to a prototypical Rough South author. He was born and raised in Mississippi. His upbringing was rural. He was born into a working-class family, practically a working-poor family, and despite his eventual literary acclaim, he remained a member of the working class. He was largely self-educated and wrote about the local landscape and its "boozy misfits," as the *New York Times* called them, capturing the general mood of existential despair that pervades the less privileged areas of rural Mississippi. I never intended the word "rough" to be a description of Larry's writing, which could be delicate or florid or seductive or minimal or whatever he needed it to be in order to get its point across. "Rough" means "less than genteel"; in fact, that's where I first came across the term, at a cocktail party, from an authentic genteel southerner, an attorney sipping a bourbon and Coke, who said in passing, "Now this is the *rough* South I'm speaking of. Not the genteel South you're so familiar with."

In the late '80s I pitched a series of one-hour shows to Wyndham Robertson at UNC-TV. I told her it would be called "The Rough South of (name your author)," and that we'd shoot twelve episodes. In the first half-hour, I explained, we'd meet an author, and in the second we'd see a dramatization of his or her work. Soon I discovered that I'd been overly ambitious, that my local television affiliate lacked the budget for dramatizations. Furthermore, I learned that twelve Rough South authors simply didn't exist—not twelve interesting ones, anyway—and of those who met the requirements, most were specialists in essays or long fiction. So I dropped the fiction element for the first two episodes, on Tim McLaurin and Harry Crews, but attacked the material with a spirit of adventure, which is always the best move when you lack the wherewithal to do it right. How would I make this stuff interesting? What would viewers actually see?

The less said about the McLaurin program, the better. For twenty-eight minutes McLaurin and I served up one failed experiment after another. One of the only moments that in any way justify the film is when Tim told a funny story about a pet alligator that bit his finger. He had jerked back and accidentally thrown the gator across the kitchen into a boiling pot of butter beans. He and his mother looked in the pot and decided to leave the gator in there for flavor. The other interesting moment was when I filmed a pit bull scuff in rural Fayetteville, North Carolina—or rather, my cameraman did. Otherwise, the McLaurin show is fairly unwatchable. One of the many mistakes I made was that I asked McLaurin to perform his own work, which requires acting ability he simply didn't have. It was less obvious to me then than now that writing and performing are two completely different talents. For every Sam Shepard or Harry Crews there are fifty bad actors reading well-shaped prose. Presently I'm suffering through a Juno Diaz audiobook, an author who reads his own work like he has a gun to his head. And even the best authors, Faulkner for one, hurry through their words. O'Connor is mousy and weird. So is Gibbons. Almost no one could do it, least of all McLaurin.

Harry Crews—my first (of two) true Rough South encounters—was a Georgia-born writer working in Florida. Larry Brown already interested me more, but in the early '90s I wasn't ready to make a film about Larry. The only other authors who looked promising were Jim Grimsley and Kaye Gibbons. I interviewed Jim, but nothing more, and I never even put a camera on Kaye. When she broke the second scheduled interview with me—leaving a twelve-man camera crew standing in her yard—I gave up on her. I gave up on Grimsley when Jodie Foster optioned his largely autobiographical novel *Winter Birds* (1984/1994).

How did I discover Larry Brown? His publicist, Katharine Walton, gave me a copy of *Facing the Music* (1988), Larry's first book of stories. I remember riding back to my house with the book in the seat beside me, practically calling to me. I drove a mile or so, then pulled into a strip mall and eased to a stop under a street light and read the entire book of stories right there. I'm not exaggerating. The whole book. But I wasn't ready for Brown. I had to make something that didn't suck first.

How did I meet Harry Crews? Well, I just called him up on the phone. He said, "Sure, come down on Saturday," then gave me directions to his house. When Friday rolled around I jumped in a van with my crew and drove from North Carolina to Gainesville, Florida. I didn't know much about Crews. I hate to admit this, but I'd read only one of his works, an essay—the one about the sniper—and that's pretty insulting when you think about it. And I was hungover pretty bad, too. I guess you could safely say that when I knocked on Crews's door I was unprepared.

Crews came to the door, and the first thing I noticed was what fantastic shape he was in. I mean, the dude was formidable. He'd just finished *Body* (1990), a novel about a female bodybuilder, and he'd been living with her, training with her, sleeping with her, and he looked twenty. Crews was sixty, I think. Anyway, he yanked open the door, and there he stood—lean and mean, with wild, blue, piercing eyes. And with those eyes trained on me he said, "Are you Hawkins?"

"Yes."

Then he threw his arms wide like a flagman on an aircraft carrier. "There's a pisser on either end of the house. We're in the back yard. Let's go."

I turned to the crew and said, "Set up in the back yard."

I've never exercised so little control over an interview. I asked one, maybe two questions, and Crews held forth for an hour and fifteen minutes, essentially asking and answering his own questions. When he announced that the interview was over, I said, "We're done?" and he said, "Yeah." And he said it like, "We're done. Now get the hell out of my yard," so we packed up and left. When I returned to North Carolina, I screened the interview and realized he'd given me one full hour of keeper footage. That's an amazing ratio, surpassed only by Shelby Foote, whom I interviewed three films later.

To assemble the Crews show I built a narrative spine from the interviews and illuminated his words with my own homespun imagery. When I reviewed the backyard interview, I realized what he'd said was interesting enough to present to audiences untouched. Crews on writing: "Writing is a moral occupation, practiced by not necessarily moral men and women." Crews on violence: "I wrote this piece called 'The Violence That Finds Us.' This young boy cut me for nothin', and I said in the piece, 'It's a good thing my ball of wax wasn't bigger because he might have felt it necessary to kill me.'" On sports: "The thing about sports, if you tell me you got 4.2 speed in the forty, we'll just put some watches on you. If you tell me you can bench four hundred pounds, we've got a bench and we've got four hundred pounds. You cain't bullshit." Roll credits. It would've worked. It would've worked, but I'd read half of *Blood and Grits* (1979) on my way to Gainesville, and those essays had hooked me. This was my kind of writing: first-person accounts with no hiding behind objectivity; edgy scenarios in which the author is wounded—physically, psychologically, or both—by the subject he's there to investigate.

I tackled the books next, but it wasn't until I reached page six of the eighth book that I found what I needed: "What has been most significant in my life had all taken place by the time I was six years old." The line is from Crews's autobiography, *A Childhood: The Biography of a Place* (1978). I read *A Childhood* in a couple of sittings and found my blueprint there. The book's structural conceit relies on a shoebox full of yellowed photographs. "I reach into the shoebox," Crews writes, "and I take out a picture of Uncle Alton. . . ." When I asked Crews for the shoebox, he told me it had burned up in a house fire. I'm not sure I believed him, but it didn't really matter. If he couldn't provide the imagery, I'd dream it up myself.

Eight months into the process, we found ourselves in need of voiceovers, so we paid Crews another visit. We drove nine hours to his house and knocked on his door, but the man who answered it this time was sixty pounds heavier and sporting a Mohawk. I'd heard that Crews was prone to slip into new identities the way the rest of us slip into and out of clothes, but I hadn't imagined anything so dramatic. When I asked why he'd affected a road warrior look, he said it was because he'd begun to feel too loved in Gainesville, like too much of a mascot. "When folks see me now," he said, "I can feel the hate comin' off 'em like heat off a stove."

We set up in his backyard and began to talk, and that's when I realized that something was fundamentally different now. The laser focus and rapid-fire delivery were gone. I'd raise a topic, and he'd address it, then he'd digress, and then he'd digress from that digression, moving further afield until he grew bored and rolled to a stop. If the first interview was a lean, mean final draft, the second was a meandering first draft. After four hours I ended the interview, and we recorded the voiceovers. At this point Crews came alive and delivered an elegant, energetic reading of his own work. "He's not just a brilliant writer," I thought. "He's also an enormously talented actor."

A year or so later we finished the show and sent it to Crews, and he liked it. When I expressed partial regret over the need to fictionalize the characters from his Bacon County childhood, he said, "No, no, Man, it might as well have been those folks. Might as well have been." When Crews died, a few from my former crew asked me if I'd stayed in touch with him over the years. I hadn't, and I don't have a good reason for it. Maybe *The Rough South* is what we were meant to do, and once it was done, we were done with each other, too. *The Rough South* belies an intimacy that Crews and I never shared. When I added up our hours together, they came to six. "There's only one thing a writer has," Crews warned me the first time we met, "and it's not money. It's time." The Crews show won an Emmy Award, and on the strength of its success I began principal photography on *The Rough South of Larry Brown*.

The first time I drove down to Oxford, Mississippi, Larry's wife, Mary Annie, had a fried chicken dinner ready when I walked in the door. I hung out for a couple of days before the crew arrived, just to get the lay of the land. When the filming began, M. A. disappeared. The second time I went to Oxford, M. A. was in a foul mood about something. She kept making passive-aggressive maneuvers like jumping up and stomping out of the room. Larry writes all night. He's on third shift, and M. A. is on first shift. So when Larry took a nap I said to M. A., "You don't want us down here, do you?"

"No, it's fine."

I said, "Then what is it?"

"What is what?"

"What's got you ticked off?"

"I'm not ticked off."

"Yes you are. What's got you ticked off?"

Finally she confessed, "You think this writing stuff is so glamorous. Let me tell you, it's *not*." I said, "Jason, set up the camera," and M. A. was in the show. When Larry trudged into the kitchen after his nap he was horrified to find his wife spilling the beans on camera. You should've seen his face. He started to yawn, and his jaw dropped.

Mary Annie actually spoke the theme of the show while Larry slept. She spoke it in two parts. At the end of the first chapter she says, "When Larry started writing we never saw him." At the end of the second chapter she says, "But when Larry writes, that's when he's the happiest. And when he's not writing that's when he's so depressed you can't stand to be around him." So put the two together, and you have a question: You can stand to be around him only when he's not around? What a wonderful paradox. That's when I glimpsed the "whole show," including how the stories would line up, how Mary Annie would figure into the mix, and how we'd revisit the conflict of Calling and Duty, a theme that stretches back at least to Odysseus. Everything became clear when she spoke those lines.

I made three trips to Oxford over the course of two years, and each visit I shot as much as our budget would allow. We often ran out of money—we had to raise more money before we could take the next step—so the show proceeded in fits and starts. On a more positive note, the huge gaps of time between interviews allowed the family to change, giving us a much truer picture of Larry's life. Each time I visited Oxford, the mood in Larry's house was different.

Even though I collected thirty hours of footage for a ninety-minute show, I didn't kill too many darlings. Docs depend on lots of footage. It's fishing. You catch a lot of stuff—not much of it edible—so you keep fishing. At some point, you've caught what you need to make a nice fish dinner. That's when you starting paring down the material.

You could argue, though, that I missed everything. After all, Larry was published before I heard of him and successful before I hustled the money together to get the film made. Most of my film looked backwards. Hearsay. Catching the unfolding moment, that's far more dynamic.

One near-miss that still haunts me—I didn't get the shot due to a camera jam—happened in M. A.'s kitchen one night. Larry and Mary Annie were arguing about an electric guitar. Larry had found a Gibson at a lefty shop down in Texas, and the price was right. Mary Annie said forget it; it's not in the budget. Larry said it was. They're arguing. Off to the side on a bar-stool, Leanne (their then sixteen-year-old daughter) is whining, "Make me a sandwich. Make me a sandwich," right on top of the argument. So, absent-mindedly, Larry—still arguing—takes out the white bread, the mayonnaise, the ham and cheese, and makes Leanne a sandwich. All the time Leanne is whining, "Make me a sandwich. Make me a sandwich." Larry doesn't even seem to know that he's making a sandwich. He's going through the motions like the factory worker he used to be. After five or so minutes of this little one-act play, Larry finishes the sandwich. He finishes the sandwich just as he and Mary Annie strike a truce. Leanne takes one small bite of the sandwich and hurries out of the kitchen to her bedroom. I didn't know what to make of that then. I still don't.

From "The Rise of Southern Redneck and White Trash Writers"[1]

Erik Bledsoe

Linda Tate has noted, with a touch of hyperbole, that "traditionally, southern literature has been understood to be that written by white men and, on rare occasions, by white women—and, in almost all cases, by and about white southerners of the upper middle class" (5–6). As recently as 1988, another critic claimed, albeit incorrectly, that Harry Crews "is absolutely unique among Southern writers in that he writes about life from the perspective of the poor white. He writes from within the class, not by observing it from without, the traditional perspective of white Southern writers" (Shelton 47). That same year, however, marked the emergence of three new voices who join Crews in writing about southern poor whites from within the class. Dorothy Allison, Larry Brown, and Tim McLaurin all published their first books of fiction: *Trash, Facing the Music,* and *The Acorn Plan,* respectively. In these and subsequent works, all three authors write about lower-class characters whose background they share. They were born in and write about the Rough South, a term coined by documentary filmmaker Gary Hawkins and more commonly referred to as the world of the redneck or white trash. In the public imagination, and arguably in reality, it is a world of excess—excessive alcohol, excessive sex, excessive violence. It is also a world that until recently has lacked its own recognized storytellers. This new generation of southern writers is giving voice to a different group of southerners, and in doing so it is forcing its readers to reexamine long-held stereotypes and beliefs while challenging the literary roles traditionally assigned poor whites.

In the race-class-gender triumvirate of much contemporary criticism, class is still the poor cousin who is often ignored while its higher-profile relatives are wined and dined by academics. Noting the critical disparity, Allison has observed that "traditional feminist theory has had a limited understanding of class differences and how sexuality and self are shaped by both desire and denial" (15). Critic Fred Hobson has identified a group of "younger southern writers [who] do not come from the privileged classes, from educated families; and . . . they do not in any way try to disguise their origins" (22). Although Hobson mentions Bobbie Ann Mason and Richard Ford as members of this group, he does not mention Brown, McLaurin, or Allison—all of whom were born a notch or two lower on the social ladder than Mason and Ford. Echoing William Dean Howells, Hobson suggests that "what is happening is simply an expansion of the franchise, part of the centuries-old progress in Western literature from a writing by and principally about the privileged—though occasionally about the lower classes, comically rendered—to a literature by, and treating seriously, the common people" (23). He also predicted that class "will be the next enlivening issue in the consideration of southern letters" (20).

Part of the difficulty of discussing southern literature from the perspective of class arises from the slippery nature of class distinctions in southern white society. The terms *redneck, white trash, cracker,* and *poor white* have all been used to describe certain white southerners, but exact categories are difficult to define. Some people, for example, casually use *white trash* and *redneck* interchangeably, while others draw distinct differences between the two. Nor is it exactly clear what the terms describe. As historian J. Wayne Flynt has observed, the phrase *poor white* "has been applied to economic and social classes as well as to cultural and ethical values" (1), thereby compounding the problem of definition. Recently, critics have begun to look at poor whites from a theoretical perspective rather than a purely historical or sociological one. The best work in this field has emerged from the growing interest in theorizing whiteness. While most critiques of whiteness seek to examine and decenter its cultural power, as Annalee Newitz and Matthew Wray point out, "the whiteness of 'white trash' signals something other than privilege and social power" (168–69).

No matter the label, lower-class whites have a long tradition in southern fiction. Sylvia Jenkins Cook points out that the poor white's role in southern literature was firmly established in the nineteenth century: "He was a confirmed object of ridicule in the works of humorists and a stock minor character in many novels, with generally villainous or pathetic tendencies according to the broader ideological sympathies of the author" (5). These three roles— comic, villain, or victim—continue into the twentieth century, although writers such as Erskine Caldwell often combine the roles to create characters like the comic-tragic Jeeter Lester from *Tobacco Road* (1932). But almost without exception, the authors of these works are from middle- or upper-class backgrounds themselves, in essence writing from the outside looking in.

The most famous representation of the lower classes in southern literature is Faulkner's mythical Snopes clan. The Snopeses often fit into the paradigm of the comic poor white; they christen their children with ridiculous names like Wallstreet Panic Snopes and Montgomery Ward Snopes. Ike Snopes falls in love with a cow and courts her as earnestly as any love-struck Italian sonneteer ever pursued his Laura. And when their amorous attentions are devoted to their own species, the Snopeses multiply at an astonishing rate. In Cleanth Brooks's index of Faulkner's characters, the Snopeses are the only family whose members fill more than one page. Even the Compsons, with their seemingly endless chronicling of ancestors, only fill just over half a page, and unlike the Compsons most of the Snopeses listed are living concurrently (481–82).

But the laughter directed at the Snopeses and their real-world counterparts is ultimately a nervous laughter. In the first decades of the twentieth century, eugenicists pointed to studies detailing the alleged prolific breeding and the proliferation of imbecility among generations of poor whites to argue for forced sterilization programs, essentially class-based slow genocide designed to protect the human gene pool from ruination. Similarly, as Faulkner shows, the proliferation of the Snopeses is be feared. The Snopes Trilogy—*The Hamlet* (1940), *The Town* (1957), and *The Mansion* (1959)—traces the rise in Yoknapatawpha County of Flem Snopes and the horde of others he brings up with him. Flem Snopes's rise to wealth and power is the culminating event in the South's decline. C. Hugh Holman has claimed that the humor in the trilogy "begins to weaken" when in *The Mansion* "Faulkner loses the distance which allows him to look without involvement at these characters, when he begins to move in close and understand Flem Snopes, and when he begins to follow Mink Snopes's determination to leave prison and seek revenge upon Flem with some admiration for his determination and persistence" (34). Holman's reading suggests how empathy and understanding can mitigate against an initial mockery born of superiority. Holman fails to note, however, that the decline in humor also corresponds to Flem's rise in power. As long as the Snopeses are easily dismissed as trash, they are comic, but as they gain economic and social power, it becomes more difficult to laugh. The narrative perspective of the Snopes trilogy is that of the middle classes, who watch in horror as they lose ground to the white trash that seeks to displace them.

Outsiders and those who consider themselves superior use pejorative labels like *white trash* and *redneck* to identify those "others" whose manners and values differ from their own and to keep those others in their proper place. Naturally, the labeled "others" usually resist such derogatory classification. Of all the slurs, *redneck* is today the most socially acceptable term used to disparage members of a particular group. As Will D. Campbell has pointed out, "Like the nouns *nigger* and *kike*, *redneck* is most often used pejoratively. And, as a descendent of people disparaged by that word, I ask why the first two terms are eschewed by even the most blatantly racist and bigoted publications, while *redneck* is used routinely in virtually every respectable, sophisticated and allegedly responsible newspaper and magazine in America?" (92). Campbell's comments were made in 1988, and unlike many other consciousness-raising movements in the last decade or so, efforts to bring a sense of political correctness to references to lower-class whites have had little effect. In 1997, after a limited survey of the way the words *nigger* and *redneck* were used in two newspapers, Jim Goad summarized that whenever the word *nigger* occurred, the writer was directly quoting someone else, but whenever the word *redneck* occurred, in more than two out of three cases the writer himself was using it as a noun or adjective to describe lower-class whites. "If the neck's red," says Goad, "the light's green" (20). (As I typed the above paragraph, I could not help but notice that the spellchecker on my word processor refused to recognize *nigger* as a word but had no such qualms about *redneck*.)

The slipperiness of the terms *poor white*, *cracker*, and *redneck* as they apply to either socioeconomic status or a particular set of ethical values often makes categorization difficult. Combined with the derogatory intent of such labels, they sometimes provoke great anxiety in those whose classification may be borderline. In "Revelation" (1964), Flannery O'Connor satirizes the attempt of certain types of people to place others into neat class-based categories:

> Sometimes Mrs. Turpin occupied herself at night naming the classes of people. On the bottom of the heap were most colored people, not the kind she would have been had she been one, but most of them; then next to them—not above, just away from—were the white trash; then above them were the home-owners, and above them the home-and-land owners, to which she and Claud belonged. Above she and Claud were people with a lot of money and much bigger houses and more land. But here the complexity of it would begin to bear in on her, for some of the people with a lot of money were common and ought to be below she and Claud and some of the people who had good blood had lost their money and had to rent and then there were colored people who owned their homes and land as well. There was a colored dentist in town who had two red Lincolns and a swimming pool and a farm with registered white-face cattle on it. Usually by the time she had fallen asleep all the classes of people were moiling and rolling around in her

head, and she would dream they were all crammed in together in a box car, being ridden off to be put in a gas oven. (491–92)

Mrs. Turpin has no problem identifying and labeling those whom she sees as being below her, the "white trash," but she has difficulty placing herself below others whose backgrounds or behaviors she finds offensive. Despite its failings to account for everyone to her satisfaction, she clings to the flawed class system. To abandon it would create a metaphorical holocaust. As critic Barbara Wilkie Tedford has suggested, while O'Connor "pokes fun at people who set themselves up to judge others" and seems sympathetic toward poor whites, "[s]he generally lets the so-called lower classes serve as comic instruments of justice. . . . [S]he describes the white-trash only through the eyes of superior women whom she is mocking because of their attitudes" (35).

When we move to the generation of writers whose own origins are among the poor whites, we not surprisingly get a shift in the awareness of labels and the presentation of those who are labeled. In Larry Brown's *Dirty Work* (1989), a character ruminates on the southern class structure: "I'd have to call Matt Monroe trash. There's nothing else to call somebody like him. You could just tell by looking at him that he was trash. But of course trash is always in the eye of the beholder. I know. There were probably some people who thought we were trash. I know there were people who looked down their noses at us because we were on welfare. That and my daddy being in the pen" (33). Unlike Mrs. Turpin, Brown's character recognizes and accepts the subjectivity off the labels. While he prefers to use "trash" as a signifier of cultural and ethical values, he knows that to others it signifies economic instability. He still resists the *trash* label being applied to him, but unlike Mrs. Turpin he does not see disaster as the result should he be labeled as such. In their fiction, Brown and others of this new generation approach class in ways that go beyond the three traditional literary roles—comic, villain, or victim—for poor whites.

In *Bastard Out of Carolina* (1992), Dorothy Allison's invocation of *Gone with the Wind* (1936), that touchstone of southern literature for masses of readers, is telling. Bone, like Allison, recognizes that the view offered by much of southern literature has been seen from the porch of the plantation house (or its ruins). Writers like Dorothy Allison, Tim McLaurin, and Larry Brown offer a perspective from the other side of the fields. None of these writers romanticize the poor, nor do they deny the validity of many of the images people have of white trash. Instead, as Queer Nation did, they have reclaimed a once-derogatory label for their own empowerment. Their characters often drink too much, fight too much, "fuck" too much, get into trouble with the law, and have trouble keeping jobs, but nevertheless many of the characters are able at the same time to transcend such stereotypes, to reveal the humanity behind the people who populate the poolrooms and bars. Unlike the Snopeses, these white trash characters are not all either idiots or scheming to take over the town. Often coming from lower-class origins themselves, the newest generation of southern writers demands that their readers reexamine their views of class in the South, demands that we make room. White trash is no longer something to sweep out the back door.

Notes

Originally published, in slightly different form, in *Southern Cultures* 6.1 (2000); reprinted by permission of the author.

Works Cited and Consulted

Allison, Dorothy. "A Question of Class." *Skin: Talking about Sex, Class & Literature*. New York: Firebrand, 1994. Print.

Brooks, Cleanth. "An Affair of Honor: Larry Brown's *Joe*." Chapel Hill: Algonquin, 1991. Print.

———. *William Faulkner: The Yoknapatawpha Country*. Baton Rouge: Louisiana State UP, 1990. Print.

Brown, Larry. *Dirty Work*. Chapel Hill: Algonquin, 1989. Print.

Campbell, Will D. "Used and Abused: The Redneck's Role." *The Prevailing South: Life and Politics in a Changing Culture*. Ed. Dudley Clendinen. Atlanta: Longstreet, 1988. Print.

Cook, Sylvia Jenkins. *From Tobacco Road to Route 66: The Southern Poor White in Fiction*. Chapel Hill: U of North Carolina P, 1976. Print.

Flynt, J. Wayne. *Dixie's Forgotten People: The South's Poor Whites*. Bloomington: Indiana UP, 1979. Print.

Goad, Jim. *The Redneck Manifesto*. New York: Simon and Schuster, 1997. Print.

Hendrickson, Robert. *Whistlin' Dixie: A Dictionary of Southern Expressions*. New York: Facts on File, 1993. Print.

Hobson, Fred. *The Southern Writer in the Postmodern World*. Athens: U of Georgia P, 1991. Print.

Holman, C. Hugh. "Detached Laughter in the South." *Windows on the World: Essays on American Social Fiction*. Knoxville: U of Tennessee P, 1979. Print.

Larson, Edward J. *Sex, Race, and Science: Eugenics in the Deep South*. Baltimore: Johns Hopkins UP, 1995. Print.

Newitz, Annalee, and Matt Wray. "What is 'White Trash'? Stereotypes and Economic Conditions of Poor Whites in the United States." *White Trash: Race and Class in America*. Ed. Wray and Newitz. Oxford: Routledge, 1997. 168–84. Print.

O'Connor, Flannery. "Revelation." *The Complete Stories*. New York: Farrar, Straus and Giroux, 1971. 488–509. Print.

Rafter, Nicole Hahn Rafter, ed. *White Trash: The Eugenic Family Studies: 1877–1919*. Evanston: Northeastern UP, 1988. Print.

Reed, John Shelton. *Southern Folk, Plain and Fancy: Native White Social Types*. Mercer University Lamar Memorial Lectures Ser. Athens: U of Georgia P, 1986. Print.

Roebuck, Julian B., and Ronald L. Neff. "The Multiple Reality of the 'Redneck': Toward a Grounded Theory of the Southern Class Structure." *Studies in Symbolic Interaction* 3 (1980): 233–62. Print.

Skow, John. "Southern Pine." Rev. of *Joe*, by Larry Brown. *Time* 28 Oct. 1991: 96. Print.

Shelton, Frank W. "The Poor Whites' Perspective: Harry Crews among Georgia Writers." *Journal of American Culture* 11.3 (1988): 47–50. Print.

Tate, Linda. *A Southern Weave of Women: Fiction of the Contemporary South*. Athens: U of Georgia P, 1994. Print.

Tedford, Barbara Wilkie. "Flannery O'Connor and the Social Classes." *Southern Literary Journal* 13.2 (1981): 27–40. Print.

Harry Crews: Progenitor

David K. Jeffrey

HARRY Eugene Crews was born June 7, 1935, in Alma, a rural town in Bacon County, Georgia. He was the second surviving son of Ray and Myrtice Crews, who married in 1928 and worked as sharecroppers until Ray died, probably from a congenital heart defect exacerbated by overwork, in 1937. Myrtice soon married Ray's brother Pascal, another a tenant farmer—and a violent alcoholic. Crews described the poverty and despair of his upbringing in *A Childhood: The Biography of a Place* (1979): "The world that circumscribed the people I come from had so little margin for error, for bad luck, that when something went wrong, it almost always brought something else down with it. It was a world in which survival depended on raw courage, a courage born out of desperation and sustained by a lack of alternatives" (40).

One of the many factors that "went wrong" in Crews's childhood happened when he was five and contracted a fever. His legs began to draw up until his heels touched his buttocks. Doctors told him he would never walk again, and as word spread through the county, relatives, neighbors, even total strangers came "to stare at me where I lay in a high fever . . . to stare at my rigid legs. . . . I hated it and dreaded it and was humiliated by it. I felt how lonely and savage it was to be a freak" (78–79). The sickness was either the result of infantile paralysis or a hysterical reaction to violence in the home. Crews recovered the use of his legs, but less than a year later, during hog-killing time, he was popped off the end of a pop-the-whip into a vat of boiling water used to scald the hair off hog carcasses. Plucked out at once, he watched his skin fall off, forming steaming puddles on the ground. He spent several months scabbing and healing, but until he was fifteen, his back, legs, and right arm carried scars. Crews claimed that most of the people in Bacon County suffered from one deformity or another, and that he "became fascinated with the Sears catalogue because all of the people in its pages were perfect" (54). He credits that catalogue with sparking his interest in narrative and storytelling. While he recovered, he and Willalee Bookatee, an African American neighbor his age, would sit for hours making up stories about the perfect people in the "Wish Book." Myrtice and her sons eventually fled Pascal's violence and moved to Jacksonville, Florida, where she found work in a cigar factory. They later returned to Bacon County, however, and she returned to farming until she again moved to Jacksonville.

In 1953 Crews graduated from Jacksonville's Andrew Jackson High School and joined the Marine Corps, serving from 1953 to 1956, when he was discharged as a sergeant. For two years he attended the University of Florida on the GI Bill, enrolling in a writing class with Andrew Lytle, who was to become his mentor. After reading Crews's first story, however, Lytle's advice was, "Burn it, son. Fire's a great refiner" ("Andrew Lytle" 58). Crews earned a BA in English in 1960 and an MSEd in 1962. In 1960 he married a classmate, Sally Ellis. They divorced in 1961 but remarried in 1962. They had two sons, Patrick Scott and Byron. In 1964, Patrick Scott, age four, drowned. The couple again divorced in 1972.

Crews taught English at Broward Junior College in Fort Lauderdale from 1962 to 1968, during which time he also wrote for a radio show and worked on his fiction. He'd "written for ten years, and not a word had seen print." All of it, he later said, was "*fake*":

[C]ircumstances had collaborated to make me ashamed that I was a tenant farmer's son. . . . I was so humiliated by the fact that I was from the edge of the Okefenokee Swamp in the worst hookworm and rickets part of Georgia I could not bear to think of it, and worse to believe it. Everything I had written had been out of a fear and loathing for what I was and who I was. . . . [But] the next thought—and it was more than a thought, it was dead-solid conviction—was that all I had going for me in the world or would ever have was that swamp, all those goddamn mules, all those screwworms that I'd dug out of pigs and all the other beautiful and dreadful and sorry circumstances that had made me the Grit I am and will always be. Once I realized that the way I saw the world and man's condition in it would always be exactly and inevitably shaped by everything which up to that moment had only shamed me, once I realized that, I was home free. ("Television's Junkyard Dog" 145)

The epiphany led Crews to write in a more authentic voice. In 1968 he published his first novel, *The Gospel Singer*, to some acclaim, and its acceptance enabled him to return that same year to the University of Florida as an associate professor. He was promoted to full professor in 1974 and retired in 1997. Among his awards are a 1972 American Academy of Arts and Sciences Award and a 1974 National Endowment for the Arts grant.

When Harry Crews died on March 28, 2013, he had more than twenty-five titles to his credit: novels, essay collections, screenplays, and novellas. He published essays in *Rolling Stone, Sport, Playboy,* and *Esquire*; indeed, during the presidential administration of fellow Georgian Jimmy Carter, he published a monthly column, "Grits," in the last. Despite this extraordinary record of publication and his thirty-five years in academia, Crews never thought of himself as an academic—and no one who met him or took one of his classes ever confused him with, say, Stanley Fish. Crews was true to his origins, true to his people, true to his class. He's the first popular southern novelist to write from a poor white perspective, and it's telling that so many southern writers from the same class who followed him—Larry Brown and Tim McLaurin, for example—cite him as a mentor or influence. Crews is similar to other white southern writers from the middle- and upper-middle classes; however, in his concern for the vanishing rural South, his thematic use of grotesques, his fascination with man's relationship with God and the effects of a Protestant upbringing, Crews also recognizes that in the "modern" South, the traditional South of Faulkner, Caldwell, O'Connor, and Welty no longer exists. His characters—alienated, bemused, angry, often violent—seek meaning in a variety of sometimes traditional and sometimes bizarre pursuits. At their best, Crews's novels are both startlingly funny and scathingly satirical.

Works dating from the middle of Crews's career are his strongest. These include: two powerful and important novels, *The Gypsy's Curse* (1974) and *A Feast of Snakes* (1976); a fascinating collection of essays, *Blood and Grits* (1979), which sheds light on the preoccupations of his novels; and one of the best autobiographies in American literature, *A Childhood: The Biography of a Place*. As Donald R. Noble argues in "Harry Crews Introduces Himself," *A Childhood* deserves to be read alongside Benjamin Franklin's *Autobiography* (1791) and *The Education of Henry Adams* (1918)(7).

Given Crews's horror about being viewed with his legs drawn up—"I felt how lonely and savage it was to be a freak"—it will surprise no one to learn that freaks appear as important characters in his first three novels, a circumstance that led his puzzled wife to ask, "You don't intend to make a career out of midgets, do you?" ("Harry Crews: An Interview," *SQ* 72). Crews believes his grotesques are important in his novels because they so obviously lack the disguises, the facades, that "normal" humanity can hide behind, shielding themselves from self-knowledge. These grotesques exhibit values Crews admires—courage, honesty, and strength among them—and reflect the real condition of humanity in a post-lapsarian world. Freaks in Crews's works are thus paradoxically normative characters.

In *The Gospel Singer*, the titular protagonist—tall, thin, blonde, and physically perfect—returns to his hometown, Enigma, Georgia, followed by Foot, a midget with a twenty-seven-inch foot, and the members of Foot's Freak Fair. As Frank Shelton argues in "Man's Search for Perfection," Crews uses these foils to examine humanity's duality, and indeed, the Gospel Singer comes to recognize his own. His physical beauty and talent for singing contradict his corrupt and fallen nature. While his voice has "brought him into the presence of God," it has also brought him into the presence of hundreds of women, whom he has seduced and corrupted. His gift is also a curse that has "displaced him, made him uncomfortable among his own blood kin, made the place of his birth strange and unreal" (71). Near the end of the novel, he visits the Freak Fair for the first time and discovers the truth about Foot and his fellows: that they too are human; that they too have what Foot calls "a special . . . consideration under God" (208); that his sense of superiority is not unique; and that he and Foot could be friends. Finally, he confesses his sins to his congregation, after which some members lynch him in a vivid scene recalling Christ's crucifixion. His final thoughts are of sympathy for his friend Willalee Bookatee, whom a mob has also lynched, and of the mob's probable damnation, assessments that suggest his possible redemption at the instant of death and Crews's debt (which he often acknowledged) to Flannery O'Connor—"A Good Man Is Hard to Find" in particular.

In *Naked in Garden Hills* (1969), Crews chronicles the transfer of power in a Floridian Eden, a phosphate pit where thirty-six families live. Power moves from six hundred-pound Fat Man, addicted to the diet drink Metrecal, to Dolly Furgeson, a former beauty queen who transforms the phosphate plant into a discotheque. Here, too, Crews illustrates humanity's duality. Fat Man sees himself as "a man apart . . . outside the condition of those living at the bottom of the hole. After all, he lived on the hill. . . . He was a hero here in Garden Hills; outside Garden Hills he was a freak. Here he was held in reverence; he had beaten the system. Elsewhere, children laughed; adults wanted to stone him" (122). At the end of the novel, however, Fat Man is "crucified"—made to descend his hill, walk a gauntlet of sneering customers, swallow burning liquid, enter a cage that ascends when twelve men pull its golden rope, and be put on display for the mob. The novel comments satirically on the corruptive power of Mammon, and on the contemporary triumph of the shallow and ephemeral in the absence of religious values and purpose.

This Thing Don't Lead to Heaven (1970), Crews's least successful early novel, features a confusing array of characters, including: Jefferson Davis Munroe, a midget masseur; Jeremy Tetley, a dying eighty-year-old; Carlita, a Haitian voodoo priestess; Junior Bledsoe, a gravesite salesman; Hiram Peters, a preacher who denies the reality of death; and Pearl Lee Gates, owner of an old people's home. Satirizing America's preoccupation with the horror of death—Evelyn Waugh and Jessica Mitford by way of Erskine Caldwell—the novel seems to Shelton to be Crews's final rejection of both religion and any "ultimate meaning to life," any "comfort for the fact of death. Perhaps life can be made bearable through courage or love, or through the illusion . . . that magic can make one normal. But whatever resolution man finds, it must take death into account" (105).

Crews continues his satire of contemporary life in his next three novels, *Karate Is a Thing of the Spirit* (1971), *Car* (1972), and *The Hawk Is Dying* (1973). In these works he is particularly interested in our fascination with power and possessions, and with our mistaken attribution of religious, spiritual, and/or ethical value to either. All three novels comment on humanity's various dualities—spirit and body, illusion and reality, for example—suggesting as well how seldom love prevails. In *Karate Is a Thing of the Spirit*, John Kaimon finds peace in the self-discipline of karate and eventually finds happiness in his love for the former beauty queen, Gaye Nell—or "Brown Belt," as she prefers to be called. Kaimon sees her as the American "ideal" that combines the potential for sex and death. A believer in "everything" at the beginning of the novel, he comes to recognize at the end that he cannot believe that karate or heroes or gods avail in this world, or that they might affirm or transform anything in it. He does believe, however, in Gaye Nell and her ability to have their child, a view of love that has seemed to many—particularly female readers—demeaning and primitive at best.

In *Car*, Herman Mack loves cars so much that he wants—like Fat Man in *Naked in Garden Hills*—to eat one, to put everything outside himself inside himself. The novel amusingly chronicles the public spectacle that surrounds his attempt. Crowds assemble to watch Herman consume half a pound of a Ford Maverick in the evening and excrete it the next morning. The novel satirizes America's obsession with and, indeed, deification of the automobile.

Further, as Shelton has argued in "Theme and Technique in Harry Crews' *Car*," the novel

> explores man's relationship with technology and, more generally, what it means to be a human being. Although not a conventional Southern family epic, the novel also treats the role of the family and the individual's place in it, virtually all the main characters being Mack family members. The family here, as elsewhere in Crews, is not a sustaining institution; as a result, the isolated characters are desperately seeking a sense of belonging and of humanity in a landscape dominated by automobiles. (125)

The Hawk Is Dying chronicles George Gattling's quest for meaning in the traditional pursuit of falconry, a response to the banality of his life as the owner of a Gainesville, Florida, car upholstery business and to the death of his mentally handicapped nephew, the only person for whom he ever felt love. Matthew Guinn writes in "The Grit Émigré in Harry Crews' Fiction" that Gattling is one of several Crews characters who are "dislocated agrarian figures who migrate from various fictional locales in south Georgia to the Sunbelt industrial centers of north Florida." They are "strangers to the urban setting" who "embody the outsider perspective . . . as they attempt (like Crews himself) to reconcile their status as 'grits' in a changing cultural landscape" (107). Guinn notes that, as a falconer, George "affects a symbolic return to the cadences and meaning of agricultural labor; he comes to understand his place in a natural relationship as regenerative and transformative. After weeks of training, he finally flies the hawk over his nephew's grave, forging for himself a return to blood and nature, to vitality and freedom" (109).

Crews published his best works between 1974 and 1979. *The Gypsy's Curse* takes as its protagonist Marvin Molar, a deaf-mute strongman without functional legs, and tells the story from his perspective. Miraculously, the novel works; the reader credits Marvin and feels some sympathy for him. He makes his living as part of a balancing act with the body builder Russell Muscle, the "perfect" bodily antithesis to Marvin's "freak." While audiences cheer for their act, Marvin recognizes that they are applauding Russell's normalcy and their own. They are not applauding "because I was a deaf-mute who could do something besides sell pencils or apples on a street corner" (114). He takes a measure of revenge on these audiences by incorporating into his balancing act a one-fingered stand on his "society finger" (110). Eventually, however, he allows Hester Maille, the object of his hopeless love, to disrupt the family of peaceful punch drunks and gym rats with whom he lives, then cuckold him and effectually kill his surrogate father before he murders her. The novel is a powerful portrayal of the desperation and hopelessness that love can involve.

Both horrifying and funny, *A Feast of Snakes*, Crews's best novel, follows Joe Lon Mackey, a twenty-year-old illiterate redneck and former high school football hero, during the four-day course of a rattlesnake rodeo in his hometown of Mystic, Georgia. Now living in a trailer, husband to a ruined wife, and possessed of two infant sons, a psychotic sister, and a violent father who trains fighting dogs, Joe Lon despairs of his life even as the novel and the rodeo festival open. Two years earlier he had been Boss Snake of the Mystic High School Football Team; now he is reduced to dealing whiskey and ordering chemical toilets to accommodate the festival crowd. His sister's remark, "wish in one hand and shit in the other, see which fills up first" (173)—which appears in four other Crews works—crudely suggests the author's sense of humanity's duality, its longing for meaning and rootedness in a fallen world, which Joe Lon himself finally recognizes. His father's dogs, all named Tuffy, are trained by being strapped to a treadmill, and Joe Lon and his sister come to equate this cruelty with the human condition. The snakes, of course, are a traditional symbol of evil and, in this novel, of masculine power and threat. Joe Lon cannot find meaning in family, or friends, or community: "[I]t was not any one thing that scared him. It was everything. It was his life. . . . Everything seemed to be coming apart" (161–62). He comes to accept "for the first time in his life that things would not be different tomorrow. Or ever. Things got different for some people. But for some they did not. There were a lot of things you could do though. One of them was to go nuts trying to pretend things would someday be different. That was one of things he did not intend to do" (170). The morning after he experiences this insight, Joe Lon goes to the rodeo and shoots a preacher, his former girlfriend, the deputy sheriff, and a nameless member of the crowd before the mob throws him to his death in a snake pit. His targets reflect his view (and Crews's) that religion, love, law, and the crowd ultimately provide no meaning.

The late 1970s saw Crews turn briefly to nonfiction. *A Childhood: The Biography of a Place* is, in the opinion of most critics, his best work. Beautifully written and crafted, the book is a touching account of the first five brutal years of Crews's existence, and of life in the rural South during the late 1930s and early 1940s. Like *A Feast of Snakes* in the horrific black humor of some of the events it chronicles, *A Childhood* also describes poignantly and without sentimentality the hardscrabble life of farmers near the edge of ruin.

Blood and Grits contains essays Crews wrote as an *Esquire* columnist and a contributor to *Playboy*. Many of them—"Climbing the Tower" and "Carny," for example—offer straightforward statements about violence and freaks, and therefore lend important insights into his novels. "Climbing the Tower" recounts Crews's visit to the University of Texas at Austin, where the professor who invited Crews to read from his work pointed out the Texas Tower, from which in 1966 Charles Whitman shot and killed twelve people and wounded thirty-three others. Psychiatrists surmised that the brain tumor discovered during Whitman's autopsy may have caused the rampage, but Crews does not believe it: "What I know is that all over the surface of the earth where humankind exists men and women are resisting climbing the tower. All of us have a tower to climb. Some are worse than others, but to deny that you have your tower to climb and that you must resist or succumb to the temptation to do it, to deny that is done at the peril of your heart and mind" (213). In "Carny," Crews writes that after hearing a bearded lady and her husband—a man with a divided face—talking one day about eating dinner, he was "never the same again."

> I have never stopped remembering that as wondrous and special as those two people were, they were only talking about and looking forward to and needing precisely what all the rest of us talk about and look forward to and need. He might have been any husband going to any job anywhere. He just happened to have that divided face. That is not a very startling revelation, I know, but it is one most of us resist because we have that word *normal* and we can say we are normal because a psychological, sexual, or even spiritual abnormality can—with a little luck—be safely hidden from the rest of the world. (166)

Crews has said that, though he had hoped writing *A Childhood* would be "cathartic," it "took a lot out of me" ("An Interview with Harry Crews" 4). Indeed, eight years elapsed between its publication and that of *All We Need of Hell* (1987), his first novel in eleven years. The latter work recycles one of the relatively minor characters from *A Feast of Snakes*, Duffy Deeter, and although interesting and amusing for the first several chapters (which originally appeared six years earlier as the novella *The Enthusiast*), it ultimately collapses into sentimentality and narrative chaos.

The Knockout Artist (1988) and *Body* (1990) are both better novels. The former uses a glass-jawed boxer's extraordinary ability to knock himself out as a metaphor for humanity's willingness to punish and corrupt itself. Only through his relationship with an innocent Cajun fighter whom he agrees to manage does the boxer manage to redeem himself and reclaim some measure of self-respect. *Body* includes a character from *The Gypsy's Curse*, Russell "Muscle" Morgan, now the bodybuilding coach of Shereel Dupont, née

Dorothy Turnipseed. The novel satirizes the desire of contemporary men and women to remake themselves in a corrupt urban world, and calculates the painful expense of their attempts and ultimate failures. Russell has forced Dorothy Turnipseed (a name reeking of "grit") to change her name to one incorporating the supposedly urbane "Dupont" (associated with corporate wealth), and "Shereel," foregrounding her femaleness and cinematic perfection (but with a hint of cinematic fakery, as she is not "real"). Scott Romine argued convincingly in "Home and Sport in *A Feast of Snakes* and *Body*" that Shereel's chance to become somebody, a "worldbeater," via bodybuilding,

> involves the implicit premise that "the world"—conceived as such and not just a collection of opponents—can, like those opponents, be beaten. Thus, while the game permits competition that is "pure" and "clean," winning extends beyond the game to invoke metonymically a kind of mastery over the world. Such, at least, is the game's utopian aspect, which Crews ruthlessly deconstructs. (128)

Scar Lover (1992) has its critical fans, particularly Robert C. Covel, who calls the novel a "radical departure from Crews's earlier novels" because in it "he suggests, for the first time, the possibility of a catharsis that moves beyond violence and toward more constructive human interrelationships" (83). This "catharsis" involves the acceptance of one's own literal and metaphorical scars and those of others, no matter how repugnant they may appear. This is, however, a view that Crews stated less sentimentally in earlier novels and in the essay "Carny."

The Mulching of America (1995) is an embarrassing work, a largely unfunny satire of America's desire for material success, while Crews's *Celebration* (1998) chronicles the effect of a beautiful blonde, Too Much, on a Florida trailer park filled with the dying aged. While the novel returns to the subject of *This Thing Don't Lead to Heaven* and its concentration on our fear of and consequent despair about the fact that we must die, it is less fragmented than that work.

Crews said early in his career, "I always wanted twenty titles because I thought if you did . . . if you wrote as well as you could and as honestly as you could and with as much concentration, focus, diligence . . . as you could, well, then, out of twenty you might get a good one" ("Harry Crews: An Interview," *GT* 151). He got more than those twenty titles and at least four "good ones," by my count. His works are powerful tales of a world by turns violent and brutal, dangerous and darkly comic, filled with characters who are literally or metaphorically grotesque, yet whose despair and pain, need and desire frequently inspire sympathy.

Works Cited

Covel, Robert C. "The Violent Bear It as Best They Can: Cultural Conflict in the Novels of Harry Crews." *Studies in the Literary Imagination* 27.2 (Fall 1994): 75–86. Print.

Crews, Harry. "Andrew Lytle." *Rolling Stone* 367 (15 April 1982): 58. Print.

———. *Blood and Grits*. New York: Harper & Row, 1979. Print.

———. *A Childhood: The Biography of a Place*. New York: Harper & Row, 1978. Print.

———. *A Feast of Snakes*. New York: Atheneum, 1976. Print.

———. *The Gospel Singer*. New York: William Morrow, 1968. Print.

———. *The Gypsy's Curse*. New York: Knopf, 1974. Print.

———. "Harry Crews: An Interview." Interview by David K. Jeffrey and Donald R. Noble. Jeffrey 140–51. Print.

———. "Harry Crews: An Interview." Interview by David K. Jeffrey and Donald R. Noble. *Southern Quarterly* 19 (1981): 65–79. Print.

———. "An Interview with Harry Crews." Interview by Dinty W. Moore. *AWP Chronicle* 24.4 (Feb. 1992): 1–4. Print.

———. *Naked in Garden Hills*. New York: William Morrow. 1969. Print.

———. "Television's Junkyard Dog." *Blood and Grits* 134–51. Print.

Guinn, Matthew. "The Grit Émigré in Harry Crews' Fiction." *Perspectives on Harry Crews*. Ed. Erik Bledsoe. Jackson: UP of Mississippi, 2001. 105–15. Print.

Jeffrey, David K., ed. *A Grit's Triumph: Essays on the Works of Harry Crews*. Port Washington: Associated Faculty P, 1983.

Noble, Donald R. "Harry Crews Introduces Himself." Jeffrey 7–20. Print.

Romine, Scott. "Home and Sport in *A Feast of Snakes* and *Body*." *Perspectives on Harry Crews*. Ed. Erik Bledsoe. Jackson: UP Mississippi, 2001. 117–32. Print.

Shelton, Frank W. "Harry Crews: Man's Search for Perfection." *Southern Literary Journal* 12 (1980): 97–113. Print.

———. "Theme and Technique in Harry Crews' *Car*." Jeffrey 124–31. Print.

Elevated above the Real:
The Poor White Southerner in
Cormac McCarthy's Early Novels

Marcus Hamilton

IN *The Tennessee Encyclopedia of History and Culture*, Robert Benson praises Cormac McCarthy for his vivid and honest portrayal of east Tennessee and its people—the lower classes in particular. He argues that "no writer, not even Faulkner or Flannery O'Connor, to whom [McCarthy] is often compared, has written better dialogue or realized more vividly the character of the plain folk of his region" (582). The claim is high praise, especially as earlier critics, making similar comparisons, often found McCarthy lacking. The *Times Literary Supplement*'s anonymous review of his first novel, *The Orchard Keeper* (1965), for instance, suggested that McCarthy "ha[s] it in him to write a much better novel than this: but he will not do so while he confuses his Tennessee with Yoknapatawpha County" ("Americans in Debt" 185).

Such comparisons, however, tend to obscure the unique power of McCarthy's fiction and dismiss rather than highlight its divergence from southern literary tradition. Benson's implicit defense acknowledges clearly what sets McCarthy apart from southern writers of earlier generations: his almost exclusive focus on representing—in fine, though often disturbing detail—the material and spiritual deprivations of the most destitute inhabitants of the lower-class South. In fact, Benson goes on to argue that McCarthy not only accurately represents the speech and character of the "plain folk" of east Tennessee, but "without sentimentality or condescension . . . brings mountain people to life, rendering their cautious reserve, their dignity and resignation flawlessly" (582). Benson therefore accurately characterizes McCarthy's work as a critical shift in the representation of lower-class characters in southern literature. With the exception of a few minor characters, his first three novels—*The Orchard Keeper, Outer Dark* (1968), and *Child of God* (1973)—rarely even include middle- and upper-class characters, and on the rare occasions that they do appear, they are generally cold, unsympathetic, and/or morally repugnant.

This focus on exploring and illuminating the lives of those often called "white trash" suggests a direct and important link between McCarthy's work of the 1960s and early '70s and the work of later southern writers invested in recovering the poor white southerner from the margins of literary representation. Filmmaker Gary Hawkins has called these authors, most of whom came to prominence in the 1980s, writers of the Rough South. Erik Bledsoe, in "The Rise of Southern Redneck and White Trash Writers," finds their collective aim the subversion of the negative, condescending, paternalistic stereotypes traditionally applied to lower-class southerners. If we take Benson at his word that McCarthy reforms the literary treatment of this spurned demographic, McCarthy is the unambiguous and indisputable forefather of this late twentieth-century movement. It does not hurt, either, that Larry Brown, a central figure in the movement, considered McCarthy his "favorite living writer" and "probably the greatest living writer we've got" (47).

And yet, for several reasons, McCarthy's connection to later Rough South writers is decidedly complex. Unlike "true" Rough South writers, McCarthy was born in New England, grew up part of the middle-class family of a Yale-educated lawyer in Knoxville, Tennessee, and attended the University of Tennessee (though he failed to complete a degree). As his semi-autobiographical novel *Suttree* (1979) implies, though, McCarthy was well acquainted with Knoxville's seedy underbelly and hardly a stranger to the Rough South. For much of his adult life, in fact, he subsisted on grant money and odd jobs, refusing the speaking engagements that might have afforded him a reprieve from the decidedly primitive life that—unlike his protagonists (save Cornelius Suttree)—he apparently chose to lead.

But while McCarthy's biographical divergence from the Rough South bears notice—particularly when considering his treatment of lower- and middle-class interactions in later works like *The Gardener's Son* (1977/1996) and *Suttree*—the potentially troubling content of his early southern novels demands more attention. Indeed, Benson's unqualified praise for McCarthy's treatment of east Tennesseans might strike some as rather odd. Readers unfamiliar with his work might be shocked to find that McCarthy's east Tennesseans commit murder, necrophilia, and incest; hump watermelons; consume human flesh; and generally live to violent excess in every way imaginable (and some ways previously unimaginable). McCarthy occasionally counters these grotesque, violent figures with images of simple hospitality and genuine human warmth, but these moments are rare and do little to dispel the unmistakable cloud of violence and depravity that pervades his early fiction.

Unsurprisingly, not all critics have been as quick as Benson to praise McCarthy's portrayal of lower-class southern whites. Duane Carr, in "The Dispossessed White as Naked Ape and Stereotyped Hillbilly in the Southern Novels of Cormac McCarthy," charges the author with capitulating to outdated stereotypes: "The poorest of working-class whites . . . in southern literature . . . have been most often depicted, from William Byrd in the eighteenth century to Cormac McCarthy in our own, as simple-minded, shiftless, lazy and violent—a subspecies to be detested and ridiculed or, on rare occasions, felt sorry for" (3). Carr finds that "many of [McCarthy's] characterizations are neither sympathetic nor dispassionate, as has been claimed, but rather some of the most blatant stereotypes of Southern 'rednecks' in contemporary American fiction" (9). Carr is of course accurate in noting that McCarthy populates his southern novels with violent and morally reprehensible lower-class whites, and that together with his descriptions of the landscape they constitute a disconcerting vision of the South. But to take McCarthy's early novels as mimetic is to commit a fundamental mistake. Despite his darkly amoral vision, McCarthy powerfully distances himself from earlier southern authors and meaningfully prefigures the rehabilitative work of Rough South writers through a mythorealist style that in his first three novels blurs the line between realism and a Gothic, allegorical, and mythic aesthetic.[1] While this often unsettling combination culminates in *Child of God*'s treatment of Lester Ballard as both individual and symbolic everyman, *The Orchard Keeper* and *Outer Dark* also reveal similarly difficult experiments in the overlapping of these narrative modes. In all three novels, the intrusion of the mythic into the real complicates superficial criticism of McCarthy's portrayal of the lower-class white and reveals the subtle but critical identification with and compassion for the lower classes that undergird his fiction.

In *The Orchard Keeper*, a novel whose disjointed and indeterminate narrative structure and mythic overtones continue to divide critics, McCarthy introduces three primary characters: John Wesley Rattner, a young man who lives in poverty with his mother after the death of his father, Kenneth; Marion Sylder, a bootlegger who becomes an unlikely father figure to John Wesley; and Arthur Ownby, an old man who lives alone on a decrepit orchard. Temporally ambiguous and narratively complex, *The Orchard Keeper* traces the unexpected and sometimes inexplicable circumstances that connect these men as they traverse the land around Red Branch, Tennessee. McCarthy employs three primary techniques to lend the novel its mythorealist coherence: juxtaposition of realist and symbolic descriptions of the landscape; disjointed and initially opaque connections among John Wesley, Sylder, and Ownby that later unfold with an air of mythic inevitability; and the elevation of Ownby to the level of mythic symbol.

McCarthy highlights the symbolic resonance of the landscape by italicizing the novel's seemingly atemporal opening passage, in which two men cut down a tree only to find that a fence has *"growed all through"* it (3). While this image might seem a none-too-subtle symbol of modern civilization's intrusion into the pure, pastoral South, images of natural decay abound. Shortly thereafter we read, "Clay cracks and splits in endless microcataclysm and the limestone lies about the eroded land like schools of sunning dolphin, gray channeled backs humped at the infernal sky" (11). These images constitute a less than benevolent view of the natural world that subsumes the real landscape of east Tennessee. The landscape is therefore both the east Tennessee of McCarthy's childhood and, at the same time, a mythic space.

The narrative drive of *The Orchard Keeper* is still more mythic. Though McCarthy initially obscures from both readers and characters the ways in which Kenneth Rattner's murder will inevitably draw John Wesley, Sylder, and Ownby together, the quickly unfolding plot signals these mythic connections even before Rattner dies. As Sylder and his friend June Tipton at one point drive over the mountain, for instance, "[f]rom his porch Arthur Ownby had watched them pass and now he heard the slam of the car door up the road where they had stopped" (20). In fact, Sylder will continue to frequent this spot, as it is key to his bootlegging operation. And just after Sylder and Ownby's near miss on the mountain, the narrator reveals that John Wesley, walking along the same road, "looked up at the house on the sidehill, dark and abandoned-looking. He could not see the old man and the old man was asleep" (21). So even before the revelation of the death that will bring these characters together, McCarthy sets up a tight narrative structure that unfolds with a distinct sense of the predetermined and uncanny. This air of mythic inevitability stretches the bounds of realism and transforms John

Wesley, Sylder, and Ownby into chess pieces guided by narrative necessity more than individual agency.

As we soon learn, these connections trace a vaguely Oedipal trajectory, when Sylder, picking up the hitchhiking Rattner, kills him in self-defense. Immediately afterward, Ownby discovers a corpse in his orchard's spray pit—though the novel does not reveal it as Rattner's until much later. In the ensuing narrative, Sylder becomes an ironic father figure to the now father-less John Wesley, as Ownby stands ritualistic guard over the corpse: "These six years past [the pit] had served as a crypt which the old man kept and guarded" (52). Later, Ownby also becomes something of a grandfather figure to John Wesley. While McCarthy's narrative style may initially appear hazy and disconnected, the plot's quasi-mythic structure creates a dream-like co-herence of narrative inevitability.

It is particularly significant that—except for Sylder, whose bootlegging has earned him newfound and most likely temporary wealth—nearly all the characters in *The Orchard Keeper* are assuredly lower class. While McCarthy does address their material deprivation—the Rattners, for instance, "paid no tax on [their house], for it did not exist in the county courthouse records" (63)—he defines them not by their poverty, but by their participation in a drama that examines the nature of guilt, loyalty, and circumstance against the backdrop of Red Branch, Tennessee.

While Sylder and John Wesley remain partially rooted in the realist tradition, McCarthy elevates Ownby to the level of symbol. In addition to stand-ing guard over Rattner's decaying corpse, Ownby is uniquely attuned to the seasons, a repository of ancient folklore and the ways of the mountains. As Stephen Frye suggests in *Understanding Cormac McCarthy*, Ownby is "the iconic representative of an old order, a time when survival, human happi-ness, even spiritual sustenance came from cultivating a synergistic relation-ship with the untamed wilderness" (24). Even a sunset becomes a spiritual experience for Ownby: "[B]ehind the old man's chair the sun lowered, casting his head in silhouette and illumining his white hair with a prophetic translu-cence" (150).

Ownby's attack on a nearby tank erected by the Tennessee Valley Author-ity further solidifies his symbolic status as symbol. Without explanation, he one night he makes his way up the mountain and dispassionately shoots an X into the tank, an act that later leads to a violent shootout with police and, eventually, to his arrest. Mirroring the opening image of the fence grown into the tree, this symbolic act reveals how Ownby exists as a mythic relic of a bygone era, a mouthpiece for a nostalgic view of the pastoral South fighting the incursion of modern civilization. After they arrest him, authorities hand

Ownby over to a social worker, to whose questions he meets with responds with increasingly elliptical answers and blank stares. Soon fed up, Ownby tells the young man that he could consider his questions later, for "I ain't goin nowhere" (222). McCarthy then makes Ownby's estrangement from the bureaucratic world still more apparent: "[H]e sat very still with his hands on his knees, his shaggy head against the bricks, restored to patience and a look of tried and inviolate sanctity . . . and the old man felt the circle of years closing, the final increment of the curve returning him again to the inchoate, the prismatic flux of sound and color wherein he had drifted once before and now beyond the world of men" (222). McCarthy elevates and valorizes Ownby as symbolic of an older order, offering both a humanizing and mythic portrait of the lower-class southern white.

Despite the novel's juxtaposition of real and mythic, critics remain divided as to whether *The Orchard Keeper* reaches the mythic level of McCarthy's later novels, particularly *Outer Dark*. Like *The Orchard Keeper*, *Outer Dark* imbues a savagely beautiful landscape with deep symbolic resonance and—even more than McCarthy's first novel—elevates its impoverished characters above the real. Critics often cite *Outer Dark*'s utter lack of clear temporal and spatial markers as a feature that complicates a reading of the novel as a realistic depiction of early twentieth-century Tennessee, but the novel balances real and mythic in other significant ways.

In a nod to epic convention, *Outer Dark* opens *in medias res* as the impoverished Rinthy Holme is about to give birth to her brother Culla's child. Culla, consumed by guilt for his moral transgression and lacking the resources to prepare for the birth, takes the child into the woods, where he abandons it. Coincidentally, a tinker who had stopped by the cabin just before the birth later finds the baby and takes it. Culla, upon returning, tells Rinthy the baby died, but she does not believe him and sets out through the woods, alone and penniless, to recover her son. Culla soon follows. From this premise proceed two parallel narratives chronicling each sibling's separate travels.

As in *The Orchard Keeper*, *Outer Dark*'s mythorealist style emerges early, through the juxtaposition of dream-like imagery and gritty detail. Culla's dreams, nearly always haunted by guilt and retribution, encourage readers to see him as more symbolic than real. In his first dream, a few days before Rinthy gives birth, he finds himself in a crowd watching a prophet:

> The sun hung on the cusp of eclipse and the prophet spoke to them. This hour the sun would darken and all these souls would be cured of their afflictions before it appeared again. And the dreamer himself was caught up among the supplicants and when they had been blessed and the sun begun

to blacken he did push forward and hold up his hand and call out. Me, he
cried. Can I be cured? (5)

The dream's symbolic imagery bleeds into the waking world as Rinthy shakes
Culla awake "from dark to dark, delivered out of the clamorous rabble under
a black sun and into a night more dolorous" (5). *Outer Dark*, as its title indicates, abounds with vaguely Christian images of retribution and salvation;
the phrase "outer dark" itself comes from Matthew 25:30 and is often taken as
a reference to hell or to the last judgment. But throughout *Outer Dark*, Mc-
Carthy presents separation from grace as a precondition of human existence.

Though not precisely allegorical—the novel lacks the consistent and fixed
symbolic structure that defines true allegory—the pervasive use of such elemental imagery lends the novel a distinctly mythic quality that, despite the
detailed landscape, is rarely fixed in time and space. McCarthy strengthens
this mythic quality by declining to provide information about Culla and
Rinthy's past—not even about what circumstances preceded their child's
birth. When we first encounter the couple in their small, primitive cabin, it is
as if they live in a timeless hothouse of incestuous isolation.

And yet, McCarthy simultaneously emphasizes the gritty reality of their
impoverished lives. Take, for instance, the gruesome birth scene, during
which Culla momentarily thinks Rinthy dead. She lies on the bare floor,
"looking up with eyes that held nothing at all. Then her body convulsed and
she screamed. He struggled with her, lifting her to the bed again. The head
had broken through in a pumping welter of blood. . . . With his own hand
he brought it free, the scrawny body trailing the cord in anneloid writhing
down the bloodslimed covers, a beetcolored creature that looked to him like
a skinned squirrel" (14). Noting that Culla and Rinthy have no wood for a fire
and no money for even the most basic medical care, McCarthy further emphasizes the hardships of poverty.

Again, however, McCarthy complicates such realistic detail by imbuing
Rinthy with mythic subtext and portraying her as an innocent, childlike Madonna. After realizing that Culla has lied about the child's death, Rinthy sets
out "humming softly to herself . . . turning her face up to the sky and bestow-
ing upon it a smile all bland and burdenless as a child's" (53), an image made
still more innocent when she rests along the road she rests in the home of
a hospitable family: "She laid her bundle down on the bed . . . holding the
lamp votively before her. . . . She watched the ground, going with care, the
basin upright and riding her hip, slowly, processional, a lone acolyte passing
across the barren yard, face seized in the light she bore" (62–63). Despite the
incest at the heart of the tale, the religious imagery is difficult to miss. Mc-

Carthy further emphasizes Rinthy's role as innocent wanderer when, late in the novel, she says, "I don't live nowheres no more. . . . I never did much. I just go around huntin my chap. That's about all I do any more" (156). Rinthy herself seems to imply that she's trapped in a symbolic narrative; unlike a fully-formed person, she exists as a mythorealist symbol whose only function is to "hunt her chap," to stand in for some powerful though perverse vision of motherhood. In fact, near the novel's close, having returned to her home without the child, she directly confronts this narrative inevitability. "She did not know that she was leaving. She woke in the night and rose half tranced from the bed and began to dress, all in darkness and with gravity" (211), as if compelled by some uncontrollable force of narrative or myth to do so.

Again, however, McCarthy sets this mythic symbolism against references to her abject poverty and bodily necessities. In addition to her need for food and water, Rinthy's dual material/spiritual nature emerges most directly in references to the breast milk that often leaks through her ragged clothing. A doctor expresses shock upon learning that, after six months of separation, she still produces milk. Rinthy, however, takes it as a sign that her child still lives: "The doctor leaned back. You couldn't still have milk after six months. If he was dead. That's what you said wasn't it? She was leaning forward in the chair watching him. That means he ain't, don't it? That means he ain't dead or I'd of gone dry" (154). The product of a perverse Madonna, Rinthy's continued supply of breast milk symbolizes both motherhood and the endless search for her child, while simultaneously emphasizing her embodiment, her fundamental reality.

While Rinthy is welcomed by hospitable strangers and described in quasi-spiritual terms, Culla, dogged by crimes he did not commit, encounters the judgment, casting out, and subsequent "gnashing of teeth" that conclude the parable from Matthew. At one point Culla enters a small town where several graves have been robbed. As the townspeople turn to look at him, silently suspecting the poor, primitive-looking stranger, he begins to run. Again, the symbolic representation of sin subsumes the very real circumstances of his predicament: "He went faster. With full dark he was confused in a swampy forest, floundering through sucking quagmires and half running. . . . He followed it down, in full flight now, the trees beginning to close him in, malign and baleful shapes that reared like enormous androids provoked at the alien insubstantiality of this flesh colliding among them" (16–17). Ignoring such symbolism would make of Culla only another poor, shiftless hill-dweller who, also having committed incest, embodies perhaps the worst of southern stereotypes. Considered amid the context of his mythic journey toward salvation, however, his flight into the dark swamp, with its malignantly conscious plant life, elevates him to symbolic level.

More than even *The Orchard Keeper*, *Outer Dark* suffuses its landscape, characters, and plot with a mythic quality—which becomes still more apparent when a third narrative thread intrudes. In addition to Culla and Rinthy's parallel narratives, short italicized chapters trace the movements of a grim trio of primitive murderers called the triune. These chapters, one of which opens the novel, double down on McCarthy's ambiguous mythorealist style, and at the same time detail the violent crimes these men commit while traveling sometimes ahead of, sometimes behind Culla. While the triune appears throughout the novel—often crossing Culla's path long enough to commit the crimes that make him suspect—McCarthy indicates their mythic qualities most clearly in the novel's haunting conclusion, in which they appear in a dream-like manner, in true mythorealist fashion: "They wore the same clothes, sat in the same attitudes, endowed with a dream's redundancy" (231). For readers who do not yet apprehend this mythorealist style, McCarthy next describes the three as "like revenants that reoccur in lands laid waste with fever: spectral, palpable as stone" (231). In a perverse parody of the Holy Trinity, McCarthy elevates the triune from grotesque villains to symbols of divine retribution.

The scene returns, if only briefly, to real-world violence, revealing that the triune has the long-lost infant, now "naked and half coated with dust so that it seemed lightly furred" (231). Then, in a moment of gruesome horror, the infant is finally killed, completing the inevitable narrative trajectory that refuses to let Culla escape his symbolic crime. "Holme saw the blade wink in the light like a long cat's eye slant and malevolent and a dark smile erupted on the child's throat and went all broken down the front of it. The child made no sound. It hung there with its one eye glazing over like a wet stone and the black blood pumping down its naked belly." The mythorealism that pervades the novel, however, quickly overpowers the grim reality of the murder when one of the triune "looked once at Holme with witless eyes, and buried his moaning face in [the infant's] throat" (236). In this final moment of ritualistic sacrifice, the symbolic thrust of divine retribution wholly subsumes Rinthy's realistic journey to recover the child.

Rinthy's mythic narrative ends shortly thereafter. As in *The Orchard Keeper*, McCarthy concludes in distinctly anti-realist fashion as Rinthy, Culla, and the triune appear at the same undisclosed spot at nearly the same time. Rinthy retains the symbolic air that follows her throughout: "And stepping softly with her air of blooded ruin about the glade in a frail agony of grace she trailed her rags through dust and ashes" (237). Culla, similarly ends his journey in mythic terms as he walks down the road "soundless with his naked feet, shambling, gracelorn, down out of the peaceful mazy fields" where "the road went on through a shadeless burn and for miles there were only the charred shapes of trees in a dead land where nothing moved" (241–42).

A positive portrait of east Tennessee this is not, but to argue that we can or should judge McCarthy's repugnant characters as meaningfully connected to actual poor white southerners is wholly inappropriate. The South functions as but the nominal setting of this ahistorical and symbolic examination of guilt and salvation that draws some of its power from gritty realism, but is ultimately uninterested in such detail in and of itself. McCarthy ultimately avoids stereotypes by elevating lower-class southerners to the level of universal symbols, while treating their very real material deprivations seriously.

Because the protagonist of McCarthy's next novel, *Child of God*, so often tests the limits of human sympathy, it might seem difficult to attribute the book's horrific violence to mythorealism. The gritty detail with which McCarthy describes the crimes of Lester Ballard would in the hands of lesser writers likely be accompanied by condemnations of his actions. Instead, in a passage that continues to challenge readers and critics, McCarthy suggests in the opening chapter that Ballard is "small, unclean, unshaven. . . . A child of God much like yourself perhaps" (4). Though Ballard is thereby elevated as a universal symbol of human depravity, *Child of God* is a more realist work than its predecessors. In it, for the first time, McCarthy in many ways elucidates the crimes of his protagonist. While the absence of history for Rinthy and Culla in *Outer Dark* encourages symbolic or allegorical readings, *Child of God* more fully balances real and mythic—and with chilling results. Because of this doubleness, critics have wrestled with the degree to which we should sympathize with Ballard,[2] in part because his tragic history prevents the kind of unalloyed hatred and disgust his crimes would otherwise warrant. In other words, McCarthy forces us to consider Ballard as a both living, breathing human and a symbol of the most base desires and depraved potential within us all.

McCarthy offers a number of possible reasons for Ballard's crimes, among them his economic dispossession. The novel opens at an auction of Ballard's house, an event that clearly (and justifiably) troubles him. Seeing Ballard, the auctioneer calls out, "What do you want, Lester?" Ballard replies, "I want you to get your goddamn ass off my property. And take these fools with ye." After asking Ballard to watch his language, the auctioneer cautions him that he "done been locked up once over this" (7). Having nowhere else to go, Ballard holes up in a seemingly abandoned house until police arrest him for trespassing, again rendering him homeless.

McCarthy, however, offers a more thorough analysis of Ballard's development through short, first person narratives from unnamed townspeople. One takes us back to Ballard's school days, when he bullied another boy, telling him to retrieve a ball for him. When the boy refused, "he just stood there a minute and then [Ballard] punched him in the face." The unnamed speaker admits, "I never liked Lester Ballard from that day." But then again, he adds, "I never liked him much before that," even though "[h]e never done nothin to me" (18).

Given the encounters described in these first-person narratives, readers might be little surprised by Ballard's first foray into sex crimes. He approaches a car parked on Frog Mountain, finds an interracial couple having sex inside, and, leaning in to watch, "unbottomed, spent himself on the fender." When they notice him, he runs away, "a misplaced and loveless simian shape scuttling across the turnaround" (20). While Ballard's voyeurism is the least of his crimes, the description here suggests a kind of narrative sympathy—the sense that Ballard is not, at this point, evil, just "misplaced and loveless," a fate no reader would relish.

The next first-person chapter, which details his early family life, strengthens this sympathetic view. The narrator chronicles the breakdown of Ballard's parents' marriage and his father's suicide when Ballard was just nine years old. The chapter begins, "They say he never was right after his daddy killed hisself. They was just the one boy. The mother had run off, I don't know where to nor who with. . . . He come in the store and told it like you'd tell it was rainin out" (21). The narrator doesn't indicate whether we should take this information as a factor contributing to or an excuse for Ballard's subsequent behavior, or simply as another sad chapter in the story of a congenital sociopath. But since his father's suicide happened when Ballard was nine, we are called to reassess the story of his boyhood bullying and, by extension, his alienation as an adult.

McCarthy then stretches the reader's sympathy past the breaking point as Ballard's crimes escalate to include necrophilia. After finding a dead couple in the backseat of a car, he "undid his buckle and lowered his trousers. A crazed gymnast laboring over a cold corpse. He poured into that waxen ear everything he'd ever thought of saying to a woman" (88). Even in this most disturbing of scenes, McCarthy stings readers with the unexpected recognition of Ballard's loneliness, his utter inability to form a meaningful relationship. Even as Ballard's actions become increasingly grotesque, though, McCarthy does not treat him like the grim triune of *Outer Dark*: Where they seem elemental, Ballard remains real.

Events continue to degenerate as Ballard takes the woman's body home and attempts a domestic scene, even buying new clothing and makeup for the corpse. Perversely, McCarthy asks us to read the scene as a tender moment: "When he came back in he unbuckled his trousers and stepped out of them and laid next to her. He pulled the blanket over them" (92). Ballard later begins to "arrange her in different positions and go out and peer in the window at her" (103). McCarthy emphasizes that Ballard's actions aren't purely sexual; they're also social, and for that reason still more pitiable and bizarre. The scene then becomes even more bizarre as a massive house fire consumes Ballard's dead "girlfriend." In a piteously comic moment, he stands outside the burning building, holding a stuffed tiger he won at a carnival.

Ballard then embarks on a rapid series of violent crimes, among them murdering a young woman who has rejected his advances and setting her house on fire. Meanwhile, he also frequents his former home: "Ballard took to wandering over the mountain through the snow to his old homeplace where he'd watch the house, the house's new tenant. He'd go in the night and lie up on the bank and watch him through the kitchen window" (109). This voyeurism not only reminds us of Ballard's economic dispossession, but also allows McCarthy to delay revelation of even greater crimes. In another nod to epic convention, Ballard descends into mountain caves for refuge, and McCarthy finally reveals how Ballard's desire to dress up and perversely interact with his victims has escalated since fire destroyed his home. "Here in the bowels of the mountain Ballard turned his light on ledges or pallets of stone where dead people lay like saints" (135). The enormity of his crimes now revealed, Ballard's killing spree starts to unravel. After accosting a couple in a car parked on the mountain, he shoots the man, pulls the woman from their car, and then "laid the muzzle of the rifle at the base of her skull and fired. . . . He laid her down in the woods not fifty feet from the road and threw himself on her, kissing the still warm mouth and feeling under her clothes" (151). But here he makes a critical mistake: Though he leaves the man for dead, Ballard's victim is able to drive to town to initiate a hunt for his victimizer.

Knowing that authorities will organize a manhunt, Ballard returns to his cave, grabs what belongings he can, and runs until he nearly drowns in a rapidly rising creek. "He could not swim, but how would you drown him? His wrath seemed to buoy him up. . . . See him. You could say that he's sustained by his fellow men, like you. . . . But they want this man's life. He has heard them in the night seeking him with lanterns and cries of execration. How then is he borne up? Or rather, why will not these waters take him?" (156). In this stunning narrative shift, it is as if fate or even God speaks—it is a jarring break from the novel's generally realist style. The almost biblical flood that transpires while Ballard tries to escape further suggests the resonance of his descent into the underworld.

As the narrative turns to survey the flood damage in town, the narrator further emphasizes the now undeniably mythic overtones of Ballard's depravity. Lest we forget Ballard's status as "child of God," a local deputy surveying the damage asks a local man, "You think people was meaner then than they are now?" The old man replies, "No . . . I don't. I think people are the same from the day God first made one" (168). In a rather chilling way, considering Ballard's crimes in the context of original sin makes them seem less uniquely depraved and more symbolic of a universal human capacity for evil.

Just as Ballard reaches his full mythic potential, McCarthy returns to a more realist style that emphasizes his protagonist's economic dispossession and corporeality. Despite knowing that the authorities are after him, Ballard, desperately obsessed with avenge the loss of his home, goes back to his old house with a plan to murder the new tenant, John Greer. After hitting Greer with multiple shotgun blasts, Ballard is shocked to receive return fire and find "one arm flying out in a peculiar limber gesture, a faint pink cloud of blood and shredded clothing . . . amid the uproar" (173). He passes out from his injuries and later wakes at the county hospital, minus an arm. Ballard later wakes again to find a lynch mob in his room, asking for the location of his victims. He agrees to lead them to his underground mausoleum, but once he does so, he disappears deeper into the mountain, only to find himself trapped there for three days. Upon escaping, he slowly returns to the county hospital and casually tells a nurse, "I'm supposed to be here" (192).

To emphasize Ballard's essential humanity, McCarthy leaves us with the scene of his protagonist's dissection after he dies of pneumonia. The narrator notes that Ballard was "laid out on a slab and flayed, eviscerated, dissected. His head was sawed open and the brains removed. His muscles were stripped from his bones. His heart was taken out. His entrails were hauled forth and delineated and the four young students who bent over him like those haruspices of old perhaps saw monsters worse to come in their configurations" (194). McCarthy reduces Ballard to a body, the same body that we all share, in a final nod to his status as "child of God"—one "much like yourself perhaps." Significantly, the students find the "monsters worse to come" not in Ballard's tortured psyche, but in the physical structure of the human body. Because he identifies Ballard's everyman status at the level of both body and soul, McCarthy challenges and disturbs readers by carefully balancing mythic and realist techniques. In *Child of God*, even more than in *Outer Dark*, McCarthy raises (and lowers) his main character to the level of everyman. He becomes not just Lester Ballard the dispossessed, lower-class southerner, but Lester Ballard, symbol of the human capacity for unspeakable evil.

Once again, McCarthy's is no rosy image of the South or its lower classes. If anything, *Child of God*'s realism makes its violence and perspective on the human capacity for evil more shocking and affecting than those in *Outer Dark*. If we take McCarthy's lower-class white southerners as "children of God"—as perverse, latter-day everymen—we come to a much different conclusion about his representation of them than if we saw them as autonomous individuals with fully-formed subjectivities, whose motions indicate real life. Though McCarthy's lower-class white southerners commit violent and depraved acts, the way they function as symbolic children of God divorces their depravity from that of the real South they appear to inhabit. Characters like Arthur Ownby, *Outer Dark*'s triune, and Lester Ballard are presented as mythic symbols, while the landscape in each novel—particularly *The Orchard Keeper* and *Outer Dark*—has both realist and mythic qualities. William J. Schafer's "Cormac McCarthy: The Hard Wages of Original Sin" is accurate in arguing, "The tales spring from McCarthy's deep exploration of his home place—the Smoky Mountain basin southeast of Knoxville, Tennessee—*and* his intense imaginative preoccupation with the ramifications of evil" (105; emphasis added). Critically, Schafer acknowledges that these two elements are not necessarily related; instead, McCarthy's works grow as his setting collides with his interest in evil as a unifying thematic concern.

By employing such a style, of course, McCarthy risks denying his characters the individual sovereignty and subjectivity that would allow readers to consider them fully realized human beings, but it also elevates them as universal symbols. While we could surely argue over the success of this technique at fully casting off the shackles of paternalistic condescension traditionally evident in representations of the lower classes, McCarthy's application of mythorealist style to lower-class southern whites enables him to reclaim them from the trash heap of the "comic, villain, or victim" (Bledsoe 70). By taking their material and spiritual deprivations seriously—and at the same time elevating them to a level of mythic, allegorical, and/or symbolic resonance—McCarthy created an opening for later writers to examine the lives of lower-class southern whites in broader and more broadly positive ways.

Notes

1. Critics often comment upon this style, frequently disagreeing over the extent to which it is symbolic, mythic, allegorical, or some combination of the three. Georg Guillemin, in *The*

Pastoral Vision of Cormac McCarthy, for example, argues that McCarthy "is a storyteller in a parabolic sense. The secret of his symbolism is that it works not symbolically but allegorically" (10). John Cant, in *Cormac McCarthy and the Myth of American Exceptionalism*, on the other hand, suggests that myth is the defining feature of all McCarthy novels after *The Orchard Keeper*, for their characters have "characteristics [that] mark them out as mythic in the 'tall tale' American tradition" (66).

2. See in particular John Lang's "Lester Ballard: McCarthy's Challenge to the Reader's Compassion." *Sacred Violence: A Reader's Companion to Cormac McCarthy*. Ed. Wade Hall and Rick Wallach. El Paso: U of Texas—El Paso P, 1995. 87–101. Print.

Works Cited

"Americans in Debt." Rev. of *The Orchard Keeper*, by Cormac McCarthy. *Times Literary Supplement* 10 Mar. 1966: 185. Print.

Benson, Robert. "McCarthy, Cormac (1933–)." *The Tennessee Encyclopedia of History and Culture*. Ed. Carroll Van West et al. Nashville: Tennessee Historical Society and Rutledge Hill P, 1998. 581–82. Print.

Bledsoe, Erik. "The Rise of Southern Redneck and White Trash Writers." *Southern Cultures* 6.1 (2000): 68–90. Print.

Brown, Larry. "Interview with Larry Brown: Bread Loaf 1992." *Conversations with Larry Brown*. Ed. Jay Watson. Jackson: UP of Mississippi, 2007. 45–61. Print.

Cant, John. *Cormac McCarthy and the Myth of American Exceptionalism*. New York: Routledge, 2008. Print.

Carr, Duane R. "The Dispossessed White as Naked Ape and Stereotyped Hillbilly in the Southern Novels of Cormac McCarthy." *Midwest Quarterly* 40.1 (1998): 9–20. Print.

Frye, Steven. *Understanding Cormac McCarthy*. Columbia: U of South Carolina P, 2009. Print.

Guillemin, Georg. *The Pastoral Vision of Cormac McCarthy*. College Station: Texas A&M UP, 2004. Print.

McCarthy, Cormac. *Child of God*. 1973. New York: Vintage, 1993. Print.

———. *The Orchard Keeper*. 1965. New York: Vintage, 1993. Print.

———. *Outer Dark*. 1968. New York: Vintage, 1993. Print.

Schafer, William J. "Cormac McCarthy: The Hard Wages of Original Sin." *Appalachian Journal* 4 (1977): 105–19. Print.

Tim McLaurin: Universality
from Rural North Carolina

bes Stark Spangler

Timothy Reese McLaurin was born December 14, 1953, in Fayetteville, North Carolina. The second of Reese and Darlene McLaurin's six children, he spent his childhood in Beard, a small community on the outskirts of Fayetteville, where his father grew tobacco and raised livestock to supplement his earnings at a local bread company. Though the family rented a small house without indoor plumbing or central heat, Tim and his brothers enjoyed a compensating sense of freedom roaming the fields and woods nearby. These childhood explorations imbued McLaurin with a lifetime love of nature. Fascinated by the creatures he encountered while exploring, he became adept at handling snakes, a skill he would continue to cultivate. His sense of himself as part of the southern working class, with family and emotional roots in eastern North Carolina, firmly established itself during his childhood and adolescence and would last until the end of his relatively short life.

After graduating from Cape Fear Regional High School in 1972, McLaurin joined the Marine Corps. He returned to Fayetteville in 1975, married his high school sweetheart, and began collecting snakes and other exotic animals while working various short-term jobs—among them a stint as Wild

Man Mack, part of a carnival act known as the Last Great Snake Show (Mills, "Tim McLaurin" 274). Work as a reporter led him to enroll as a journalism major at North Carolina Central University, but he abandoned the effort in 1980. He soon divorced his first wife, remarried, and in 1981 traveled with his second wife to Tunisia as a Peace Corps volunteer.

Upon returning to the United States, the couple and their young daughter settled near Chapel Hill so McLaurin could attend the University of North Carolina, where in 1985 he earned a bachelor's degree in journalism. McLaurin also took creative writing courses at UNC and, encouraged by one instructor, Doris Betts, started writing narratives about the people and places he knew. In 1988 he published his first novel, *The Acorn Plan*; his second novel, *Woodrow's Trumpet*, followed in 1989. The reception these works received, and a teaching appointment at North Carolina State University, seemed to promise both financial security and recognition as an author, but before he had a chance to fully enjoy either, he was diagnosed with multiple myeloma.

After months of chemotherapy, McLaurin opted for a bone marrow transplant that allowed him—by then he was a father of two—to resume teaching and writing. He published a memoir, *Keeper of the Moon: A Southern Boyhood* (1991), and two more novels, *Cured by Fire* (1995) and *The Last Great Snake Show* (1997). In 1999, N C State awarded him a visiting assistant professorship. During the late 1990s, he struggled with alcoholism, a factor that contributed to ending his second marriage. Diagnosed with cancer of the esophagus, McLaurin continued to teach, publish, and deliver public readings, and in late 2000 he married for a third time. He died on July 11, 2002, and was buried on family land in Cumberland County, North Carolina ("Remembering Tim McLaurin").

Called a "Red-Neck Mystic" by his widow, Tim McLaurin produced works that reveal the artistry and vision of a Rough South writer who portrays, in the ordinary lives of North Carolinians, universal human stories. Conscious of language as an indicator of heritage and authenticity, he reproduces in his fiction the southern working-class speech he grew up hearing and speaking, but he is equally skilled at writing almost poetic prose. In his posthumously published novel, *Another Son of Man* (2004), for instance, the character Junuh remembers days in his childhood when "sunset was upon the water, the reed thickets like stalks of dried corn, the sky dappled with high clouds turning pink" (48).

McLaurin similarly yokes self and regional identity. Protagonists, often orphaned or reared by single parents, struggle to reconcile inherited identities and personal aspirations. *The Acorn Plan* foregrounds an identity crisis in the life of twenty-two-year-old Billy Riley, son of a local World War II hero whose rise from mill worker to mill manager led to an early death from a heart attack. Billy returns home after a stint in the Marine Corps to resume his role as a Riley, but feels despondent and claustrophobic walking familiar streets lined with houses that seem to express the lost dreams of their inhabitants. Ultimately, to avoid coming to terms with his heritage and future, Billy gives up the wild ways he has resumed. With the help of his lawyer, a family friend, he accepts work in a pet store.

Still troubled by the question of identity, which he believes a matter of chance, Billy meets a young topless dancer determined to make her way to New York, where she anticipates having a career in ballet. As they sit talking under a large oak tree one afternoon, she challenges Billy's fatalism by reminding him that though some acorns fail to germinate, others become trees and produce more acorns. Offering Billy this cyclical "acorn plan," she leaves town soon thereafter to "germinate." Billy comes to recognize that regardless of the degree to which his background has shaped him, he can reject the limitations inherent in his perceived local identity; loyal to but not owned by his heritage, he can risk attending the university that has accepted his application.

Identity looms large in McLaurin's second novel as well, but more as a regional than an individual concern. Having often voiced opposition to the influx of educated professionals in eastern North Carolina's Research Triangle, McLaurin makes land development the central issue of *Woodrow's Trumpet*. He also introduces the first of his innocents—characters, often simple-minded, whose goodness makes them vulnerable. In this novel, Woodrow's innocence (he is a man who does not need a mirror to know himself) cannot survive the modern world of suburban housing developments. His habit of roaming a local wooded ridge, blowing his trumpet and calling his hounds, has been accepted by residents of Oak Hills and the surrounding area, all of whom know he's the brother of the area's two largest landowners.

When Woodrow creates a beach, complete with palm tree, swimming pool, imported white sand, and plastic pink flamingoes for Nadean, a young African American woman and former drug addict for whom he feels love and compassion, his new neighbors protest. The question of property rights evolves into a countywide conflict about whether homeowners can display on their property anything they choose, or whether the community should designate a standard. The new residents win the vote, and in their haste to get rid of the unsightly palm, two neighbors try to cut it down. A local veteran, angry to see power passing to outsiders, opposes them, and as a skirmish develops in Woodrow's yard, Nadean grabs the veteran's gun to prevent accidental injury or death. It discharges, mortally wounding her.

McLaurin narrates much of the novel through the eyes of Ellis McDonald, an orphan, small for his age, who runs away but returns to Oak Hills and moves in with Woodrow and Nadean while completing high school. Somewhat like Melville's Ishmael, Ellis alone remains to tell the tale. Late in the novel, having chosen the life of a wanderer, he passes through Oak Hills one final time, noting additions to the development. He blows Woodrow's trumpet, then lays it on Nadean's grave. With its haunting overtones, the novel reflects the all too real demise of the region's traditions and inhabitants, a process McLaurin found distressing, for customs, like language, contribute to regional identity.

In his third book, the memoir *Keeper of the Moon*, McLaurin frames his recollections with a river journey. Beginning with the final night of a one-hundred-mile canoe trip down the Neuse River, he recalls earlier times on the waterway and youthful experiences with his family and friends in and around Fayetteville. As is true of all memoirs, recollection joins imagination, and he dramatizes such family scenes as a typical Thanksgiving dinner and a local cockfight (justified by rooster owners as no worse than deer hunting). Written soon after McLaurin's bone marrow transplant, the book balances dramatic scenes with descriptive detail, evoking a palpable sense of time and place, as in the passage describing a walk with his father from their house to the barn the night they saved a piglet's life:

> I walked beside my father in the orb of light from the lantern. A waning
> moon was already high in the sky, and an owl hooted from the top of a pine
> at the wood's edge. . . . Cows were huddled near the barn, the hogs were
> sleeping in layers under shelter. We stooped and entered the door of the
> birthing shed. I spied the sow lying on her side in a bed of straw. Her belly
> rose rapidly with short breaths. The glow of the lantern reflected off walls
> and tin roof and lit the shed in a pale yellow glow. (99)

Such memories of his early years give clear evidence of McLaurin's talent as a writer and his awareness of life's fragility.

In 1995, McLaurin published *Cured by Fire*, a technically ambitious novel organized into sections titled "Spark," "Flames," "Inferno," "Ashes," and "Phoenix." These five sections advance both literally and symbolically through flashbacks experienced by two main characters, who relate their respective trials by fire. Beginning in the present, as they rest together under the stars, awaiting dawn. This event foreshadows the final moment of the novel, when Elbridge Snipes will die a peaceful death, and Lewis Calhoon will rise from the "ashes" and return home. The forward movement of the sections and flashbacks reinforces thematically the cyclical nature of time. The narratives reveal that both men were branded with negative labels as children: Snipes felt the sting of being called a "half-breed nigger bastard" (32), while Calhoon absorbed taunts of "white trash" (45). Both men rise above these labels—and both men fall, unwittingly contributing to their wives' deaths. Their losses bring religion to the foreground of the novel, tying fire to redemption. Horribly scarred by the fire that almost claimed his life, Calhoon literally foregoes his humanity by allowing himself to be displayed as a "freak" in a carnival side show (186); he travels west, hoping that an unfamiliar setting and his daily dose of vodka will help him erase memories.

Elbridge's Christian faith and practice become so unbearable for his wife that she begins to drink excessively. When she fails to put out a cigarette and accidentally sets fire to the bedroom where she and their children sleep, Elbridge travels west in the belief that God is sending him to rescue someone to make amends for failing to save his family.

The two men come to recognize their shared humanity as they talk and comfort one another in a Seattle hospital. Near death, Elbridge yearns to see mourning doves, which he associates with his Kentucky home and his grandfather's love. The night vigil is Calhoon's gift to Elbridge, for they await dawn and the doves. Calhoon, however, has received the greater gift in the restoration of his humanity. He will rise from the ashes of his despair and return to North Carolina and his young daughter.

Two years after *Cured by Fire*, McLaurin again set characters on the road. *The Last Great Snake Show* begins in North Carolina, where Darlene Murphy's House of Joy brings pleasure-seeking members of Wilmington's newly established movie industry to see Gloria Peacock, an African American striptease dancer, and Jubal Lee, a local snake handler. Darlene's long-time suitor and friend, Clinton Tucker, a retired army captain called "Cappy," believes that "these customers are getting stranger all the time. Perverted. Damned country is getting like Rome before the fall" (10). After a tornado destroys the House of Joy and leaves Darlene with an inoperable sliver of glass working its way into her brain, the motley group decides to travel to Oregon, where Darlene hopes to die and be buried on land she owns. Traveling in an old school bus called the Jubilee Express, they begin their odyssey, soon discovering a stowaway who calls herself Kitty. As Kitty secretly calls her housekeeper, readers learn that Kitty is actually Cornelia Monroe, daughter of a prominent Wilmington developer, and is running away from an impending socially acceptable marriage. Kitty adds a romantic thread to the novel, for she and Jubal will fall in love along the journey.

True to epic form, McLaurin both develops relationships among travelers and exposes them to adventures that allow him to satirize much of American culture. The two threads come together here as the travelers, confronting the ways people try to take advantage of them, learn more about themselves and the values associated with their North Carolina heritage. Darlene is close to death when they reach Oregon, but she and Cappy marry before she dies. A near drowning, during which the remaining four "save" one another, cements the relationship among the four. As they turn to the east, Cappy tells them,

> [H]ome is changing, and for the worse, I think. You have a proud heritage, and you can't be the generation to lose it. The South has her problems, but Goddamn, she's clung together through it all. She's stood because of a mixture of people thrown in together with dirt under their fingernails and clay on their soles. The future ain't pretty little white subdivisions and black housing projects. (221)

Cappy speaks for McLaurin, who continues to dramatize various ways in which the old gives way to the new. He never produces local color fiction, exaggerating to support myths positive and negative. McLaurin's narratives, focusing instead on working-class townspeople or small farmers and rural inhabitants, confront complex conflicts and dramatize the necessity of coming to terms with one's self, one's identity, a necessity not only for his characters, but for himself—as his second memoir, *The River Less Run* (2000), reveals. Whereas *Keeper of the Moon* is episodic and descriptive, this record is more meditative. In it, McLaurin has already begun treatment for his second bout with cancer and is determined to spend time with his family and friends while he is still strong. He embarks on a personal odyssey of sorts, as he, his two children, his mother, his brother Bruce, and his brother-in-law Donnie travel west in a Winnebago.

Having two weeks to visit points of interest, they drive by historic sites, stop at campgrounds, interact with other travelers, share conversations, recollect past events, and admire the landscape through the windows of their vehicle. As the title suggests, this memoir is associated with a river, itself an image of time. Driving through Montana, McLaurin thinks of how ironic it is that he has recently bought a house in Hillsborough—something he had sworn never to do—but now believes that the purchase is "right for now, and now is all of existence" (83). Earlier in the narrative he acknowledges, "I have already opened so many doors, and now I am content to circle through the rooms I already know" (14). Near the end of the book, he recounts a reading he delivered in a private home in California. Always nervous when reading publicly, he anticipates that the questioners will be so unfamiliar with his southern speech and background that he will be hard put to explain them. Deciding to bypass such questions, he simply says, "I write to understand my own existence, rather than to help others understand" (218).

In 2000 McLaurin completed two major works. In addition to his memoir, he published the dramatic narrative poem *Lola*. Divided into five sections, the poem is occasioned by the burial of John Wesley Stewart. Lola is another of McLaurin's innocents, the "touched one born from an ancient womb," and her memories are of "love and the companionship she shared with her father in their understanding of the natural world" (Mills, "Tim McLaurin and the Narrative-Dramatic Poem" 187). As family members walking behind the coffin reflect on the significance of this passing, they are seen by a serpent that, owing to his vantage point in a tree and his inability to close his eyes, offers a panoramic view of the procession. *Lola* is "a starkly tragic parable of the passing of the land and the human culture it supported into careless and self-serving hands" (Mills, "Tim McLaurin and the Narrative-Dramatic Poem" 186).

In *Another Son of Man*, completed in 2002 and published posthumously, McLaurin again unites characters from different backgrounds and racial identities to confront a crisis. The narrative allegorically develops the question of salvation in terms of both lives and souls. Initially, an African American oncologist named Junuh, a reformed alcoholic and newly converted preacher named Reese, and a nurse named Ruth with New Age faith in Mother Earth are drawn to a dying patient named Nate. Each regrets not being able to save Nate from the cancer claiming his life, while Nate himself experiences a vision that reassures him he will return home. Having no family that he knows of, he asks his three friends at the hospital to carry his ashes to the far shore of Alligator Lake and await a sign indicating when and how to scatter the remains.

Arriving at the seemingly habitable island, the trio sets up camp, having taken everything necessary in two canoes. They are not prepared, however, for the hurricane that is about to batter the North Carolina coast. While they consider their options, a stranger calling himself Son of Man offers to take them to Paradise. Junuh recognizes him as an autistic savant, and Ruth intuitively trusts the stranger's innocence and goodness, but Reese, adhering to his understanding of Christian doctrine, believes that Son is the devil, come to take their souls. The three do accept the food and other assistance Son brings them in his battered rowboat before and after the first phase of the hurricane.

Barely surviving the storm, the three friends see that it has destroyed their canoes and scattered their tents and supplies in the woods; they are marooned, facing another, much stronger storm. Son returns and offers to take them all to the safety of Paradise, but only Ruth goes. The two men, having absolved the guilt that haunts them for not having saved comrades in battle or family members in peril—and having accepted, furthermore, their personal legacies—opt to stay on the island and tie themselves to trees. Ruth discovers that Paradise is a log home built by Son's mother, who spent her life protecting and nurturing her autistic son, having given up his twin Nathaniel. After showing Ruth the underground storm shelter where she can safely wait out the hurricane, Son returns to the island with rope to share with Reese and Junuh.

As the winds rage, Ruth briefly opens the door of the shelter and releases Nate's ashes into the storm, understanding that he is for, in death, Son has made a willing sacrifice. Ruth survives, with the hope that her union with Reese, initiated as they sought to comfort one another, will produce the child she has always wanted. She has trusted in the goodness of Son and of the source of life (whether called God or not) throughout the ordeal and will continue to live. This allegorical narrative brings into striking relief themes developed in his earlier novels.

During his career, McLaurin received North Carolina's highest literary honors, including the Mayflower Cup, the Sir Walter Raleigh Award, the Regan-Rubin Award, and the R. Hunt Parker Award for Lifetime Contribution to the Literary Heritage of North Carolina. In July 2003, North Carolina legislators declared Tim McLaurin Day, honoring him as a writer and native son. At the "Remembering Tim McLaurin" program organized in October 2010 by Marvin Hunt, a former colleague, Lee Smith spoke for many when she said she had never known a person "who lived his life as fully and intensely as Tim, right up until the moment of his death. . . . Always close to the earth, the water, and the whole natural world, Tim was a man like a force of nature himself" ("Remembering Tim McLaurin").

McLaurin ends his second memoir, *The River Less Run*, with a statement of faith and anticipation:

One day for certain I will die. My heart's thump will shudder and stop, my lungs will cease to rise. And the great mystery will finally be known, all the secrets opened. I believe the answer to all of creation will flower in an instant, the riddle so complex, yet so incredibly simple that I will open my ghost mouth into an oval and say "Ohhh, so that was it!" (258)

McLaurin's statement is a fitting summary of his quest to find his way through a world of both natural beauty and social change to an ultimately transcendent reality.

Works Cited and Consulted

Cornett, Sheryl. "Like a Brother: Profile of a Literary Friendship." *North Carolina Literary Review* 12 (2003): 160–63. Print.

McLaurin, Tim. *The Acorn Plan*. New York: Norton, 1988. Print.

———. *Another Son of Man*. Asheboro: Down Home P, 2004. Print.

———. *Cured by Fire*. New York: Putnam, 1995. Print.

———. *Keeper of the Moon: A Southern Boyhood*. New York: Norton, 1991. Print.

———. *The Last Great Snake Show*. New York: Putnam, 1997. Print.

———. *Lola*. Asheboro: Down Home P, 1997. Print.

———. Papers. Louis Round Wilson Special Collections Library. University of North Carolina at Chapel Hill.

———. *The River Less Run*. Asheboro: Down Home P, 2000. Print.

———. *Woodrow's Trumpet*. New York: Norton, 1989. Print.

Mills, Jerry Leath. "Tim McLaurin: Fayetteville, December 14, 1953—Morehead City, July 11, 2002." *North Carolina Literary Review* 12 (2003): 164–65. Print.

———. "Tim McLaurin." *Southern Writers: A New Biographical Dictionary*. Ed. Joseph M. Flora and Amber Vogel. Baton Rouge: LSU P, 2006. 274–75. Print.

———. "Tim McLaurin and the Narrative-Dramatic Poem." *North Carolina Literary Review* 9 (2000): 185–87. Print.

"North Carolina Lawmakers Honor Tunisia RPCV Tim McLaurin." *peacecorpsonline.org*. Peace Corps Online, 19 July 2003. Web. 13 May 2013.

"Remembering Tim McLaurin." *indyweek.com*. Indy Week, 24 July 2002. Web. 13 May 2013.

"Tribute to Honor Author Tim McLaurin, Nov. 7 at Fearrington Village." *http://blogs.lib.unc.edu/news/*. UNC Library News and Events, 20 Oct. 2010. Web. 13 May 2013.

Larry Brown: A Firefighter
Finds His Voice

Joe Samuel Starnes

O XFORD, Mississippi, firefighter Larry Brown had not yet embarked on
a writing career when a call to the firehouse in the late 1970s sent him
to Rowan Oak, the Oxford estate of the late William Faulkner. "I had never
gone there," Brown wrote, until a New York film crew "was shooting something, probably a documentary, in the yard and wanted some rain" (*On Fire*
172). Brown and another firefighter opened a hydrant in the front yard and
attached a hose, so "the New Yorkers had their rain. While we were waiting
on them to get through, I took a good first look at Rowan Oak" (173).

By the time he had five unpublished novels, more than one hundred short
stories, and some long-awaited critical acclaim to his credit, Brown had often
returned to Faulkner's stately home, tucked behind oaks only a few blocks
from Oxford's town square:

> I like to walk around the old wooden fence, and look at the trees, and think
> about what he did with his life. I figure he didn't pay much attention to what
> the world thought. He just went on and wrote his novels and stories and
> eventually won the Nobel Prize. I was born in this town, still live here, but

it's something to stand in that yard, maybe a block from where I'm sitting now, and think about that, about all those novels and stories that came from inside that house. (174)

Larry Brown was born in 1951 and grew up in rural Lafayette County, Mississippi, the land on which Faulkner based his fictional Yoknapatawpha County. Brown's father, a World War II veteran haunted by memories of combat, worked as a sharecropper, the original occupation shared by Faulkner's Snopes family, notorious for burning barns and other "white trash" transgressions. When Brown was three, his family moved to Memphis, Tennessee, where his father, a heavy drinker, bounced from one job to another, and moved his family from one rented house to another. The family returned to Mississippi when Brown was in his early teens, and his father died a few years later.

After high school, Brown, a weak student who graduated only after retaking twelfth-grade English, enlisted in the Marines. He wrote that he withstood the grueling physical tests and the abuse of superiors because if he failed to pass recruit training he would have been too ashamed to return home. He had no desire to serve more than his two-year enlistment, but for that period he was committed. "I had discipline, by God. I had it. I loved my Marine Corps" ("Discipline" 180).

Brown returned to Mississippi in 1972, married, started a family, and landed a position in the Oxford Fire Department. He would spend seventeen years as a firefighter, rising to the rank of captain. On days off from his primary job, he held several part-time positions: "Grocery store sacker, house painter, hay hauler, pulpwood cutter-and-hand loader, fence builder, bricklayer's helper, carpenter, carpet cleaner man, truck driver, forklift driver, dock worker . . . pine tree planter, timber deadener, surveyor's helper, plumber, answering service employee" (qtd. in Day 192). Even this long list omits his early employment in the stove factory where his father once worked and his job picking cotton as a child.

Although he lacked a college education and performed poorly in high school English, Brown inherited the habit of reading from his mother. His family visited public libraries frequently, and Brown read avidly, including *Of Mice and Men*, Faulkner's hunting stories (Day 191), and the western novel *Shane* (Bjerre 58). Some of his favorites in the '70s were commercial novels by Stephen King, Louis L'Amour, and John D. MacDonald (Cash 46). He later discovered Harry Crews's novel *A Feast of Snakes* (1976), even though he didn't remember precisely when: "It was probably way back in some dim year close to the time when I started writing, and that was in 1980" (*Billy Ray's*

Farm 17). He would go on to devour all the Crews he could find. His own narrative voice would come to follow a sparse, rough, direct style more like Crews's than the circumlocutory style of his fellow Lafayette County native, Faulkner.

Applying his blue-collar work ethic, Brown sat down at his wife Mary Annie's Smith Corona typewriter, following a pursuit she initially thought a passing whim. It wasn't. Five years later, he had churned out sizable stacks of written work, but had published only three stories—his first not in a literary journal, but in the biker magazine *Easyriders* in 1982. His breakthrough came in 1986, when *Mississippi Review* published "Facing the Music," the short story Shannon Ravenel of Algonquin Books would publish in the 1988 edition of *New Stories from the South: The Year's Best.* Ravenel would become Brown's editor, and over the next two decades Algonquin would publish nine of Brown's ten books. In 1990 he left the fire department to write full time, an occupation that brought with it travel to promote his work and sporadic college teaching appointments. A heavy smoker who struggled with his drinking, Brown died from a heart attack in 2004 at the age of fifty-three.

As in Crews's writing, working-class characters stand at the center of Brown's fiction, and in works dating from the beginning of his career, they frequently speak in the first-person. In the opening, title story of his first collection, *Facing the Music* (1988), a boozing, philandering, but likable husband speaks of coming to terms with his wife's mastectomy, and in the final story, "The End of Romance," the male half of a hard-drinking couple describes witnessing a shooting at a convenience store. *Dirty Work* (1989), Brown's first novel, relies on a pair of first-person voices, alternating between the story of a younger white veteran of the Vietnam War and an older black veteran, whose arms and legs have been amputated. The novel, a penetrating look at what war can do to men, earned Brown critical acclaim and national press coverage, including a guest spot on NBC's *Today* with Jane Pauley. The stories in *Big Bad Love* (1990), Brown's second collection of short fiction, are also told in the first-person, some plunging into autobiographical territory with tales of struggling, working-class writers who fight to rise above circumstances. These stories are often laugh-out-loud funny; one narrator's wife, an agonized and aspiring writer, labors over a short story entitled "The Hunchwoman of Cincinnati."

Brown was never afraid to write humorous stories that dealt with sexual content in a way that would be unfit for garden and Rotary clubs. The title story in *Big Bad Love* features an oversized vagina, and another story revolves around a small penis. The narrator of "Big Bad Love" is unable to satisfy his wife, confessing, "I just couldn't do anything with her big Tunnel of

Love. I could hit one side at a time, but not both sides" (53). In "Waiting for the Ladies," the narrator tells the story of a man who contemplates his wife's being flashed:

> My wife came home crying from the Dumpsters, said there was some pervert over there jerked down his pants and showed her his schlong. I asked her how long this particular pecker was—I was drinking beer, not taking it half seriously—and she said it sort of resembled a half-grown snail, or slug, she said, a little hairy. It was so disgusting, she said, and gave off this little shiver, doing her shoulders the way she does. (79)

The narrator gets drunk and goes to his father's house, where they watch Humphrey Bogart in *The Caine Mutiny* and discuss his wife's encounter. "Then [my father] looked back around to me, swung his old flat gray eyes up there on my face and said, Son, a little dick's sorta like a Volkswagen. It's all right around the house but you don't want to get out on the road with it" (84).

The year the collection appeared, Brown was a fellow at Vermont's Bread Loaf Writers' Conference. He wondered in a letter to Clyde Edgerton if "this crowd can handle" the frankness of "Waiting for the Ladies" (Cash 106). Brown, however, was well received, and the conference invited him back to New England three more times.

After about a decade of writing and three successful books written in first-person mode, Brown turned to third-person narration in the novel *Joe* (1991), where the narrative voice departs from the rural speech of his earlier hardscrabble characters, taking on a lyrical elegance and marching rhythm inspired by Cormac McCarthy, whom Brown had come to revere as a successor to Faulkner. Brown often describes the rural southern landscape through the perspective of Joe Ransom, a whiskey-drinking ex-convict who works for a timber company, supervising crews who poison scrub trees that will be replaced with stands of new pine. Even though Joe has inherent flaws and holds a despicable job, his character is sympathetic, especially in the concluding scene, when he prepares to kill a man who paid a ne'er-do-well alcoholic to have sex with the drunk's mute, prepubescent daughter. Joe and the reader understand that he'll go back to prison, but that he's doing the right thing.

Characters who drink more than is good for them, as Brown often did, populate his work, and beer and liquor frequently fuel characters' bad decisions. Drinking, it seems, for many of his troubled characters—held down by circumstances, lack of discipline, and the inability to rise above their stations—is the only balm they have to address the overwhelming weight of their lives. In "Economics of the Cracker Landscape: Poverty as an Environmental Issue in Larry Brown's *Joe*," Jay Watson writes, "[W]e might say that alcohol leaves the novel's human landscape as poisoned and deadened as Joe's chemicals leave the forest landscape" (54). A river of alcohol runs through not only through *Joe*, but also through all of Brown's work.

In *Joe*, as in much of Brown's writing, characters frequently drive country roads, and his narratives are filled with descriptions of the lush but troubled land. Unlike in his earlier work, however, *Joe* takes on a beauty of sentences not spoken by characters, but narrated by an author with a refined and perfected voice. As Brown describes what Joe Ransom sees through the windshield of his pickup, we are in Ransom's head through close third-person narration, but at the same time we see the land through Brown's eyes:

> The woods thinned and opened up into green hills dotted with horses and cows and cultivated land gleaming wetly under the weak sun trying to break through the clouds. Tarpaper shacks and shabby mobile homes, actually no more than campers, lined the road, the yards full of junked autos and stacked firewood overgrown with weeds and pulpwood trucks and the windows smashed out and the rear ends jacked up and propped on oil drums, El Dorados with mud halfway up the sides parked before porches of rough sawmill lumber. (73)

Just as McCarthy's Cornelius Suttree ambles about Knoxville, Tennessee, and its environs, and just as the violent ragtag band in *Blood Meridian* (1985) roams the United States-Mexico borderlands, Brown's characters are often in motion. And again, as in McCarthy's work, Brown's third-person voice favors conjunctions over commas. His sentences often move—even march—as in *Joe*'s opening: "The road lay long and black ahead of them and the heat was coming now through the thin soles of their shoes" (1).

This shift to third-person allowed Brown to move out of his characters' voices and take on larger themes using an authorial voice reminiscent of McCarthy's. Rural Mississippi comes alive in *Joe* in a way that it had not in Brown's previous, more personal works. Brown told interviewer Kay Bonetti that the novel was

> a great opportunity to show the landscape, and to set my characters against it. And to have this larger thing, even larger than the lives that are going on, which is the land. The ground is so ancient. It's the oldest thing we've got. I like to have people picture what it looks like—that distant watershed where all the line of trees fade into this little blue line that's the end of the horizon.

That's what I love. This is my country, and I love this place. I try to re-create it on the page. (qtd. in Cash 128)

The use of third-person narration and the ability to enter the heads of more than one character (though *Dirty Work* reaches into the heads of two) allowed Brown to expand the scope of his work and paint a broader canvas than he had before. This new approach also creates dramatic irony, allowing the reader to know more than the characters know, and gives the reader an overall view instead of hearing the voice of just one character.

Brown also uses multiple points-of-view masterfully in his 1996 novel *Father and Son*, arguably his finest work. From beginning to end, the novel is compelling and beautifully written, shockingly violent on the one hand and peaceful and serene on the other. Suspense grips the reader until the final pages. The novel takes place over a few days in the late 1960s in Oxford and the surrounding county, which Brown views through the lenses of several interrelated characters: Glen Davis, a bitter man fresh off a three-year sentence in Parchman, Mississippi's state penitentiary, for driving drunk and killing a little boy; his father Virgil, an aging but peaceful drinker with much to regret; Puppy, Glen's better-adjusted brother; Jewel, a waitress and the mother of Glen's four-year-old son, born shortly before he went to prison; Bobby Blanchard, the sheriff and a rival for Jewel's affection; and Mary, Bobby's mother, with whom he lives and with whom Virgil had an early affair. Hanging over the narrative like ghosts are Glen and Puppy's brother Theron, whom Glen accidently shot and killed when they were boys, and Emma, Virgil's wife and Glen's mother, who committed suicide while Glen was in prison.

Brown enters into close third-person perspective and takes the reader inside the heads of all these characters, moving deftly from one to the next in short, unnumbered chapters. These viewpoints explore interwoven connections, deep-seated love, and long-brewing resentments, weaving a complex tapestry of the town and the landscape and presenting both through the eyes of the interrelated cast. Like a puzzle whose pieces come together slowly, the entire picture eventually falls into place. Halfway through the book, the reader realizes that Glen and Bobby, the lawman responsible for sending Glen to prison, are not only rivals for Jewel's love, but unacknowledged half-brothers. Bobby is Virgil's illegitimate son.

Moving within the characters' close third-person points-of-view—as Brown does at the end of the novel, for instance, when Glen abducts and rapes Mary, his father's mistress and Bobby's mother—creates tense, cinematic moments when readers know more about what's going to happen than characters do. When we see Bobby going into his house, we know that Glen has Mary tied up in the barn outside. Bobby wonders where his mother is, but, assuming she is out on an errand, he takes a nap. We see Jewel placing a phone call to Bobby that goes unanswered while he sleeps. *Father and Son* is not unlike a horror movie—"Turn around!" or "Wake up!" we want to yell—though it's much more elegantly told.

Thomas Ærvold Bjerre, in "The White Trash Cowboys of *Father and Son*," argues that westerns—on both page and screen—inspire the novel, an insightful argument considering Brown's early fondness for Louis L'Amour and the novel *Shane*. While Brown employs techniques common to westerns and horror movies, his deft characterization sets the novel on a higher plane. His portrayal of Glen, whose transgressions are extreme—in the course of a few days he denies his young son, kills a pet monkey, commits a murder and two rapes—paints him not simply as a one-dimensional evildoer, but as a complex man burdened by ignorant mistakes, a scarred past, and a river of whiskey and beer. He's a tragic character, a man who seems to want to do right, but just doesn't know how—and even if he attempted to do right, his inner demons wouldn't let him.

In one scene, Glen has wrecked his car and passed out beside it:

> A long time later, or so it seemed, he came to in a yard. He was on his back on the wet grass and the sky above him had not changed. He rolled over onto his side and looked at the car. A bush was hanging out from behind the back wheel. He found an empty beer bottle in his hand and lifted it and sucked at it, but nothing came out. The world did not love him and he knew it. He sucked at the bottle and then he laid it down. (162)

Brown's insight into Glen's world—and into that of all the characters in *Father and Son*—comes by way of a perspective Gustave Flaubert introduced into nineteenth-century fiction: free indirect discourse, now more commonly called free indirect style. This approach, which Brown first used in *Joe* and then brilliantly employed in *Father and Son*, expanded the scope of his novels until the end of his career. *Fay* (2000), *The Rabbit Factory* (2003), and the posthumously published *A Miracle of Catfish* (2007) employ the same viewpoint. This technique works perfectly for the stories he wants to tell, dipping into the hearts and minds of working-class characters, but allowing him space for lush, lyrical language. If he had written *Joe* or *Father and Son* from the first-person perspectives of the taciturn Joe Ransom or the angry Glen Davis, they would be vastly different novels, far more limited in breadth and depth, because even though these characters sense what's wrong with themselves and the world around them, they don't have the will, ability, or vocabulary to articulate their malaise it. In third-person, though, Brown's powerful authorial voice blends into the consciousness of the rough-edged characters and presents them in a fuller, more sympathetic light.

And depicting blue-collar characters with care and honesty was one of Brown's primary concerns: "I have great sympathy for the good people of the working class. . . . The little man is kept down by the big man, and it's always been that way, and it always will probably. The factory worker can't find anything better, or figures he has no right to hope for anything better since that's what his daddy did and what all the people around him do. I was exactly of that mindset, but I changed over the years" ("That Secret Code" 192–93). Brown told Day that his working-class background "helps to make things realistic." He cited scenes he was working on from *A Miracle of Catfish*, his unfinished final novel, that take place in a stove factory. He said he knows "what kind of people work there, so it surely helps to make the characters real. The food they eat, the cars and trucks they drive and the things that are wrong with them, the kind of beer they drink, the music they listen to. What they do on the weekends. Not just the way they talk, but that's important, too. Real dialogue. Those people have hopes and dreams, too" (194).

Only in his nonfiction books *On Fire* (1994) and *Billy Ray's Farm* (2001) would Brown return to the first-person. *On Fire*, as much as any of his nonfiction, reveals Brown's standing as a man of the world, a man who liked to drink and who worked hard, a man who had seen much of life and death and wrecks and rescues. While Brown characterized himself in the collection as a writer without education, he had no shortage of what many academics now call "experiential learning." I once heard Brown's friend Barry Hannah decry many of today's writers as "air-conditioned sissies," something Brown certainly was not. When Brown wanted a new house for his family, he and his friends designed and built it themselves. He often was out on the road in a fire truck—or, when off-duty, a pickup truck, driving around drinking and listening to music, watching the rural landscape through his windshield. When he wrote about violence or death or the landscape or a dive bar or a stove factory, he had been there and seen it. He lived his research.

Though Brown frequently recounted the story of his late start as a writer and his years of collecting rejection letters, his legend as the toiling artist has taken on a trace of mythological quality. In reality, there's less than a decade elapsed between the day he first sat down at this wife's typewriter and the day he appeared on *Today* to tout his second book, an apprenticeship with a length that many longer-suffering writers would envy. And while he was self-taught and lacked a college degree, Brown was fortunate to be an aspiring writer in Oxford, the most literary small town in the South, if not the nation. A statue of Faulkner sits outside city hall, across from Square Books, an independent bookstore that has long brought in writers from all over the country. While many such businesses have been shuttered, Square Books has thrived, and its owner, Richard Howorth, a close friend and ardent supporter of Brown's, even served as Oxford's mayor for two terms. In his nascent years, Brown took a writing workshop at the nearby university from novelist Ellen Douglas, who guided his reading toward Flannery O'Connor and more literary fare. And he was encouraged by Hannah. While all writers live to some degree in isolation, grinding out the pages behind closed doors, Brown had the support of a vibrant community of writers and readers, a community that is nonexistent in places like Alma, Georgia, and Morgan City, Louisiana.

We should be eternally grateful to the literary oasis of Oxford, Mississippi, which gave us not just William Faulkner, but Larry Brown. Brown's legacy as a southern working-class writer who achieved much-deserved critical acclaim will only continue to grow as new readers discover his timeless work and vivid explorations of the rural landscape and life's joys and hardships. His intentions were as true as the day is long, and that honesty comes through in every line he wrote.

Works Cited

Bjerre, Thomas Ærvold. "The White Trash Cowboys of *Father and Son.*" *Larry Brown and the Blue-Collar South: A Collection of Critical Essays*. Ed. Jean W. Cash and Keith Perry. Jackson: UP of Mississippi, 2008. 58–72. Print.

Brown, Larry. *Big Bad Love*. Chapel Hill: Algonquin, 1990. Print.

———. *Billy Ray's Farm*. Chapel Hill: Algonquin, 2001. Print.

———. "Discipline." *They Write among Us: New Stories and Essays from the Best of Oxford Writers*. Ed. Jim Dees. Oxford: Jefferson, 2003. 177–90. Print.

———. *Facing the Music*. Chapel Hill: Algonquin. 1988. Print.

———. *Father and Son*. Chapel Hill: Algonquin. 1996. Print.

———. *Joe*. Chapel Hill: Algonquin. 1991. Print.

———. *On Fire*. Chapel Hill: Algonquin. 1994. Print.

———. "That Secret Code." Interview with Orman Day. *Conversations with Larry Brown*. Ed. Jay Watson. Jackson: UP of Mississippi, 2007. 190–96. Print.

Cash, Jean W. *Larry Brown: A Writer's Life*. Jackson: UP of Mississippi, 2011. Print.

Watson, Jay. "Economics of the Cracker Landscape: Poverty as an Environmental Issue in Larry Brown's *Joe.*" *Larry Brown and the Blue-Collar South: A Collection of Critical Essays*. Ed. Jean W. Cash and Keith Perry. Jackson: UP of Mississippi, 2008. 58–72. Print.

Dorothy Allison: Revising the "White Trash" Narrative

Emily Langhorne

OROTHY Allison knows about growing up "white trash." On April 11, 1949, in Greenville, South Carolina, she was born "the bastard daughter of a white woman from a desperately poor family" (*Trash* vii). Her unwed mother, only fifteen at the time, worked as a waitress. When Allison was five, her mother married a route salesman who sexually abused Allison until she was sixteen. As a result of this abuse, she contracted an undiagnosed sexually transmitted disease that rendered her infertile.

Poverty forced Allison's family to leave South Carolina for central Florida in search of a better life. Although the family's economic status did not improve, for the first time in her life Allison was not plagued by her family's "white trash" reputation. Her new high school placed her in college preparatory courses, and she became the first member of her family to graduate from high school and college, attending Florida Presbyterian College on a National Merit scholarship.

During college, Allison became heavily involved in the women's movement. She moved into a feminist collective, discovered her sexuality, and began writing about her experiences. After graduating in 1971, Allison held a variety of jobs—substitute teacher, maid, Social Security Administration clerk—before moving to New York in 1979 and completing a master's degree in anthropology at the New School for Social Research. During this time, she worked as a writer and editor for lesbian and feminist journals, including *Quest* and *Outlook*. She published a collection of poetry, *The Women Who Hate Me*, in 1983, followed by a short story collection, *Trash*, in 1988.

In 1992, Allison published *Bastard out of Carolina*, a largely autobiographical novel about growing up in the Rough South. Both a mainstream and a critical success, the novel was a finalist for the National Book Award in 1992 and was adapted into an award-winning film in 1996. Allison's other works include essays, a memoir, and fiction. She now lives in northern California with her partner, Alix, and their son, Wolf Michael.

Although Allison has published only one memoir, *Two or Three Things I Know for Sure* (1995), all of her work draws heavily on her upbringing in the working-class South. The intense poverty and harsh conditions of her childhood and adolescence are her central themes, and her work is largely concerned with the myth of poverty versus its reality. Through her characters and stories, she works to replace stereotyped images of poverty with the real ones conveying the difficulties of working-class existence. Her writing thus exposes the truth behind growing up "trash," calling attention to the façade that is white America's supposedly classless society.

Allison considers the poverty into which she was born not only the central theme of her work, but also the "central fact of [her] life." As she says, "That fact, the inescapable impact of being born in a condition of poverty that this society finds shameful, contemptible, and somehow oddly deserved has had dominion over me to such an extent that I have spent my life trying to overcome or deny it" (*Trash* vii). Allison's keen observation of how outsiders view her class remains one of the most compelling aspects of her work. From a young age, she felt despised because of her social status; moreover, she recognized that such contempt coincides with a belief that the poor are to blame for their poverty. She writes, "I have learned with great difficulty that the vast majority of people believe that poverty is a voluntary condition" (*Skin* 15). By viewing poverty as self-inflicted, the upper and middle classes shame and stigmatize "white trash," instead of trying to understand or empathize with them. In "What is 'White Trash'? Stereotypes and Economic Conditions of Poor Whites in the United States," Annalee Newitz and Matthew Wray write that in "a country so steeped in the myth of classlessness . . . the white trash stereotype serves as a useful way of blaming the poor for being poor" (1). Upper and middle classes gain security by creating these stereotypes, distancing themselves from the working class not only financially, but also culturally and intellectually.

"White trash" stereotypes reinforce the idea of upper- and middle-class superiority without creating understanding, thereby perpetuating a damaging system of class stratification and prejudice. Allison explains: "The horror of class stratification, racism, and prejudice is that some people begin to believe that the security of their families and communities depends on the oppression of others, that for some to have good lives there must be others whose lives are truncated and brutal. It is a belief that dominates this culture. It is what makes the poor whites of the South so determinedly racist and the middle class so contemptuous of the poor" (*Skin* 35).

In a stratified society, such stereotypes have created a myth of poverty that differs vastly from the reality of working-class life. Mainstream images of poor whites fail to depict three-dimensional human beings, thereby perpetuating this myth and creating "acceptable" prejudice against poor whites—"white trash"—in a society that preaches tolerance and equality. Indeed, in "Who Are These White People?: 'Rednecks,' 'Hillbillies,' and 'White Trash' as Marked Racial Subjects," John Hartigan Jr. comments on the natural way in which the term "white trash" perpetuates itself socially, generating "loathing and disgust" among the upper classes (105). Although openly acknowledged as a pejorative, the term "white trash" and its prevalence demonstrate society's tolerance of stereotyping poor whites.

Allison writes to combat this myth and these prejudices. By deconstructing the myth of the poor, she grants her audience access to three-dimensional, working-class characters, rather than flat stereotypes. Such stereotypes not only portray to outsiders a false image of the working class, but are reinforced within the working class itself. With no alternative image of themselves, poor whites often accept negative views generated by others, creating a narrative cycle with no alternative outcome.

Throughout her childhood, Allison searched for books containing genuine portraits of her people. Poor white southerners have been staples of literature since the nineteenth century, with their appeal tied in their depiction as "either comic or contemptible" (MacDonald 16). Allison found her family represented nowhere, "not on television, not in books, not even comic books" (*Trash* vii). She knew her family was neither evil nor villainous, neither saintly nor noble, and even as a child, she understood the false portrayal of poverty created by those romanticizing an ugly condition: "[T]hat is also one of the things that hurt me a great deal as a child, where you encountered this romantic notion, 'Oh they're ragged, but they're clean!' Because you know, we weren't always clean and you could get seriously depressed about yourself if you did not even meet the romanticized notion" ("An Interview with Dorothy Allison" 44). As an adult, she reflected upon her experiences and the idea of honorable suffering, concluding, "I know that suffering does not ennoble. It destroys" (*Skin* 38). Allison suggests that only those who have not suffered characterize suffering as a source of dignity.

In much of her work, Allison revisits the lack of realistic working-class characters: "All of my life, I have hated clichés, the clichés applied to people like me and those I love. Every time I pick up a book . . . I do so with a conscious anxiety, an awareness that the books about us have often been cruel, small, and false" (*Skin* 165). In a poignant scene in *Bastard out of Carolina*, Bone Boatwright, the young protagonist, receives a beautiful copy of *Gone with the Wind* "with tinted pictures from the movie." An avid reader, Bone at first loves the book, but then, "one evening I looked up from Vivien Leigh's pink cheeks to see Mama coming in from work with her hair darkened from sweat and her uniform stained." The sight makes Bone indignant, for she knows that her mother would not be Scarlett O'Hara, but Emmy Slattery, "part of the trash down in the mud-stained cabins, fighting with the darkies and stealing ungratefully from our betters" (206). Bone realizes that, in fiction, there is no sympathy or justice for people of her class.

In *Skin: Talking about Sex, Class & Literature* (1994), Allison writes of discovering Morton Thompson's *Not a Stranger*, a book that changed her feelings about herself, poverty, and "the belief that there was no connection between my life and the lives of the people in fiction" (78). At age eleven, she finally encountered characters she recognized; moreover, Thompson's young protagonist's ambition to escape poverty mirrors Allison's own. "For the first time," she writes, "a book showed me a part of my life in someone else's story in a way that I could believe" (79).

Throughout her writing, Allison makes clear that her childhood revolved around the narrative others had written for her: She was lazy, good-for-nothing, stupid. In response, Allison examines the way in which society's reinforcement of this narrative encourages children to regard it as inescapable. One of the most tragic and compelling parts of her writing is the way she describes how her people think of their situation and themselves. Demoralized by poverty and contempt, many of her characters suffer a deep-rooted shame; moreover, because they believe their futures are predetermined by their circumstances at birth, they do not expect anything better. Allison writes, "We were not noble, not grateful, not even hopeful. We knew ourselves despised. What was there to work for, to save money for, to fight for or struggle against? We had generations before us to teach us that nothing ever changed, and that those who did try to escape failed" (*Trash* vii). Despite any desire for social mobility, Allison's people begin to see themselves as outsiders do, as "trash." Furthermore, they internalize this sense of worthlessness as a predictor of their future, which they have come to regard as a fate to endure. Indeed, in much of Allison's work, she refers to the poverty-afflicted adulthoods of her characters as their "fate," claiming that she "grew up trying to run away from the fate that destroyed so many of the people I loved" (*Skin* 13).

Poverty, therefore, was not an obstacle to overcome, but a condition to suffer—like a disease. Allison reflects on the deep-seated fear, shame, blame, and hopelessness that come with being born poor and believing in the narrative of poverty as fate. Allison, too, fell victim to this type of thinking, believing herself worthless and unworthy of love. Despite her talent and the clear proof of her intelligence, she admits that she "never went after a grant, never believed I could get one" (*Trash* xiv). She acknowledges that this lack of self-love partially comes from the narrative of shame and pride that defined her childhood: "We had not been raised to love ourselves, only to refuse to admit how much we might hate ourselves" (*Skin* 237).

Putting an end to such thinking requires realizing that one is an active participant in one's own narrative, rather than a passive victim of fate. When society emphasizes only one narrative and uses it to justify prejudice, stereotyped subjects struggle to rewrite their narratives. Only when a different narrative emerges does it become possible to envision a different future. In *Skin*, Allison writes about the moment she first realized she could rewrite the narrative of her life. Of her family's move to Florida, she writes,

> The first time I looked around my junior high classroom and realized I did not know who those people were—not only as individuals but as categories, who their people were and how they saw themselves—I also realized that they did not know me. In Greenville, everyone knew my family, knew we were trash, and that meant we were supposed to be poor, supposed to have grim low-paid jobs, have babies in our teens, and never finish school. . . . Suddenly I was boosted into the college-bound track, and . . . there was also something else I had never experienced before: a protective anonymity, and a kind of grudging respect and curiosity about who I might become. Because they did not see poverty and hopelessness as a forgone conclusion for my life, I could begin to imagine other futures for myself. (20–21)

Allison thus began writing a narrative no longer predetermined by her birth or her stepfather's abuse—no matter the shame and hopelessness of the former, or the physical and psychological trauma of the latter.

Allison redefines the narrative of her people to encompass the full story of their situation. She does not romanticize their circumstances; neither does she attempt to distance them from stereotypes that reveal truths about their behavior. Although stereotypes and caricatures present one-dimensional portraits, she regards them not as absolute falsehoods, but as half-truths. Allison shows the whole truth about growing up as "poor white trash" in the Rough South by creating three-dimensional characters able to evoke affection and empathy, as well as disgust.

Although all of Allison's work offers glimpses into working-class lives, *Bastard out of Carolina* paints the fullest portraits of her characters as survivors of a broken class system. Born a certified bastard in Greenville, South Carolina, to fifteen-year-old Anney Boatwright, Bone grows up victimized by the physical and emotional abuse of her stepfather, Daddy Glen. The strength of the novel comes largely from Bone's narration, through which readers come to appreciate the profound and destructive psychological impact of social prejudices against the working class. The pride and shame Bone feels for her family seep into her narration and prompt readers to understand the complicated love that exists in an environment plagued by violence and poverty. Allison uses this understanding to create empathy for her characters, rather than relying on stereotypes that promote contempt and overlook insight into circumstances.

Because Bone is a sympathetic narrator, readers regard her as intelligent and kind. Bone, however, begins to define herself by the labels others place on her and her family: *"No-good, lazy, shiftless"* (3). Born a Boatwright, she understands from an early age her stigmatized status. The designation on her birth certificate merely reifies prejudices that will define the rest of her childhood. Bone thus develops a sense of worthlessness, and Daddy Glen's abuse only furthers her self-loathing and contempt. Societal prejudices lead Bone to believe that she deserves her poverty; similarly, Daddy Glen makes her feel that she deserves his abuse. In both instances, Bone accepts blame for the injustices she suffers, experiences shame as a result, and mentally links poverty, violence, and broken homes. When her Aunt Raylene tries to tell her, "People are the same. . . . Everybody just does the best they can," Bone shouts back angrily, "Other people don't go beating on each other all the time. . . . They don't get falling-down drunk, shoot each other, and then laugh about it" (258). Because of her experiences in a "white trash" environment, Bone accepts society's opinion that her people are not like others, and that she should be ashamed of them.

Truly a victim, Bone believes herself responsible for Glen's beatings because social stereotypes have helped destroy her self-worth. "[W]hy couldn't

I be pretty? I wanted to be more like the girls in storybooks, princesses with pale skin and tender hearts" (206). Bone's longing is less for true physical beauty than for the security and love inherent in representations of middle-class lifestyles, which popular culture associates with beauty. Scrutinizing herself, she decides she is nothing like the girls in "white nylon crinolines and blue satin hair ribbons. They were the kind of little girls people really wanted. No part of me was that worshipful, dreamy-eyed storybook child, no part of me was beautiful. I could see why Daddy Glen was hateful to me" (208). Believing in a predestined "white trash" life, Bone concludes, "[t]his body, like my aunts' bodies, was born to be worked to death, used up, and thrown away" (206).

Through Bone's voice, Allison depicts poverty as both a financial state and a psychological condition. The latter proves as difficult to overcome as the former—especially in the Boatwright family, for whom the cycle of poverty has lasted for generations. Children become deeply affected by the poverty and shame-filled environment in which they live. Michael Lewis, in *Shame: The Exposed Self*, observes that they "are likely to learn to experience shame through empathic shame induction" (qtd. in Bouson 106). Bone's family exposes her to their shame by telling her repeatedly not to *act ashamed*, that she has nothing *to be ashamed of*. In "Talking Trash, Talking Back: Resistance to Stereotypes in Dorothy Allison's *Bastard out of Carolina*," Kathlene MacDonald writes about this struggle of experiencing and denying shame. The Boatwrights "maintain fierce pride and loyalty towards their family, but they also suffer deep feelings of shame and hopelessness. Much of this shame and self-hatred of poverty derives from the contempt of those in middle and upper classes" (20). In a telling scene, Bone and her sister Reese lie to a bill collector, telling him Anney is not home. Bone understands this lying as a protective device, for she already knows the truth of their situation: "We knew what the neighbors called us, what Mama wanted to protect us from. We knew who we were" (*Bastard* 82). They are poor, and being poor means being bad. If the neighbors' opinions have not already confirmed it, Bone's experience of poverty—lying to the bill collector, suffering name-calling at school, moving to a new house every few months—does.

Bone's interactions with Daddy Glen's family also exemplify the prejudice she suffers. Daddy Glen comes from a middle-class family he has shamed by marrying Anney. Ironically, Daddy Glen, the only major middle-class character in the novel, remains the character most deserving of condemnation, as he continuously assaults his stepdaughter. But his family intentionally makes Bone and Reese feel ashamed of themselves: "They served us tea in the backyard, just us—Anney's girls, they called us. Their kids went in and out of the house, loud, raucous . . . tracking mud in on the braided rugs" (101). Despite exhibiting better behavior than her step-cousins, Bone sits isolated in the garden, the segregated victim of her socioeconomic background. She wants to be accepted for who she is, but she resents that her character and intelligence are not enough to let her prove herself, and she therefore considers accepting the "white trash" fate society has prophesied for her. By understanding the injustice of her situation as independent of her actions, however, Bone manages to hold on to a sense of self, fueled by rage and hunger.

Allison's depiction of Bone's hunger emotively reflects the frustration of poverty. Although Bone only sporadically experiences physical hunger, Allison's illustration of her spiritual hunger—fueled by the frustration and helplessness of her "white trash" status—creates empathy in the reader. Continually trying to resist the negative labels applied to her, Bone develops a hunger for all she has been denied. This hunger revolves around material objects as representations of opportunities she has not received. Primarily, it reflects her resentment of outsiders, who see her poverty instead of her humanity. She first experiences this hunger when the manager at a Woolworth's humiliates her for stealing candy: "I looked around at the bright hairbrushes, ribbons, trays of panties and socks, notebooks, dolls, and balloons. It was hunger I felt then, raw and terrible, a shaking deep down inside me, as if my rage had used up everything I had ever eaten. . . . It was a hunger in the back of the throat, not the belly, an echoing emptiness that ached for the release of screaming" (98). Her helplessness transforms into hunger, then develops into a defensive rage.

While Bone is only beginning to flout society's vision for her future, the love of her family daily enables her to survive poverty and abuse. In the Boatwright family, Allison creates believable characters full of passion, tragedy, and flaws that embody the struggles of being human and the reality of living poor in the Rough South. By way of Bone's extended family, readers develop full pictures of the kind of working-class southerners who have often been society's faceless villains. "I want my writing to break down small categories," Allison says. "The whole idea in *Bastard out of Carolina* was to give you a working-class family that had all the flaws, but to also give you the notion of real people and not of caricatures" ("An Interview with Dorothy Allison" 44). In breaking down these categories, Allison rewrites the story of poverty through characters who experience limited choices, complex emotions, and complicated relationships.

Allison hides nothing in the novel. The graphic violence, sexual abuse, and alcoholism that plague Bone's childhood reflect Allison's own experiences. Allison, however, does not want only these qualities to define her characters. The Boatwright family creates its own community. The aunts become a source of comfort and strength for Bone as Glen's abuse worsens and her relationship with her mother deteriorates. Unlike her relationship with Anney, which is based on secrets and shame, Bone's relationship with Aunt Raylene is based on trust and love. By taking pride in her and praising her to Anney, Raylene instills in Bone a sense of self-worth. Bone relishes this praise: "I loved her praise more than money, loved being good at something." Raylene not only helps Bone redefine herself as valuable, but places no stock in her alleged "fate," seeing Bone's potential and encouraging her to use it: "I am so tired of people whining about what might happen to them, never taking no chances or doing anything new. I'm glad you an't gonna be like that, Bone. I'm counting on you to get out there and do things, girl" (182). But Allison's characters are never so one-sided. Despite supporting Bone, the aunts, too, have flaws. Aunt Ruth suspects Glen's abuse but remains silent about it because she knows that she has not properly loved her own many children; for example, Ruth shows care and love for Bone, but her interactions with her own daughter Deedee are strained. After Ruth dies, Deedee says that her mother told her "time and time again" that "I was ruined already" (236).

Bone also finds support and love in her relationship with her uncles. Allison's own uncles provided her with fascinating and complex characters who suffer the tragedy of believing in their "fate." They represent the true image of the Rough South; they "went to jail like other boys go to high school. They took up girls like other people choose a craft" (*Two or Three Things* 28). Bone worships her uncles, even though they are rough, boisterous men who can't hold jobs and drink heavily. Unlike Daddy Glen, Bone's uncles take pride in her and show her innocent affection: "[T]heir hands never hurt me and their pride in me was as bright as the coals on the cigarettes they always held loosely between their fingers" (*Bastard* 23). Mean and reckless, Bone's uncles encompass all the stereotypes of the poor white male, yet their love for their families creates an alternate identity for these men. When Aunt Raylene discovers Bone has been beaten, it is the uncles who avenge the girl, nearly killing Glen with their fists. Such a show of violence reflects stereotypical "white trash" behavior; however, in their violence, the uncles enact their own code of honor and love, thereby reshaping such violence in the minds of readers.

The bond between the siblings demonstrates the strength of their community. In a touching scene, Uncle Earle and his sister Ruth hold each other, as Ruth comforts him over the wife who left him. When, after the death of her baby, Aunt Alma creates a classic "white trash" scene—smashing everything in the house and threatening to kill her husband—Anney is the one who calms her, holding her "like a little girl, and rock[ing] her back and forth" as she cries (272). While the uncles beat Glen for his abuse of Bone, Raylene and Anney hold one another as "if their lives depended on each other" (247). By creating such demonstrations of humanity, Allison keeps readers from passing judgment on her characters.

Nowhere does Allison present more complex human emotion than in Anney Boatwright. Anney tries to remove her family from the shame of poverty, but her marriage to Glen results in the emotional and physical abuse of her daughter. Anney, frightened of what might happen if the abuse is discovered, keeps it a secret and thereby assumes a large portion of the responsibility for Glen's destructive behavior. Yet on some level, Anney clearly loves her children. In a scene that accurately represents the desperation of poverty, one evening after having to serve Bone and Reese ketchup on crackers, Anney leaves the house to work as a prostitute. Anney longs to break the cycle of poverty for her children, yet she cannot break the cycle of abuse. Thoroughly flawed, Anney stays with Glen and acknowledges her need for him as her weakness. Upon Raylene's discovery of Bone's bruises, Anney cries, "Oh God. Raylene, I love him. I know you'll hate me. Sometimes I hate myself, but I love him" (246). Allison juxtaposes this image of Anney against the Anney who sacrifices herself during the ketchup scene. And yet, after Glen brutally rapes and nearly kills thirteen-year-old Bone, Anney still cannot leave him. In a moment of weakness, when Bone lies bleeding in the car, Anney perpetuates the cycle of abuse when she turns and embraces Glen as he cries for forgiveness. Knowing she cannot leave him, Anney pleads, "Help me, God" in "a raw, terrible voice" (291).

Rather than break the cycle, Anney removes Bone from it, abandoning her with Raylene and leaving town with Glen and Reese. Readers condemn Anney for her choice, but Allison makes us understand that her choice has less to do with Anney's status as "white trash" than with the human condition. She is neither good nor evil, but a character with deep flaws and complicated emotions that influence and are influenced by her choices and struggles. Likewise, Bone's deepest desires are not different because of her lower-class status—they are just made more difficult by it. She concludes, "We had all wanted the simplest thing, to love and be loved and be safe together, but we had lost it and I didn't know how to get it back" (307).

Bastard out of Carolina illustrates Allison's ability to create characters who transcend stereotypes by acknowledging their strengths *and* weaknesses. "I have a theory about writing fiction," Allison says. "[I]f you create a character and if you tell enough about that character, even if you are creating someone who is a villain or someone who does terrible things, if you tell enough about them, then you have the possibility of loving them" ("An Interview with

Dorothy Allison" 41). In "tell[ing] enough," Allison creates a world of terrible stories and troubled people, but she also inspires understanding and concern. She asserts, "That our true stories may be violent, distasteful, painful, stunning, and haunting, I do not doubt. But our true stories will be literature. No one will be able to forget them, and though it will not always make us happy to read of the dark and dangerous places in our lives, the impact of our reality is the best we can ask of our literature" (*Skin* 166). Readers cannot dismiss Bone's rage or excuse Anney's abandonment. They cannot pass judgment on the aunts and uncles. But they will not forget the Boatwrights. And they will never again be able to hear the words "white trash" without thinking of Allison's people in their full humanity.

Works Cited and Consulted

Adichie, Chimamanda. "The Danger of a Single Story." TED Conferences, Oct. 2009. Web. 7 May 2013.

Allison, Dorothy. *Bastard out of Carolina*. New York: Dutton, 1992. Print.

———. "An Interview with Dorothy Allison." Interview by Susanne Dietzel. *Conversations with Dorothy Allison*. Ed. Mae Miller Claxton. Jackson: UP of Mississippi, 2012. 40–52. Print.

———. *Skin: Talking about Sex, Class & Literature*. Ithaca: Firebrand, 1994. Print.

———. *Trash*. 1988. New York: Penguin, 2002. Print.

———. *Two or Three Things I Know for Sure*. 1995. New York: Penguin, 1996. Print.

Bouson, J. Brooks. "'You Nothing but Trash': White Trash Shame in Dorothy Allison's *Bastard out of Carolina*." *Southern Literary Journal* 34.1 (2001): 101–23. Print.

Doane, Ashley "Woody," and Eduardo Bonilla-Silva, eds. *White Out: The Continuing Significance of Racism*. London: Routledge, 2003. Print.

Hartigan, John Jr. "Name Calling: Objectifying 'Poor Whites' and 'White Trash' in Detroit." Newitz and Wray, *White Trash* 41–46. Print.

———. "Unpopular Culture: The Case of 'White Trash.'" *Cultural Studies* 11.2 (1997): 316–43. Print.

———. "Who Are These White People?: 'Rednecks,' 'Hillbillies,' and 'White Trash' as Marked Racial Subjects." Doane and Bonilla-Silva 95–111. Print.

MacDonald, Kathlene. "Talking Trash, Talking Back: Resistance to Stereotypes in Dorothy Allison's *Bastard out of Carolina*." *Women's Studies Quarterly* 26.5 (1998): 15–25. *JSTOR*. Web. 7 May 2013.

Newitz, Annalee, and Matthew Wray. "What is 'White Trash'? Stereotypes and Economic Conditions of Poor Whites in the United States." *Whiteness: A Critical Reader*. Ed. Mike Hill. New York: New York UP, 1997. 168–84. Print.

———. *White Trash: Race and Class in America*. New York: Routledge, 1997. Print.

Sandell, Jillian. "Telling Stories of 'Queer White Trash': Race, Class, and Sexuality in the Work of Dorothy Allison." Newitz and Wray, *White Trash* 211–30. Print.

A World Almost Rotten:
The Fiction of William Gay[1]

William Giraldi

WHEN William Gay died at his home in Hohenwald, Tennessee, on February 23, 2012, age seventy, American literature lost one of its most authentic chroniclers of life in the Rough South. He was good because he had lived that life and had taught himself to write, reading work by the best American authors who preceded him. In its obituary of Gay, the *Washington Post* wrote, "[H]is characters were often hardscrabble carpenters, as he once was. They lived in trailer parks, as he once did, or in log cabins in the west Tennessee wilderness, like the one outside the town of Hohenwald where he died" (Shapiro). Achieving recognition fairly late in life, Gay continued to live in the privacy of rural Tennessee and showed little interest in self-promotion. In 2001, he told the *Tennessean*, "I never wanted a lot of money out of it, or to be a literary lion. I just wanted to be a writer" (qtd. in Shapiro). Gay was a genuine writer of the Rough South, one whose career, like that of Larry Brown, ended too soon.

In William Gay's scorched world, Flannery O'Connor is less a looming ghoul than an elderly aunt who lives in his house and will not die. And yet despite O'Connor's strong presence—and the unavoidable presence of the

Yahweh of southern literature, the god from whom no male writer in the South can ever hope to flee—Gay's work is wholly its own, pulsing with both tradition and novelty. His books were crafted from darkness: *The Long Home* (1999), *Provinces of Night* (2000), *Twilight* (2006), and the short story collection *I Hate to See That Evening Sun Go Down* (2002)— were crafted from darkness. Gay was, along with Barry Hannah, Cormac McCarthy, and Harry Crews, one of the four horsemen of the southern apocalypse, all of which wrote about the lives of the underclass with both understanding and sincerity.

There was not a single pocket in Tennessee in which Gay could hide from Faulkner's commanding influence. For an aspiring writer in working-class Lewis County, Faulkner existed in the very air. He was a kind of Delphic oracle for new scribes; without him, nothing even remotely literary came to pass. Gay read Faulkner in the thirty-five cent Signet editions he bought at the local drugstore in Hohenwald. He had been buying notebooks and pens since childhood, but, late in high school— charged by O'Connor's and Faulkner's doomed visions of the South—he began to formulate his own fiction, began to heed the insistent voices calling from within. His parents contemplated the boy something of an anomaly. Though Gay was the first in the family to finish high school, his mother and father weren't sure that writing was a prudent choice as an occupation. Gay's father toiled as a sharecropper and at whatever blue-collar drudgery came along. Gay's two younger brothers fell in line; they and their father had enough Southern machismo to fire a rocket. They hunted and fished. Gay, on the other hand, "wasn't much interested in killing things." About his mother, Gay offers one word only: "Loyalty" (Interview).

A vigilant teacher in high school noticed that the boy was reading Zane Gray westerns in his extra time, and thinking Gray too inferior for his thriving intellect, the teacher passed him a copy of *Look Homeward, Angel* (1929). Gay considers this gift the turning point of his life: Wolfe's novel ignited him to his core; it offered him the insight that *this can be done*, that a writing life was not a drunken pipe dream. Alongside J. T. Farrell's *Studs Lonigan* trilogy (1932–35), Wolfe's *Look Homeward, Angel* is the one of the quintessential American novels of experience, of growing, of how home fashions a psyche for good or for ill. It gave Gay the confidence to tell stories of his own experience, and the certain knowledge that those experiences were valuable even though they lacked privilege and swagger. Wolfe lit the green lantern at the end of the dock; O'Connor and Faulkner provided him the vessel to get there.

"The Paperhanger" is a horror story, a masterpiece of brutality and loss worthy of O'Connor. The story tempts you to classify it, explain it, wonder at its majesty and terror. The story is "The Tell-Tale Heart" (1843), written by the bastard offspring of Wilkie Collins and Charles Manson, in a prose part Hebrew Bible, part Hemingway—and then defies such feeble attempts at comprehension, at reduction. The story breathes, enigmatically, as if just born; the odors of blood, beer, and birth fluid waft up from the page. Gay's story offers almost no information about its characters—not where they come from, not their fevered dreams, not what they yearn for at first light. In his short fiction, Hemingway—an early, necessary influence on Gay—famously withholds motives and histories. Gay learned from Hemingway never to clarify what readers can clarify themselves; verbosity maims, insults the dignity of narrative. In "The Paperhanger" we know only how the characters react in the midst of an unexpected mystery, how their language reveals their warped psyches—and with that alone Gay enables us to know them for life, to taste their sweat.

The paperhanger is simultaneously ominous sprite and veritable everyman. When a little girl jabs out her tongue at him, his hand shoots from his side "like a serpent" and snaps the child's neck. Fragile as a Christmas bulb, she is tiny enough to fit inside his toolbox. What psychological explanation does Gay give for the paperhanger's crime? None—not boyhood trauma or possession by devils—because he knows that such explanations are trite, exhausted, imaginary, that human beings commit acts of abrupt barbarity that no therapist, no writer, can ever adequately explain. When the paperhanger appears with the frozen body in his arms, the moment is outrageous, satanic, inevitable. As the girl's mother sleeps, the paperhanger whispers, "Sometimes . . . you do things you can't undo. You breaks things you just can't fix. Before you mean to, before you know you've done it. . . . There are things only a miracle can set to rights" (91). Does he regret the murder, the devastation he delivered to a family? Regret is possible only when one has not accepted one's nature or the cruelty of the wilderness from which we emerged naked and panting like beasts. The paperhanger is too much himself, too comfortable with Hobbesian analyses of human destiny—or what Hume aptly called "the natural depravity of mankind"—to wonder if he ought be a more benevolent man.

He departs in the mother's Mercedes, "tracking into wide-open territories he could infect like a malignant spore" and thinking about "not just the possibility but the inevitability of miracles" (92). He will beget more carnage, to be sure. The miracle he ponders: the rabid injustice of this business called living, God's abandonment of his creation, lunatics set loose. It seems a miracle that a place designed by a loving deity could be thoroughly polluted by such monsters. The man knows he's an abomination; he's made his peace with that fact. The second miracle: how Gay can massage your morality into feeling miniature sparks of sympathy for this child-killer, a lonesome and forsaken recluse who suspects that his own birth was a cosmic error.

"The Paperhanger" turns V. S. Pritchett's definition of the short story, "something glimpsed from the corner of the eye, in passing" (qtd. in Siebert 103), into something that confronts you head-on, always. O'Connor accomplishes the same magic throughout *A Good Man Is Hard to Find and Other Stories* (1955), the collection Gay read as an adolescent. He bought the Signet paperback and knew—immediately, instinctually—that inside were the best American stories ever written. He marveled over her packed sentences, her perfect endings. Gay studied O'Connor the way an evangelical studies Genesis, and from her brilliance he learned how short fiction is shaped, how a character can come alive in just a few lines—and, more important, how to tell a story that matters.

When he published *The Long Home* in 1999, William Gay was fifty-six years old, and right away was compared to both Barry Hannah and Larry Brown. Where did those years go between the teenager who read Wolfe and the middle-aged man who published his first novel? They went to the navy, to Vietnam, and then after the war to stints in Chicago and Greenwich Village (he once bumped into Janis Joplin in a pub). Back in Tennessee, the years went to marriage, to children, to a mortgage, and to the construction work that paid for it all. But Gay's time also went to reading and writing, to accumulating experience that no campus could provide, to honing his craft into a diamond tip. The chasm of those decades widened because Gay didn't know writers, hadn't made academic connections, wasn't given feedback. But when *The Long Home* finally appeared, it felt like a masterwork and not a first novel because it was the product of forty-odd years of practice. In a time when twenty-two-year-olds scribble sensational memoirs badly disguised as serious novels, it humbles one to think of William Gay in Hohenwald, Tennessee, patiently tapping the keys of his typewriter for four decades.

The Long Home takes its name from Ecclesiastes—"Because man goeth to his long home, and the mourners go about the streets"—and commences with a boom. In the undulating green environs of 1940s Tennessee, the earth has burst open with the muscle of an atom bomb, the result of either a seismic disturbance or the dawning of judgment day. This groaning gorge sits center stage as the four principal characters—Nathan Winer, Amber Rose, William Tell Oliver, and Dallas Hardin—circle it in a contest of reckoning. Hardin murdered Winer's father in a dispute over illegal whiskey and then dropped his body into the gorge. Winer was only a child at the time; he doesn't know what dirty fate befell his father. Dallas Hardin earns his fortune bootlegging and presides over the countryside like an ex-Baptist mafioso. Old man Oliver takes the teenage Winer into his tutelage, and by the time Hardin and Winer are done scrapping over Amber Rose, there is blood.

Like Milton's dazzling Satan, Dallas Hardin makes off with all the applause. Gay's reader becomes a pubescent lass from a good family who falls for the foulmouthed bad boy with a switchblade. In his villainy and hunger for destruction, Dallas Hardin is first cousin to the title character of Pete Dexter's *Paris Trout* (1988), another masterpiece about a southern psychopath with a fondness for bullets and blades. Hardin traverses his conquered territory with suave assurance, always in control, always self-righteous. He speaks like a backwards Jesus and probably reeks of fifty-dollar cologne. His name indicates his worldview: hardheaded, hard in the heart—only the hard survive. Furthermore, he is hard for Amber Rose, the teenage girl he helped raise after he stole her and her mother from the dying man whose property he confiscated and now occupies.

Where is the law? In Gay's world, the law lies mostly impotent and shriveled on the other side of town. It can be cajoled without much effort or else ignored altogether. In Hardin's case, he has paid the scoundrels in uniform to turn their backs on his criminality. If the law does come knocking, as it does in Gay's story "Sugarbaby," the knock seems a callous affront to an individual's right to freedom. In that story, Finis Beasley blasts his wife's little dog from the back porch with a large-caliber handgun because its "yip yip yip" (193) makes him batty. His wife deserts him, then sues for divorce, and Beasley ignores the letters from lawyers and summonses to appear in court. The law arrives to apprehend him, and when it does, Beasley simply cannot muster the incentive to go quietly. He tells his son-in-law at one point, "I've always minded my own business. . . . Kept my own counsel. I've always believed if a man minded his own business everybody would leave him alone" (198). Beasley's actions are less a case of gun-toting southern insurrection than of fed-up exhaustion in the face of authorities mightier than the individual. The aggravation of so many inconveniences piles up to the point that Beasley feels disgusted by his own powerlessness. This disgust for his own pathetic, diminutive place in the cosmos fuels his violence. He would have chosen peace if he had been given the opportunity to choose, if he had been left alone. Dallas Hardin, however, stomps through *The Long Home* choosing sadism and savagery because he knows no other method of being.

In Gay's able hands the archetypal characters of *The Long Home* spring to life as if for the first time: the young man on a quest; the gray sage who guides him; the comic sidekick who aids him; the gorgeous damsel who inspires him; and the villain who tries to thwart him. Their language is so authentic it seems not written at all; you *listen* to their dialogue as they sit in the same room with you. It's speech that smells of Coca-Cola and cool beer belches and early morning conversations held amidst the aroma of black coffee drunk from jars. Midway through the novel, Hardin and Winer stand out in the afternoon sun on Hardin's property. Hardin had hired Winer to help him build a honkytonk, and the boy notices that Hardin clutches his father's knife. Hardin had taken it from Winer's father the night he murdered him; when the boy asks how Hardin came by the knife, he claims he found it in a cedar grove.

> "Your pa lit out, didn't he?"
> "I don't know what happened to him. I never did believe he lit out and I don't believe it now."
> "Well, folks is funny. I don't care how close you think you know somebody, you don't know what wheels is turnin in their head. Course you don't remember but times was hard for folks back then. Times was tightern a banjo string. Lots of folks was on the road. He might've just throwed up his hands and said fuck it and lit out."
> "No."
> "Well. I ain't tryin to tell you what to think about your own daddy. But seems to me me and you's a lot alike." (134–35)

Hardin tells the boy that his own father abandoned him as well, which may or may not be the truth. Hardin, like Milton's Satan, is the great deceiver. Winer then offers to pay for the knife.

> "Hell, take it. You said it belonged to your pa."
> "Well, you've had it all these years. Decide what you want for it and hold it out of my pay."
> "Hell, no. If it means something to ye, take it on. Seems to me it's a damn poor substitute for a pa but such as it is you're welcome to it." (136)

You will not locate written speech more authentic than that, every syllable in its place, the cadence as smooth and firm as the skin on a drum. The lines also suggest the ambivalence of Dallas Hardin's character—the killer, rogue, and corrupter of Amber Rose who nevertheless attempts to give Winer honest employment, world-wary advice, and a free knife. One roots for Hardin's comeuppance, while at the same time wishing for his repentance. This is testament to Gay's tremendous skill as a craftsman. His South contains no cartoon drawings, no simplistic Zoroastrian division of darkness and light.

In Gay's world, as in ours, the wicked are laced with good, and the good are always part devil.

The Long Home owes its intricacy of assembly to *The Sound and the Fury* (1929), the book Gay received from his high school teacher when he finished *Look Homeward, Angel*, and yet the novel never feels as convoluted as Faulkner's because Gay has a Dickensian aptitude for densely woven patterns of plot and character that cohere without seam or effort. The dense, verdant prose, sweet and slow like sap—a vibrant language of poetic intensity—achieves newness in every paragraph.

> Then lightning came staccato and strobic, a sudden hush of dryflies and frogs, the walls of the attic imprinted with inkblack images of the trees beyond the window, an instantaneous and profound transition into wall-less night as if the lightning had incinerated the walls or had scorched the delicate tracery of leaf and vine onto the wallpaper. Then gone in abrupt negation to a world of total dark so that the room and its austere furnishings seemed sucked down into some maelstrom and consigned to utter nothingness, to the antithesis of being, then cool wind was at the trees, the calm eddying away like roiled water. (20)

If Gay shares with McCarthy a rich vernacular packed with flair, he also commands sentences composed of simple independent clauses strung together with the conjunction "and," sentences that would feel at home in any of the Nick Adams stories. Hemingway's reliance on concrete nouns is a lesson in the accuracy of the five senses, but it is Faulkner's and O'Connor's mythoreligious storytelling sensibility that infuses *The Long Home* from start to finish.

During one of our numerous phone conversations, Gay clarified what first struck him about Faulkner: "He took ordinary people and gave them mythic dimensions. Wolfe's people are loftier, more aware of themselves. But Faulkner's people are in the middle of it all, buffeted and battered by life." In *The Long Home*, the narrator remarks that the men and women who frequent Hardin's honkytonk—soldiers, drifters, wastrels with something to hide—are turned grand by their circumstances: "The songs and the lights and the quickened pulse of their lives made them larger than life so that they saw themselves as figures of myth and tragedy" (47). Later, when Oliver tells Winer the violent history of their region, the boy "wondered what the truth was, secretly doubted there was any truth left beneath the shifting weight of myth and folklore" (80). But of course Gay knows that myth and folklore *are* truth, or at least one way of arriving at truth—the stories we tell ourselves in order to live. Winer's wondering about the plausibility of truth does not amount to a trendy relativism, since the boy is "buffeted and battered" and thoroughly confused. In his preface to the revised edition of *Brother to Dragons* (1979), Robert Penn Warren writes, "Historical sense and poetic sense should not, in the end, be contradictory, for if poetry is the little myth we make, history is the big myth we live, and in our living, constantly remake" (xiii). Warren precisely captures Gay's mission in *The Long Home*, locating the intersection of myth and history and revealing how the truth makes itself known through living.

McCarthy's wasteland mingles history and poetry to produce a bloody modern mythology that always approaches the Old Testament in its potency. Gay has an encyclopedic knowledge of McCarthy, as he does of Faulkner, Wolfe, and O'Connor. He can recall scenes and sentences as easily as he can the names of his children. In the early 1970s, before relocating to New Mexico (and long before the globe knew of his genius), McCarthy lived in Knoxville, Tennessee. Gay, staggered by McCarthy's early novels—*The Orchard Keeper* (1965), *Outer Dark* (1968), *Child of God* (1973)—fanned through a phonebook one afternoon and discovered that the writer's number was there waiting for him to dial it. McCarthy had no interest in expounding on his own work, but as soon as Gay mentioned Flannery O'Connor, McCarthy perked up and was delighted to talk. They share in their work a violent vision of a postlapsarian South. They spoke by phone for a year, and McCarthy corresponded with Gay about the younger writer's stories. It was the only feedback available for an isolated upstart.

Gay maintains that in the 1970s the world of literature seemed to him controlled by ivory towers strewn from Boston to Manhattan. Barry Hannah was the first southern scribe of Gay's generation to be taken seriously. The publishing mecca's ostensible disinterest in new southern voices—a mystery as profound as quantum mechanics, considering that the Great American Novel, *Adventures of Huckleberry Finn* (1884), is a southern story—coupled with Gay's remoteness from anything even resembling a coterie of writers, made for dim prospects. He forged on just the same, teaching himself the craft, reading and revising, sending stories out to magazines and journals when he felt ready (one publication returned his handwritten manuscript with a note insisting on typed material only). Then, in the 1990s, two books incited a reevaluation of Gay's region and material: Cormac McCarthy's *All the Pretty Horses* (1992) and Charles Frazier's *Cold Mountain* (1997). The tremendous success of those novels shifted Gay's luck: "Things got easier for me after that" (Interview).

In writing *The Long Home*, Gay flushed McCarthy's stylistic dazzle from his system: "That language and those metaphors were all backed up in me. I just let it loose" (Interview). By the time Gay sat down to compose *Provinces of Night*, the orgasmic splendor of language à la McCarthy had spent itself—although the title comes from *Child of God*: "Were there darker provinces of night he would have found them" (23). Gay lighted on a soberer style, yet one recognizably from the same hand that penned *The Long Home*. The novel divulges the lives of three generations of Bloodworth men from Ackerman's Field, Tennessee. The district in which they live has been slated for inundation by a dam-building project, and those imminent floodwaters hover over the narrative like God's promise of annihilation. When E. F. Bloodworth returns home after thirty years on the road playing banjo and hiding from his crime—killing a deputy—long-dead sentiments and scores will be resurrected. He is another of Gay's clever, irascible old-timers: from Oliver in *The Long Home*; to Meecham in "I Hate to See That Evening Sun Go Down"; to Scribner in the story "Those Deep Elm Brown's Ferry Blues." No one matches Gay's expertise with unforgettable old men.

Of E. F.'s three sons, only Brady remains in Ackerman's Field. He cares for his demented mother and practices voodoo against deserving enemies. Warren, alcoholic and lecherous, lives over the state line in Alabama. Boyd has left for Detroit to trail his faithless wife and her lover. As in *The Long Home*, the twin heroes of this novel are the old man and the teenage boy, E. F.'s grandson Fleming—Boyd's sovereign son—an aspiring writer and one of Gay's most compassionate creations. *Provinces of Night* includes no archetypal evildoer like Dallas Hardin, but the vixen-heroine is present in the form of Raven Lee Halfacre, a cagey wit at sixteen years old. Her heat snags Fleming in a net of longing; she smells of possibility, liberation. The relationships Fleming shares with Raven, his grandfather E. F., and his close friend Junior Albright—an endearing jester who illuminates every room he walks into—allow this novel a pouring forth of affection. The hostility of Gay's universe has not diminished—storm of blood follows when Boyd finally uncovers his wife and her lover in Detroit, and E. F., too, comes to an untidy end—but in *Provinces of Night* Gay has tempered the brutality with tenderness. Here he has surpassed O'Connor—you will not come upon many moments of tenderness in her blazing Georgia. For her sanctimonious one-armed conmen, atheistic one-legged damsels, and half-naked children who crawl from the forest filthy and starved for destruction like fairy-devils, tenderness is but a rumor, the unicorn of her God-forsaken netherworld.

And then there's the comedy of the novel. Of all of Gay's characters, Fleming comes closest to approaching Nick Adams—his civility, moral code, grace under pressure, desire to write, and distressed union with his father—

but Fleming differs from Nick (and from so many O'Connor and McCarthy characters) in his appreciation of humor. Kingsley Amis once remarked that "the rewards of being sane are not many, but knowing what's funny is one of them," and Fleming is nothing if not sane, especially when compared to his volatile parents and witchdoctor of an uncle, Brady. At one point Fleming's uncle Warren jars him awake in the middle of the night to chauffeur him and his sex-scented drunk accountant over the state line, because Warren himself is too intoxicated to know north from south. Fleming says,

> "I don't have a driver's license."
> "I'm drivin on a revolted, a revoked driver's license myself and if they catch me it's my ass. I'll pay your fine if you get caught. You're not drunk are you?"
> "No."
> "That's a start then. You furnish the sobriety and I'll furnish the car and the money and we might just get organized here."
> "What about the accountant?"
> "Well, yeah, I'm furnishin her too." (105)

The drunk accountant wants a hamburger, Warren can't remember where he wants to go, and Fleming doesn't make a congenial match with an automobile. They find themselves stalled in the scrub.

> "Now you're catchin on," Warren said. "This flat black thing, I think that's what we're supposed to be drivin on. Those woods and shit, I believe I'd just try to stay out of them as much as I could."
> "We turned over in the woods three or four times," the woman said in an awed voice.
> Fleming slid his hands under his thighs to halt their shaking. "We never turned over," he said.
> "The hell we didn't," she said. "You blackhearted little liar. You tried to kill us. We turned over three or four times in the bushes and I seen every bit of it through the glass. I'm wet all over myself and I ain't ridin with you crazy sons of bitches one foot more." (107)

Twelve pages of riotous humor, with Fleming exasperated by the silliness of the circumstances, the scene reveals Gay's almost Cervantean facility with the coalescence of tragedy and comedy.

To those who know only *The Long Home* and "The Paperhanger," Gay's humor in *Provinces of Night* might seem uncharacteristic, but comedic play has been his staple all along. Most of the stories in *I Hate to See That Evening Sun*

Go Down are distinctive precisely because Gay can bend types, can marry heartbreak to hilarity in a single paragraph. Gay claims to have been influenced by the humor of Harry Crews, but Crews's comedy is almost entirely satirical, as in the "Night of the Living Dead" finale to *Celebration* (1998), or his mockery of muscle-heads in *Body* (1990). Satire has the heavy but playful hand of fabrication, while Gay's humor always touches softly, always stems from characters behaving believably in unexpected quandaries. In the title story of Gay's collection, Meecham has fled from an old-age community and returns home to discover that his son has rented his house to an insolent lout named Choat, who will not budge. Meecham handles this predicament as only an obstinate, iconoclastic eighty-year-old can: He irritates Choat to no end.

In "Bonedaddy, Quincy Nell, and the Fifteen Thousand BTU Electric Chair," sixteen-year-old Quincy Nell makes it her life's ambition to acquire as a husband Bonedaddy Bowers, a Tennessee Casanova who has a difficult time domesticating. When she finally relents and allows Bonedaddy what he's been scratching after, "came then hot honeysuckle nights of eros" (55). Bonedaddy gives Quincy Nell a stuffed panda, but then takes another girl to a dance. Quincy Nell "beheaded the panda with a single-edge razor and set the truncate corpse on the bureau, poor piebald panda with its jaunty air of yard-sale innocence" (62). By story's end, Bonedaddy Bowers will wish he had never toyed with the virginal allure of Quincy Nell Qualls.

In *The Long Home*, women are merely wagers in a gory contest for masculine dominance, but in *Provinces of Night* and most of Gay's stories, the women are shrewd operators who see men as the bumbling brutes they are. Fleming's grandmother tells him, "If sense was gunpowder ever one of you men put together wouldn't have enough to load a round of birdshot" (232). Raven Lee informs Fleming, "You men are always breaking things you don't know how to fix" (217). In "Crossroad Blues," when a grotesque little man teleported from O'Connor Country tells the main character that "a woman'll warp your mind worse than whiskey" (156), he says it in admiration, as if he were contemplating gamma rays from a supernova. Gay's story "The Lightpainter" begins, "Jenny's mother once shot her husband in the thigh with a small-caliber pistol" (263). Demonstrable logic in Gay's world is simple: If a man behaves himself and treats a woman with courtesy and compassion, he will not have his will crushed on the righteous anvil of femininity. Raven Lee Halfacre arrives as Fleming's deliverance, not his demise—and Fleming deserves this deliverance because his kindness has earned it.

Fleming Bloodworth's fight is against his testosteroned family, not a female. In *Provinces of Night*, the central struggle announces itself in the family name. What, exactly, is blood worth? What does one owe to family members, and for how long? In *Twilight*, the protagonist's sister offers him this on family: "Once you're in one, you're in it for life. You can't turn away from blood" (14). Gay's great theme throughout his work is not men against women and the agonies of that competition, but a Homeric man-against-man and the life-or-death outcome of that battle. His story "Charting the Territories of the Red," about an Achilles-like brawler who cannot let pass a slight about his wife, culminates on a riverbank in a mess of brain matter, blood soaked into the soil as into the sands of Ilium.

Twilight is the crown of Gay's oeuvre, a taut, sweat-inducing thriller so horrifying that both John le Carré and Stephen King should rethink their enterprises and revise their blueprints. The storytelling sets a new standard for darkness and depravity. Readers will find no humor here; like *Oedipus Rex*, the novel is so unrelenting in its sinister vision that any hope of light or comedy gets sucked back into the story as if by a black hole. The year is 1951, and Fenton Breece and Granville Sutter, both murderers, are every bit as psychopathic as McCarthy's Lester Ballard, from *Child of God*, and Anton Chigurh, from *No Country for Old Men* (2005). Breece and Sutter's diabolism and nihilistic designs sink so far beneath the everyday evil of men that they make Dallas Hardin look like Saint Peter. What's more, they make God look like an inebriated lunatic who holds stock in carnage, "some baleful god remonstrating with a world he'd created that would not do his bidding" (145).

Fenton Breece—a corpulent, wealthy undertaker and necrophile, who quotes Auden and listens to Mahler—surgically desecrates the bodies of the dead before interring them. He removes genitalia or positions men and women in sexual congress within the same casket, "arm in arm in eternal debauchery" (12). In some instances he does not inter them at all, but rather stores them for his own carnal bliss, dressing them in lingerie and snapping photos as he copulates with them. When siblings Kenneth and Corrie Tyler suspect Breece's deeds—Breece had violated their father's body—they unearth several caskets in the cemetery and discover for themselves the heinous mutilation. They sit "cataloguing these forbidden exhibits. From a carnival freakshow wended here from the windy reaches of dementia praecox. [Kenneth] hadn't known there were perversions this dark, souls this twisted" (12). Kenneth spies on the undertaker, manages to steal a briefcase containing photos of him with dead women, and then Corrie attempts to blackmail Breece for fifteen grand.

Enter Granville Sutter, a merciless murderer who at one point in the novel uses a switchblade to slaughter an entire family: mother, father, daughter, sons—even the dog. Breece hires Sutter to persuade the Tylers to return his property. When the siblings refuse, Sutter causes Corrie's death in a truck crash and then pursues Kenneth Tyler through the wintered wilderness like an iniquitous hound. While Breece has his way with Corrie's corpse, the cat-and-mouse competition between Tyler and Sutter reaches deep into a gelid wasteland inimical to life.

As in all of Gay's fiction, the weather and landscape become characters of their own, except that his Wordsworthian nexus to nature becomes the worship not of God's presence in the natural world, but the worship of nature's lethiferous command over human life. Gay's nature swirls in the same Tennessee towns: Ackerman's Field, Centre, Clifton, and a mostly uninhabited expanse of unkind, fabled forest called the Harrikin, the very ex-mining land into which Tyler and Sutter plunge headlong and hell-bent. Tyler

> thought he must have crossed some unmarked border that put him into territories in the land of Nod beyond the pale where folks would shun him for the mark laid on him to show that he'd breeched the boundaries of conduct itself and that he'd passed through doors that had closed softly behind him and only opened from the other side of the pale and that he'd gone down footpaths into wilderness that was forever greener and more rampant and ended up someplace you can't get back from. (154)

Gay might not appear at first glance to share O'Connor's preoccupation with religion, but every novelist with Gay's mythic, dramatic vision is religious in his own way. Gay's language owes much to the Pentecostal South and the Christianized folklore of his region, allusions and metaphors that Gay—and his characters—could not help absorbing. By *Twilight*'s end, both Breece and Sutter will be smitten by angry angels of the earth, but not before they have brought brimstone to this patch of Tennessee. *Twilight* is one of the most intrepid American novels ever written, absolutely audacious in its confrontation with hell on earth, as terrifying as medieval torture: "It is true this world holds mysteries you do not want to know. Visions that would steal the very light from your eyes and leave them sightless" (145).

Many important southern writers who came before—Peter Taylor, Eudora Welty, Carson McCullers, Walker Percy—seem timid in comparison to Gay and his nightmarish depictions. As a reader, Gay never took to Taylor or Percy. The gentility of southern aristocracy could not communicate with his rural, underclass experience, and the white-collar writers of the new South were not gritty enough for what he knew of the human animal. Tom Franklin, a dear friend to Gay, tells a story about how Gay was so poor when he was a youth that he had to mix water with crushed walnut shells in order to make ink. Gay admits that his family couldn't afford a car when he was growing up, but he doesn't boast of poverty. The writer with unflinching portrayals of human cruelty in his fiction was in life a mild and dignified man. Franklin spoke of Gay's "purity," his indifference to celebrity and the hurly-burly of New York publishing. For such an astoundingly natural talent, Gay sometimes sounded surprised that he was a writer, able to earn a living from his work for the last twelve years of his life. Surprised or not, Gay continued to beget stories and novels that help splinter the early twentieth-century fairytale of an Edenic South, that shear humankind down to the bone to lay bare the original sin and the sporadic warmth beating beneath our ribs—and for that readers should thank whichever god they call their own.

Notes

Originally published, in slightly different form, in *Southern Review* 45.2 (Spring 2009); reprinted
   by permission of the author.

Works Cited

Gay, William. "Bonedaddy, Quincy Nell, and the Fifteen Thousand BTU Electric Chair." *I Hate to
   See That Evening Sun Go Down* 50–71. Print.

———. "Crossroads Blues." *I Hate to See That Evening Sun Go Down* 148–67. Print.

———. *I Hate to See That Evening Sun Go Down.* New York: Free Press, 2002. Print.

———. "The Lightpainter." *I Hate to See That Evening Sun Go Down* 263–89. Print.

———. *The Long Home.* Denver: McMurray and Beck, 1999. Print.

———. "The Paperhanger." *I Hate to See That Evening Sun Go Down* 72–92. Print.

———. Personal interviews. June–Dec. 2008.

———. *Provinces of Night.* 2000. New York: Anchor, 2002. Print.

———. "Sugarbaby." *I Hate to See That Evening Sun Go Down* 192–215. Print.

———. *Twilight.* San Francisco: MacAdam/Cage, 2006. Print.

McCarthy, Cormac. *Child of God.* 1973. New York: Vintage, 1993.

Shapiro, T. Rees. "Author William Gay dies at 70." *washingtonpost.com. Washington Post,* 1 Mar.
   2012. Web. 17 June 2013.

Siebert, Hilary. "Raymond Carver." *A Reader's Companion to the Short Story in English.* Ed. Erin Fal-
   lon. Westport: Greenwood, 2001. 95–104. Print.

Warren, Robert Penn. Foreword. *Brother to Dragons: A Tale in Verse and Voices—A New Version.*
   New York: Random House, 1979. xi–xlv. Print.

"Recover the Paths":
Salvage in Tom Franklin's Fiction

Joan Wylie Hall

THOUGH the *Dallas Morning News* once joked that he writes like the product of a drunken tryst between Raymond Carver and Flannery O'Connor, Thomas G. Franklin was in fact born the son of Gerald and Betty Franklin in Dickinson, Alabama, in 1963. Growing up, he watched horror films, created stories for toy action figures, and wrote and illustrated his own comic books. His family, devout Pentecostals, demonstrated its faith through healings and speaking in tongues—"everything but [taking up] snakes," Franklin told an interviewer ("Tom Franklin"). At book burnings to ward off sin, he threw his beloved Tarzan paperbacks into the flames.

When Franklin was eighteen, his family moved to Mobile, where he attended the University of South Alabama, earning a BA in English. To pay tuition, he worked at a sandblasting grit factory, a chemical plant, and a hospital morgue. In 1998 he earned an MFA. at the University of Arkansas, where he met and married poet Beth Ann Fennelly. His first book, *Poachers*, appeared the next year, and he has since published three novels—*Hell at the Breech* (2003), *Smonk* (2006), and *Crooked Letter, Crooked Letter* (2010)— and in late 2013 published *The Tilted World*, a novel co-written with Fennelly.

A veteran of several teaching appointments (he has taught at Selma University, the University of South Alabama, Bucknell University, Knox College, and Sewanee: the University of the South) he is currently associate professor of English at the University of Mississippi. The essay that prefaces *Poachers* introduces Franklin's entire body of work. His title, "Hunting Years," refers to both his boyhood quest for an elusive buck in the Alabama woods and his ongoing effort, as an author, to recover lost times. In the first sentence, he revisits a scene that mirrors his younger self: "Standing on a trestle in south Alabama, I look down into the coffee-brown water of the Blowout, a fishing hole I loved as a boy." The juxtaposition of adulthood scrutiny ("I look") and past emotions ("I loved") suggests a loss he quickly underscores. Franklin and his brother once heard a panther scream while they fished this spot, but now he hears only "the groan and hiss of bulldozers and trucks on a new-cut logging road a quarter-mile away" (1). The Proustian sense of *temps perdu* is strengthened by the vivid account of early passion: the teenager's shaking hands and incipient tears when he shoots an eight-point buck at dusk, his pride when the family gathers back home to congratulate him. Most Proustian of all is Franklin's abrupt shift in time and place, from a chilly autumn in the rural South to a sunny street in France: "When I tell this story, I end by saying that nothing except Beth Ann accepting my marriage proposal on a warm wine-and-cheese afternoon in Paris has surpassed the feeling I had that night" (10–11).

"Hunting Years" relates the distance Franklin has traveled from his southwest Alabama roots. Although not "the fancy-rifled lawyer in face paint and new camouflage" he encounters upon returning to the woods, he nevertheless returns as "a kind of stranger": "I've left, gotten educated, lost some of my drawl. I even married a Yankee" (15). Poaching emerged as his motif only when the stories were almost completed: "I thought the main theme was contamination, how we're screwing up our environment. The book was originally going to be called 'Don't Touch the Ground,' after a story that we took out" ("Interview with Tom Franklin [2002]"). In "Hunting Years," Franklin compares himself to the various thieves in *Poachers* because, "coming back like this to hunt for details for my stories feels a bit like poaching on land that used to be mine." He poaches "because I want to recover the paths while there's still time, before the last logging trucks rumble through and the old, dark ways are at last forever hewn" (16). In the *Poachers* stories and the novels that followed, Franklin draws on more than a century of Alabama and Mississippi history to recover these paths.

Poachers is set in a contemporary South whose landscapes have long been under assault. "Grit," the first story, opens in a pine forest north of Mobile, with the "chugging and clanging" sounds of the "rickety" Black Beauty Minerals plant. The company manager, a hard-drinking gambler named Glen, sees himself as "captain of a ragtag spaceship that had crashlanded, a prison barge full of poachers and thieves, smugglers and assassins" (17). While the abusive Frank Bennett in Fannie Flagg's *Fried Green Tomatoes* (1987) becomes barbecue at Alabama's Whistle Stop Café, the bookie who threatens Glen with a pistol and a trench knife is baked into sandblasting grit. Roy Jones's former cohort—the white giant, Snakebite, and the stunning black Jalalieh, the only woman in the plant—help Glen process the body, and the three survivors take over Roy's scam, running the plant through the night to make a contraband product. "Tonight would be busy," Glen reflects. "You'd think, from all the sandblasting grit they were selling, that the entire hull of the world was caked and corroded with rust, barnacles and scum, and that somebody, somewhere, was finally cleaning things up" (44). The story ends as it began, with the image of a messy ship—but now the whole world is in need of cleansing, and Black Beauty grit will meet the demand, with a real black beauty in charge.

Starting with its title, "Grit" displays many conventions of Rough South literature. As Larry Brown's *Big Bad Love* (1990) likewise reveals, grit lit romance is volatile. Glen has four ex-wives and unsuccessfully flirts with Jalalieh, who drives heavy machinery on the surreptitious night shift. Set in July and August, the story emphasizes the heat of a southern summer. The Yankee owners and inspectors of the plant are outsiders, oblivious to the existence of an additional shift. Alcohol, casinos, dog tracks, hookers, cockfights, and betting on Atlanta Braves games are local diversions. Vulgarity and violence predominate, especially in the characterization of Snakebite, who threatens to cut off Glen's finger, boasts about the size of his penis, and greets an armadillo in the trash as "old armored dildo" (29). The African American Roy Jones calls Snakebite a "Texas redneck" (41), but interracial relationships in Franklin's fiction are less tense than they are in much Rough South writing. When Jalalieh takes offense at Roy's reference to "nigger-rigging" a television cable, he refuses to say "African-American" instead. "'Fuck that,' he said. 'I ain't no got-damn African-American. I'm *American* American!'" (35).

Although grit lit is generally male-centered—and Franklin regrets that *Poachers* is short on powerful females ("An Interview with Tom Franklin" 94)—Jalalieh is the first of several women in his works who show remarkable strength. Introduced as the girlfriend of Roy Jones, she quickly learns to drive loading equipment, unflinchingly helps with the grotesque disposal of Roy's body, and becomes a major partner in the illegal side-business. She later moves north, where she jogs in snowy mountains and lives alone in a cabin.

Jalalieh phones Glen with directions for banking her share of the profits, noting that she now drives a loader at a logging plant "for the fun of it" (44). Jalalieh escapes the control of Roy, who had pressured her sexually because of her brother's gambling debts; she breathes cool air hundreds of miles from the South.

In his preface to *Grit Lit: A Rough South Reader*, Franklin says grit lit is "not the hundred-pound bags of sandblasting grit I loaded onto trucks for four years in my early twenties at a plant in southern Alabama (a setting I later used in my story 'Grit'), though that's certainly part of it." He recalls what it was like "to be worked like a mule for wealthy plant owners in Detroit, underpaid, sweating, breathing silica dust alongside men with ruined backs, men whose fathers had worked at the same plant, men who never even considered college, men who used racial epithets" (vii). Such memories sum up the physical labor and economic struggle common to generations of rural southerners. Being "worked like a mule" in grit plants, poultry plants, chemical plants, and other industries of the modern South is the equivalent of back-breaking field labor in previous eras, portrayed in Franklin's later volumes. After a day of work, Glen is "so covered with sweat, grit and dust that the lines in his face and the corners of his eyes and the insides of his ears were black, and his snot, when he blew his nose, even that was black" (27). Any difference between the manager and his lowliest black worker is obscured by Glen's new duties, which expose him to every risk in the business. Conditions are so dangerous that plant employees must wear an arsenal of protection: "hard hats, safety glasses, steel-toe boots, leather gloves, earplugs and, depending on where they worked, a dust mask or respirator" (21).

Franklin admires Harry Crews, Larry Brown, William Gay, and other "practitioners of Grit Lit" who "come from the very landscape they describe" and "bring an authenticity to the page that can't be invented" (vii, viii). Although he credits these authors with sensitivity that most of their characters lack, Franklin says that "second- or third-generation Grit Litters" with creative writing degrees (like himself) "know we're a level less pure than our older, grittier counterparts." Grit lit portrays the "dirty South," without "moonlight and magnolia." Its protagonist is "a man with little hope of salvation trying to salvage what he can, even if it's only beers from the side of the highway as log trucks rumble by, carrying off the forest one shivering load at a time." The vulnerability of both the people and the land makes any effort at salvage both noble and pitiable. Yet Franklin applauds the "audacity" of "somebody up from the ground saying, 'Hold on. I ain't dead yet.' That's Grit Lit" (viii). The South of *Poachers* and Franklin's subsequent books is a dirty South in every sense, from muddy swamps and grimy plants to illegal transactions on small and large scales. And the plant manager in "Grit" is certainly up from the ground. At a climactic moment, Glen balances on a catwalk and saves his own life by pushing the armed Roy to the concrete floor one hundred feet below.

While no one mourns Roy's passing, most of the stories in *Poachers* are death-haunted. After a recent break-up with his girlfriend, the suicidal narrator of "Shubuta" says, "The pistol to the head's an option, but you need a creative twist" (45). He contrasts the slow dying of his elderly uncle to the dramatic death of a watermelon farmer who taped eyeglasses to a row of melons and shot each one through the left lens before shooting himself through the right. A stillbirth in "Triathlon" threatens to end a marriage. Internalizing these losses, the husband imagines racing a friend up a hill and finding dozens of sawed-off deer legs in kudzu at the base of a fire tower, the work of poachers. On their way to work shortly before Christmas, two men in "Blue Horses" take a pistol to a friend with a brain tumor, a gift that will allow him to kill himself. In "Reclaiming Identity, Reimagining Place: Characterizations of the White Southern Underclass in Grit Lit," Jacob Sullins writes that these anxious visitors "bear witness" to "the emptiness and loss that have taken up residence" in their friend's sad house (40). A trained geologist named Steadman in "Dinosaurs" is another witness to fatal losses, demoted for his attack on the engineer who concealed a chemical plant's discharge of "blood red chemical by-products into the Alabama River" (109), killing fish and polluting the water supply. Steadman currently checks gas stations for environmental compliance, but he is distracted by thoughts of his father, whose dementia is worsening.

Franklin tempers the devastation of body, mind, and nature with occasional notes of grace. But the blessings are secular, unlike the divine "moments of grace" that offset the grotesque in Flannery O'Connor stories. Steadman, for example, tows a taxidermied rhinoceros to a nursing home to delight his father, who has miscalculated his birthday by months. Franklin told one interviewer that the structure and themes of *Poachers* were greatly influenced by the short story collection *The Watch* (1989), by Rick Bass, an environmental activist whose first career was in petroleum geology ("An Interview with Tom Franklin" 90). Since Bass's father was also a geologist, Steadman and his geologist father are apt nods to one of Franklin's literary mentors. Steadman can picture the elderly nursing home residents "touching and stroking the dangerous beast with lust in their fingertips, a birthday gift ancient, faithful, unforgettable. Birds would collect on the rhino's back and Steadman knew his father would impress everyone by identifying them" (117).

Imaginative passages like this are a distinctive and poetic feature of Frank-

lin's grit lit. Invariably, however, the most lyrical flights and the most gener-
ous actions have a dark, even dirty shadow. Betraying his rigorous standards
for protecting the land, Steadman secures the coveted rhino from a gas station owner in exchange for a clean report on the man's defective tanks. Despite his longing "to touch something undeveloped, uncontaminated" (111),
he installs a fake leak detector in the polluted land. At least he rescues the
rhino from international poachers, who would grind her horn into aphrodi-
siac powder. In Franklin's fiction, the lovesick are likely to consult a voodoo
woman, the narrator's source for a Mason jar of murky liquid in "Shubuta":
"The love potion. It looks like plain river water, infested with bacteria and
sludge from chemical plants. Sewage" (55).

"Poachers," as its 1999 Edgar Allan Poe Award for Best Short Story implies,
concludes the collection with a strong element of mystery. A conjure woman
makes a brief appearance, but the real intrigue is a game warden's obsessive
pursuit of three orphaned brothers who are highly skilled poachers. The boys
forge a lean livelihood dynamiting catfish and trapping animals in the woods,
activities that create a lasting connection with their father, Boo Gates, who
killed himself when the oldest boy was fourteen. Kirxy, a country storekeeper, remembers that "After Boo's wife and newborn daughter had died, he'd
taught those boys all he knew about the woods, about fishing, tracking, hunting, killing. He kept them in his boat all night as he telephoned catfish and
checked his trotlines and jugs and shot things on the bank" (142). Improvis-
ing a symbolic umbilical cord, "Boo would tie a piece of rope around his sons'
waists and loop the other end to his own ankle in case one of the boys fell
overboard" (142). In his rough caretaking, the father anticipates several parents and surrogate-parents in Franklin's novels.

Years later, after the brothers kill a game warden who killed their dog, they
are stalked by Frank David, the legendary new warden and onetime poacher,
"the best poacher ever, the craftiest, the meanest" (149). Kirxy takes extreme
efforts to protect the boys. To lure David to an ambush, the storekeeper ag-
gressively poaches deer, but the warden ignores the obvious bait. On his way
to a cockfight to hear gossip about David, Kirxy passes a sign that has hung
in the woods "as long as he could remember, nailed to a tree. It said JESUS
IS NOT COMING" (152). As if to emphasize the bleak message, the warden
grotesquely kills two of the brothers and blinds the youngest with a venom-
ous snake. Dan, the maimed brother, survives, and for years he walks the
woods "seeking out each noise at its source and imagining it: an acorn nod-
ding, detaching, its thin ricochet and the way it settled into the leaves. A
bullfrog's bubbling throat and the things it said" (188–89). The story does not
end with this peaceful scene, because the lone brother periodically identifies

a more ominous sound: the "soft, precise footsteps of Frank David. Down-wind. Not coming closer, not going away. Circling. . . . A strange and terrify-ing comfort for the rest of Dan Gates's life" (189).

There is a different comfort in the legacy of Kirxy, who dies of cancer after naming Dan his beneficiary. The storekeeper had fed the boys, read them Tarzan stories, and tried to send them to school after their father died. Frank David is a much more disturbing replacement for the lost poacher-father. When he unleashed the poisonous snake on Dan, he whispered, "Goddamn, son . . . I hate to civilize you" (185). With this terrible revenge for the death of a fellow warden, the man's violence runs its course, a pattern that Frank-lin repeats in the bloodbaths of his first two novels, *Hell at the Breech* and *Smonk*. In these depictions of an earlier Rough South, the violence threatens destruction that reaches far beyond a family. Social networks are so badly damaged that one reviewer describes both books as "dark, violent tales filled with characters who had no redemption" (Talbott). This comment makes too little of Franklin's concluding scenes. His characters may be as seriously wounded as Dan Gates in "Poachers," but against all odds, each book ends on a redemptive note. However tenuous, the chance for recovery is an essential feature of Franklin's plots.

Hell at the Breech was inspired by events that tore apart a rural Alabama community in the late 1890s. With the Civil War still a bitter memory, a lo-cal feud brought bloodshed and betrayal to a new generation. Franklin grew up hearing stories about the clash and was intrigued by conflicting accounts of the Hell at the Breech gang. In his acknowledgments, he cites Harvey H. Jackson III's *The Mitcham War of Clarke County, Alabama* for historical con-texts. In an interview, he credits a facsimile of an 1897 Sears & Roebuck cata-logue for the accuracy of his descriptions: "You can't write convincingly un-less you know the tiny details of a place, of people, buttons on their britches or zippers, how much their snuff costs, the caliber of their sidearm, and this Sears catalogue's got it all" ("Tom Franklin").

Franklin also took care with physical settings, picturing "lush deep ra-vines with sprawling water oaks in the bottoms and hollows crowded with pine and other evergreens, limbs hung with Spanish moss, ivy, wisteria, and honeysuckle, creeks where cool water smoothed the surfaces of wide white rocks" (*Hell* 23). He knew the woods from his childhood in south Alabama, but cotton fields are just as prominent as pines in the novel because Franklin learned that the crop covered wide areas of Clarke County in the 1890s ("Au-thor Interview: Tom Franklin on *Hell at the Breech*"). Some of his research into the ecosystem was more unusual. Franklin told one interviewer that he planned to have a character kill an armadillo, until he discovered that "They hadn't crossed the Mississippi yet. There were no coyotes or egrets. So that

kind of thing handcuffed me again and again and again," slowing the completion of the book four years ("Author Interview: Tom Franklin").

Franklin was constrained further by the reality of his characters. "It wasn't
until I, on a whim really, changed a character's age that I realized I could do
what I wanted: it was a novel after all" ("Tom Franklin"). In making Sheriff Billy Waite a generation older than his 1890s original, Franklin provided
a perfect foil to the two young orphans who come of age in the novel. He
wanted to call the lawman Farnsworth, a name he especially likes, but county
residents urged him to retain the names of the past. Franklin adds, "If I were
making a name up, I would never call him Waite because that's what he does.
If he had acted quicker things would have come out a lot different" ("Author
Interview: Tom Franklin"). In contrast to William and Mack Burke, the im-
patient country boys, Waite is a settled man of the town, nearing retirement
and burdened by duties and regrets.

After Macky misfires a gun in the dark and shoots the country storeowner
Arch Bedsole, the brothers' naïveté leads to their dangerous liaison with the
Hell at the Breech gang, which swears to avenge Bedsole's death. The hooded
gang members capture the sheriff's attention when they fight for control of
Mitcham's Beat. Franklin agrees with his literary agent, Nat Sobel, that his
fiction has, "at its center, an innocent who's drawn into violence." The novelist
confirms that "The journey—it can last a second—from innocence to cor-
ruption/guilt fascinates me" ("Tom Franklin: Exploring the Journey from Innocence"). Young though they are, the teenagers feel their childhoods recede
as they serve the gang's violent purposes. William is initiated into the group
before the younger boy, and he taunts Mack for feeling guilty about Arch's
death. Told to bury the gang's victims, the sixteen-year-old Macky "ached
with longing for how things used to be, the two of them fishing in the creek
or playing croquet with the widow watching and Arch alive and up on the
porch giving one of his speeches" (*Hell* 89). Widow Gates is the boys' adopted
mother, a midwife who has delivered most of the county—including Tooch,
the murderer who lets the boys think that Mack's stray shot was the one that
killed Arch. The widow's famed second sight fails to detect the full extent of
Tooch's treachery, though she knows he would like to kill the brothers.

William and Mack are not the only vulnerable children in *Hell at the
Breech*. Three little Norris brothers work the land along with their father and
are reminiscent of the Gates boys in "Poachers." The sharecropper Floyd Norris is persuaded that Hell at the Breech represents the county's poor, but he is
afraid to antagonize landowners by joining the gang. Harvest time for cotton
is near, and Norris can pick almost three hundred pounds a day—too much
of an investment to lose. After his wife falls dead in the field, Floyd Norris
despairs and is later killed by Ardy Grant, an outsider who tries to massacre

the gang for political advantage. In a gruesome scene, the tow-headed Norris children take pleasure in torturing the wounded Grant, punishing him for their father's death.

Franklin's several references to fog and obscured vision suggest the moral ambiguity of the situation, as all forces gather to slaughter each other near the end of the novel. Ardy Grant wounds Macky Burke, who is in Sheriff Waite's custody, but the sheriff kills Grant before he can murder the boy. To share the responsibility and the guilt of executing Tooch, the chief remaining villain, the sheriff commands all the men in his posse to shoot together. Afterward, "Fingers and half-fingers were strewn about him and a piece of an ear lay by his head and his chest was collapsed in. He had no face, just a mass of bone and hair and gore" (298). Macky runs to his adopted mother's house and hides in her chimney, and Waite lets him go. Franklin repeats the word "hope" twice in the final paragraph, as the sheriff heads home. He looks forward to talking with his wife that night and welcoming their grown son for a visit at Christmas, a few weeks away. After so many deaths, the novel closes with the prospect of innocent new life. Waite wishes "that the future would let him hold a baby boy named Billy Waite, who would grow to manhood and obey and endure the laws of man, who could survive the world the world was becoming" (318).

Much as the Burke brothers come of age through violence in *Hell at the Breech*, two teenagers in Franklin's next novel, *Smonk*, have a comparable experience. Willie and Evavangeline encounter even more mayhem and mutilation, including zombies, castration, dynamite, incest, rabid people and dogs, and a witch who can control tornadoes. The chief setting is again Clarke County, Alabama, near the start of the twentieth century, and *Smonk*, too, concludes with hopeful references to Christmas and a baby. Franklin surprised himself by tackling historic fiction again so soon after the slow writing of *Hell at the Breech*. But *Smonk* is an even less conventional period novel, despite its references to the Civil War, wounded veterans, and post-war racism. Franklin is open to such terms as "industrial gothic" and "rural noir" for his brand of grit lit and crime fiction. His favorite "crime writers" include Elmore Leonard, Dennis Lehane, and others who challenge the ways genre fiction "seems to insist on boundaries" ("Tom Franklin"). Moreover, as he told one interviewer, *Smonk* is the novel "that I most wanted to read. I loved writing it" ("Interview with Tom Franklin").

Franklin's playfulness begins with the title, inspired by his young daughter's "mishearing of 'skunk,'" as he explains in his acknowledgments (*Smonk* 253). An ardent reader of Cormac McCarthy, another coiner of words, Franklin acknowledged in an interview, "Early versions of *Smonk* were a parody of *Blood Meridian*." He also admitted that he retained several features of McCarthy's style in the published novel: omitting quotation marks from dialogue; identifying characters by their professions instead of their names; prefacing chapters with short headings (sometimes comic, sometimes cryptic); and belatedly calling characters by their full names, as McCarthy does in naming John Joel Glanton only upon his death. Franklin names E. O. Smonk at the start, but readers do not find the meaning of "E. O." for several pages, when the judge calls Eugene Oregon Smonk to the dock ("Tom Franklin").

Smonk rivals Pushkin's Eugene Onegin for cruelty and vanity, but the ambience of Franklin's novel is more Wild West than Russian—or even Rough South. Near the end of *Smonk*, the apocalyptic "red moon blazing over all" (246) is a visual echo of McCarthy's full title, *Blood Meridian: The Evening Redness in the West*. The same archetype of disaster occurs in "The Fall of the House of Usher" (1839) and "An Odor of Verbena" (1938), works by two more authors with whom Franklin has been compared. With its hyperbole, verbal energy, and bawdiness, *Smonk* also evokes the tall-tale legacy of southwest humor, a tradition much in evidence in the outrageous plots of two of his colleagues at the University of Mississippi, the late Barry Hannah—to whom Franklin dedicated *Smonk*—and Jack Pendarvis. Franklin admits to multiple borrowings in his novel. While Charles Portis's Mattie Ross, from *True Grit* (1968), is a likely influence on the cross-dressing Evavangeline, the fifteen-year-old prostitute's namesake is Longfellow's Acadian heroine, whose long quest for her beloved is memorialized in the epic "Evangeline" (1847).

The satire in *Smonk* is scatological, sexually explicit, and profane, but Franklin does not abandon the lyricism that qualified the horror in *Hell at the Breech*. There is "harmonica music in the air" when the dwarfish, syphilitic, one-eyed title character arrives in Old Texas, Alabama, for his murder trial: "Ten after three o-clock in the afternoon according to the shadows of the bottles on the bottle tree" (*Smonk* 1). Tom Franklin's Alabama is as desiccated as T. S. Eliot's Waste Land, and Franklin, too, turns sterile soil into poetry: "It was October the first of that year. It had been dry and dusty for six weeks and five days. The crops were dead. It was Saturday and hot" (1). In the parched air of 1911, a boy grips a balloon that becomes a fragile token of innocence. By the end of the book, Willie loses his father, his home, and his balloon. He is lucky to leave town with his life when he escapes an exploding house, along with several purported orphans and Evavangeline, who was earlier run out of Louisiana. Old Texas is purged by fire after most of the residents die by gunfire and dynamite.

Together, the small band of young people flees north, and rain falls for the first time. In seven weeks on the road, Willie and Evavangeline return the boys and girls to the remote homes from which they had been kidnapped after the children of Old Texas were lost to rabies. The homeless Willie is adopted "near Christmastime" by a Mississippi family that offers a refreshing change from the withered sugarcane and ruined cornrows of Clarke County: "The house he would live in had indoor plumbing, and there was a big sweet gum tree to climb, right outside the window of his bedroom" (250). Evavangeline's parting gift to Willie is his sexual initiation. Three months later, in Memphis, she realizes she is pregnant, and she finds employment in "an upscale house of harlotry for men who desire girls in a family way." The pay is good, and so are the champagne and shrimp. For the adventurous Evavangeline, who has longed for a baby for much of the novel, pregnancy is "a goddamn miracle" (251). "A Prayer" is the final phrase in the sardonic heading for this last chapter; much like Sheriff Waite at the end of *Hell at the Breech*, Evavangeline looks to the future with customary cynicism, but also a new sense of peace.

Franklin planned to set his next book, *Crooked Letter, Crooked Letter*, like its predecessors, in southwest Alabama, but the title phrase was so appealing that he moved the action west to Mississippi. In an appendix for the Harper Perennial paperback edition, Franklin describes several autobiographical elements of this *New York Times* bestseller. A suspense novel and a coming-of-age story, *Crooked Letter* takes place in the late 1970s and early '80s—when Larry Ott and Silas Jones are schoolmates—and in the post-9/11 twenty-first century, when the men meet after two decades of estrangement. Although the mob violence of *Hell at the Breech* and *Smonk* does not recur, crimes and other mysteries are once more central to the plot.

When Larry Ott is in high school, his date disappears in the middle of the night. No body is found, and Larry is innocent, but more than twenty years later he is still suspected of her murder. The recent disappearance of a college coed has placed him under police scrutiny again, a scrutiny that intensifies when Larry is shot in his own home. Police chief Roy French is convinced that Larry killed both young women and that his wound is self-inflicted. The subsequent discovery of the coed's body on the Ott farm almost pushes the confused Larry to confess to murder.

The first several chapters of *Crooked Letter* alternate between past and present. The second half of the book is set mainly in the present century, but the past intrudes repeatedly. When Silas, now the constable of Chabot, Mississippi, cleans an old rifle from his childhood, he "was a boy again, the world the world it had been a long time ago, a world full of unknowns, a world full of future and possibility" (265). Hospitalized with a bullet near his heart, Larry considers "how time packs new years over the old ones but how those old years are still in there, like the earliest, tightest rings centering a tree, the most hidden, enclosed in darkness and shielded from weather" (251). Gradually, Franklin exposes the old growth—the darkest, most hidden secrets—while also recovering scenes of childhood innocence. Trees are more than metaphors to Larry, who, with no steady source of income, has been selling the family's acreage to the local pulpwood plant. Franklin's descriptions of the shrinking South are reminiscent of Larry Brown's portrayal of Joe Ransom "deadening" trees in the novel *Joe* (1991) and Janisse Ray's account of her ancestors cutting ancient-growth forests in *Ecology of a Cracker Childhood* (2000), works that illuminate Jay Watson's insight that southern poverty is an environmental issue (49).

So many issues are relevant in Franklin's book—from cold legal cases and domestic violence, to alcohol abuse and nursing home standards—that the University of Mississippi chose the novel for its 2012–2013 Common Reading Experience. *Crooked Letter* is Franklin's most detailed treatment of race relations in the South, a major aspect of his coming-of-age plot. The middle-school friendship of the white Larry and the black Silas, rare for its time and place, ends in a shocking scene of racial violence. At first, both boys resist as Larry's father tries to goad them into fighting for possession of a gun that Larry has loaned Silas. "White to colored," the drunken racist urges (89). The athletic Silas reluctantly knocks Larry to the ground, and Carl hits Larry with a belt to spur him to hit harder. In his defeat, Larry's old speech impediment returns, and he stutters a racial insult at Silas, whose eyes suddenly glare with "the same fierceness the other black boys at school had." Franklin adds that Larry "was already sorry but knew it was too late" (90).

A few years later, as a high school student, Silas, too, has regrets. His secret girlfriend, Cindy Walker, asks Larry for a date so that she can meet Silas. Although Silas's mother, Alice, had warned him not to get involved with a white girl, his star quality on the baseball field captivates Cindy for months. To convince Larry she must talk with her boyfriend, she lies, saying she is pregnant; unaware that the lover is Silas, he swears to keep her secret. When Cindy vanishes, the police assume Larry was the last person to see her. Silas does not reveal that he dropped her off at her house the night of her disappearance. For a long time, he thinks the rebellious Cindy ran away to escape boredom and her salacious stepfather. As a constable, though, he believes Cecil Walker was angry enough to kill the girl that night, especially if he suspected she was seriously dating Silas, who had once confronted Cecil in Cindy's defense.

Silas plays baseball at the University of Mississippi and travels around the world in the navy, while Larry tends his father's moribund auto repair shop.

Both are scarred by their memories. When Larry is shot, Silas discovers that a sociopath named Wallace Stringfellow is both Larry's attacker and the recent murderer of the local coed. Searching for evidence, the constable also discovers an old photograph that convinces him he is Larry's half-brother. His dead mother never told him that the Otts had hired her as Larry's baby nurse and then sent her away when she became pregnant. Franklin had planned to write a story of "two white brothers, one well-to-do, one on the down-and-outs" until his friend David Wright, an African American author, suggested that Silas should be black ("Interview with Author Tom Franklin"). Larry is so upset by Silas's revelation that he does not want to share a hospital room after Wallace's pit bull attacks the constable.

Before Larry returns home, however, the movement toward healing begins. The recuperating Silas and Angie, his girlfriend of a few months, scrub the floors, stock the refrigerator, and return the old rifle that Silas has kept since their childhood fight. When Larry walks away from the hospital before his formal discharge, Silas finds him and drives him to the farm. "It was country dark, as Alice Jones had called these nights, the absence of any light but what you brought to the table" (272). Light and dark imagery is abundant in the concluding paragraphs of *Crooked Letter*, the most vivid image a cinnamon candle Angie leaves on the kitchen table as a homecoming gift. Larry is pale and limping, Silas's arm is in a sling, but when Larry opens the door and switches on the light, he sees "his house made ready, washed of blood and smelling like Angie" (272).

Franklin, as he told one interviewer, is "drawn to lyrical writing," and "nature seems appropriate for this type of writing." Denying any "special understanding" of the natural world, Franklin instead claims "a working knowledge. I'm just writing what I know; since that's where I grew up—a hamlet in Alabama, very rural—it's what I have" ("Tom Franklin: Exploring the Journey from Innocence"). On the other hand, as he told another interviewer, the impact of his wife, award-winning poet Beth Ann Fennelly, is "on every page" of *Crooked Letter* ("Interview with Author Tom Franklin"). The conjunction of influences is even stronger in the couple's first co-authored book, *The Tilted World*. Set in the era of bootleggers, revenue agents, and the Great Mississippi Flood of 1927, the novel incorporates elements of the epic as well as the lyric, the national as well as the local. In her commentary for *Oxford American*'s play-list of flood songs, Fennelly describes the huge forces of nature and the wrenching social forces that gave birth to blues classics by Bessie Smith, Charlie Patton, and others.

Readers of *The Tilted World* will also find analogues in Faulkner's *Old Man* (1939), Richard Wright's "Down by the Riverside" (1938), and other fictionalized treatments of the natural disaster. Like Franklin's earlier volumes, *The Tilted World* depicts catastrophic losses and hard-fought gains. The twenty-two-year-old bootlegger Dixie Clay Holliver combines the law-breaking spunk of Evavangeline with the maternal love of the Widow Gates or Alice Jones. The most fully developed of Franklin's female characters, Dixie Clay can heft a twenty-five-pound sack and is a better shot than her husband Jesse, but after two years, she is still shaken by the loss of her baby to scarlet fever. With the flood bearing down on Hobnob, Mississippi, revenuers approaching the Hollivers' still, and sabotage threatening the levee, *The Tilted World* describes a different Rough South than any of Franklin's previous work.

Franklin says he has "never lost the need to tell of my Alabama, to reveal it, lush and green and full of death" (*Poachers* 16). So full of death are *Poachers, Hell at the Breech*, and *Smonk* that the landscapes of Clarke County and surrounding areas are hard to see for all the bloodshed. Central characters are rescued at the end of Franklin's first three books—just barely. Dan Gates of "Poachers" is alive but blinded, and he is forever stalked among the lushness. Young Mack Burke escapes a rural massacre, but he plans to go west: "Hell's breech had opened, and the closing, when it came, would come slowly" (*Hell* 317). Willie McKissick and Evavangeline leave the rabies, rapists, and religious fanatics of *Smonk*'s hyperbolically rough South for the comforts of indoor plumbing in Fulton, Mississippi, and a big paycheck at a high-class Memphis brothel.

Blood also stains the rural Mississippi landscape of *Crooked Letter, Crooked Letter*, but prospects for recovery are more lasting in this fourth book. Surviving near-death at the hands of the same killer, Larry and Silas work to recover their lost friendship and accept their brotherhood. Only Sheriff Waite of *Hell at the Breech* achieves a comparable sense of homecoming. Originally set in Alabama, *Crooked Letter* is a transition to the inherently Mississippi story *The Tilted World*, where nature itself harbors both life and death, like the wilderness Franklin knew as a boy. Rick Bass describes young Gary Jones's expulsion from a rural storm culvert as a "birth-like passage" to "redemption" after a thunderstorm in *Brown's Joe* (xv). The sense of danger and deliverance is magnified in Franklin and Fennelly's Great Flood of 1927. Many are lost in the waters. Yet when Dixie Clay retrieves a little coffin-shaped trunk from a snag on the shore, she finds a mandolin, not a child's body. In this Rough South, the salvage can be sweet.

Many thanks to Whitney Hubbard and Beth Spencer of the University of Mississippi Department of English for generously sharing their ideas on

Franklin's work. I am also grateful to Franklin himself for visiting my southern literature survey class for an unforgettable discussion of *Crooked Letter, Crooked Letter.*

Works Cited

Bass, Rick. "Foreword: A Tribute to Larry Brown." *Larry Brown and the Blue-Collar South.* Ed. Jean W. Cash and Keith Perry. Jackson: UP of Mississippi, 2008. vii–xvii. Print.

Fennelly, Beth Ann. "3 More Great Songs about the Flood." *oxfordamerican.org. Oxford American,* 9 Dec. 2011. Web. 17 May 2013.

Franklin, Tom. "Author Interview: Tom Franklin." Interview by Robert Birnbaum. *identitytheory. com. Identity Theory,* 31 July 2003. Web. 17 May 2013.

———. "Author Interview: Tom Franklin on *Hell at the Breech.*" *harpercollins.com.* HarperCollins Publishers, n.d. Web. 18 May 2013.

———. *Crooked Letter, Crooked Letter.* New York: Morrow, 2010. Print.

———. *Hell at the Breech.* New York: Morrow, 2003. Print.

———. "Interview with Author Tom Franklin." Interview by Karen Spears Zacharias. *patheos.com.* Patheos, 17 Jan. 2011. Web. 19 May 2013.

———. "An Interview with Tom Franklin." Interview by Joy Wilson. *Yalobusha Review* 7 (2002): 89–96. Print.

———. "Interview with Tom Franklin." Interview by J. C. Robertson. *southernlitreview.com. Southern Literary Review,* 5 May 2009. Web. 18 May 2013.

———. "Interview with Tom Franklin (2002)." Interview by Amber Breland. *Mississippi Writers & Musicians.* Starkville High School, 17 Dec. 2002. Web. 17 May 2013.

———. *Poachers.* New York: Morrow, 1999. Print.

———. "Preface: *What's Grit Lit?*" *Grit Lit: A Rough South Reader.* Ed. Brian Carpenter and Franklin. Columbia: U of South Carolina P, 2012. vii–viii. Print.

———. "Tom Franklin." Interview by Rob McClure Smith. *Allan Guthrie's Noir Originals.* Noir Originals, 2008. Web. 18 May 2013.

———. "Tom Franklin: Exploring the Journey from Innocence." Interview by Louis Mayeux. *Southern Bookman: A Literary Blog for All Seasons.* Typepad, 27 Aug. 2009. Web. 18 May 2013.

———. *Smonk.* New York: Morrow, 2006. Print.

———, and Beth Ann Fennelly. *The Tilted World.* New York: Morrow, 2013. Print.

Sullins, Jacob. "Reclaiming Identity, Reimagining Place: Characterizations of the White Southern Underclass in Grit Lit." MA thesis. University of Mississippi, 2006. Print.

Talbott, Chris. "Tom Franklin's New Novel: Twisting Tale of Completion." Rev. of *Crooked Letter, Crooked Letter. huffingtonpost.com. Huffington Post,* 11 Jan. 2011. Web. 21 May 2013.

Watson, Jay. "Economics of the Cracker Landscape: Poverty as an Environmental Issue in Larry Brown's *Joe.*" *Larry Brown and the Blue-Collar South.* Ed. Jean W. Cash and Keith Perry. Jackson: UP of Mississippi, 2008. 49–57.

The Rough South of Ron Rash

Thomas Ærvold Bjerre

R ON Rash hails from the southern Appalachian Mountains, where his an-cestors settled in the mid-1700s. He was born in Chester, South Caroli-na, in 1953, and grew up in Boiling Springs, North Carolina. Rash sets almost all of his work—poems, short stories, and novels—in this region and focuses on the people who live or have lived there. While not a direct heir to the "Southern Redneck and White Trash" tradition that Erik Bledsoe discusses in his seminal essay, he fills his work with characters firmly embedded in the Rough South. Brian Carpenter describes this demographic in his intro-duction to *Grit Lit: A Rough South Reader* as "mostly poor, white, rural, and unquestionably violent" (xxvii), and Rash's characters are unquestionably that. He peoples his fiction with mostly lower-class whites from Appalachian North and South Carolina. In a 2006 interview that opened with a division of southern writing into the same two groups Tony Early has cited—those on the right side of the tracks (heirs of Eudora Welty) and those on the wrong side (the hell-raising, hard-drinking, violent group)—Rash was asked if he considers himself a member of the latter. He answered in the affirmative: "Yeah, in the sense of the kind of world that I depict and the language of that world as well. And also just being outdoors, being out there among the may-hem at times" ("Renegade Writers").

Rash's work illustrates his concern with working-class characters and their struggles, with poor whites and their violent conflicts. He writes both out of and against the southern agrarian tradition; he uses his own escape from the Rough South through education to explore the experiences of various characters. Many characters in Rough South literature, such as the eponymous character in Larry Brown's *Joe* (1991), do not need to escape or "overcome" their poor white origins. To do so "would be to give up all that he knows and cares about" (77), Bledsoe writes. But many of Rash's characters long to escape their poor backgrounds. Those who succeed in doing so, however, encounter resentment from members of both lower and upper classes and struggle with guilt for leaving their backgrounds behind.

Rash's interest in the working poor reflects his own family background. His grandfather worked in the textile mill that gives its name to Rash's first collection of poetry, *Eureka Mill* (1998). In fact, the grandfather is a recurrent figure in the poems, which present a poignant and unflinching portrait of North Carolina cotton mill workers in the early 1900s. The poems depict both the physical hazards and the grueling labor involved in working the turn-of-the-century mills. At the time of Rash's birth, his parents, too, worked in the mill. His father would later attend night school, complete a college degree, and eventually teach at Gardner-Webb University in Boiling Springs, where Rash would later earn his bachelor's degree ("Biography: Ron Rash"). But while Rash did attain some higher education, his family toiled in the Rough South, a fact that perhaps explains his ability to write "from *within* the class," as Bledsoe describes Harry Crews's perspective on the poor white (68). As Rash explained in "The Natural World Is the Most Universal of Languages: An Interview with Ron Rash," "I think I'm close enough, I've known enough people who farm, including my own family, not to sentimentalize that life. It's a hard life. . . . It's a little too easy to idealize it. It's a tough, tough life, and one I obviously didn't choose" (222).

Rash's background thus affords him the kind of authenticity that Carpenter and Tom Franklin stress in *Grit Lit*. Franklin claims that Grit Lit writers "have more often than not come from the very landscape they describe; they've fought their way up from the ground. . . . They bring an authenticity to the page that can't be invented" (ix). This inside knowledge and identification with poor southerners formed the basis of Rash's first novel, *One Foot in Eden* (2000). The genesis of the novel was a poem about a farmer standing amid a field of dying crops. Rash realized, however, that "what I wanted to write, *what that farmer wanted me to write*, could not be contained in a poem. . . . I knew that if I were to give him and his story their due I would have to write a novel. . . . All I knew was that I had to try, because for some inexplicable reason I owed it to that man in the field" ("The Story Behind the Book: *One Foot in Eden*"). Thus Rash's becomes the voice of forgotten farmers whose culture has all but vanished in today's technological society. In poetry, short fiction, and novels, Rash is determined to tell *their* story.

By questioning industrial progress and re-creating a lost rural culture, Rash situates himself beside the Southern Agrarians, particularly Andrew Nelson Lytle, who wrote melancholically of a lost era, a rural, backward-looking place of farms and small towns. But whereas Lytle's Agrarian paradise was an elitist (or at least middle-class) utopia, Rash's lost world is one of poor mountain people struggling to make ends meet. This life would not sit well with the Agrarians, who often marginalized such populations. Richard Gray, in *Southern Aberrations: Writers of the American South and the Problems of Regionalism*, describes how, in the 1930s, the accepted view of poor whites was that they "did not exist; or if they did, they existed outside of 'civilization.' They were irredeemably 'others,' marking the outer limits of the culture" (160). Discussing Agrarian Donald Davidson's omission in "A Mirror for Artists" of literature about poor whites, Gray writes that for many of the Agrarians, "to write of the 'unknown people' of the Southern countryside was not to write as a Southerner; it was doubtful if it was even to write as an American" (161). This marginalization of poor whites has, to a large extent, continued until recently. As Matthew Guinn notes in "Writing in the South Now," Crews shocked the literary establishment with his novels of the late 1960s and early '70s, their poor-white perspectives leaving southern critics "unequipped to evaluate" them. And the "virulently anti-pastoral images" of Cormac McCarthy's novels of the period left traditional critics furious at what they considered an all-out attack on tradition and culture (571). In 1999, Fred Hobson, in *But Now I See: The White Southern Racial Conversion Narrative*, stated that class was the "least openly and honestly addressed" aspect of southern culture (134). While Rash belongs to the group of writers who empathize clearly with poor southerners, he does not romanticize them. This more realistic perspective appears in his many depictions of physical labor—as we will see—and the violence looming over his characters' lives.

Violence, Carpenter asserts, "is an ever-present threat" in Rough South works like Rash's (xxi). *One Foot in Eden* features rowdy bar fights. A man guns down another at point-blank range; later, he and his wife drown in a flood. In *The World Made Straight* (2006), both a 1970s Appalachian bildungsroman and a meditation on the role of the past in the present, seventeen-year-old high school dropout Travis Shelton moves in with a local drug dealer, Leonard Shuler, after being maimed by the brutal farmer and local drug lord Carlton Toomey. The conflict between the two men builds to a violent climax in which three people are killed. In *Serena* (2008), an Appalachian retelling of Shakespeare's *Macbeth* and a condemnation of the ruthless lumber industry that destroyed a large part of the western North Carolina wilderness, the title character and her husband rule their lumber empire by brute force—including their use of the henchman and killer Galloway. Ultimately, Serena's ruthless ambition drives her to kill her own husband. In *The Cove* (2012), set during World War I, the cowardly army recruiter Chauncey Feith orchestrates a violent mob that ultimately commits several murders.

Carpenter also addresses the Rough South concern with "understanding the how and why, the cause and consequence of what Crews called the 'need to bleed'" (xxii). Holland Winchester, from *One Foot in Eden*, is a good example of this concern. He tells the high sheriff, "Sometimes when a man's hurting on the inside a good bar fight can help him feel some better" (5). Later, Holland finds himself at the wrong end of a shotgun. Having impregnated the wife of Billy Holcombe, a sterile tobacco farmer, he now has to face a grim reckoning. On the surface, this is an iconic scene of macho violence, rooted in the southern tradition of male honor, but Rash shows us how Billy's violent action to a certain extent results from a "domineering and suffocating" tradition (Bjerre 244). In fact, in losing the confrontation, Winchester is even more locked into this tradition. Pushing the barrel against Winchester, Billy's hands shake, "but Holland steadied the barrel against his chest. 'Settle it now one way or another,'" he tells Billy, "'because this here is the only way to keep me from claiming what's mine'" (126). The scene demonstrates how Rash's approach to violence follows that of other Rough South writers.

The two men, acting out an age-old script, point to one explanation for violent excess in the Rough South. Crews referred to these confrontations as "blood moments," in which you "find out who the hell you are, what you really are, what you really believe" (97). In a similar vein, every time he was criticized for his use of violence, Barry Hannah gave a variation of the same answer, such as: "[I]t puts your back up against the wall. People tend to lie less in conditions of violent behavior. . . . There's a more straightforward reaction" (113). The confrontation between Billy and Winchester perfectly exemplifies the epistemological aspects of violence that Crews and Hannah employed, but Rash also uses violence so as to gain insight into characters and move them forward.

The scene also echoes Crews's explanation of the sometimes seemingly constant violence in the Rough South, what Carpenter calls "a vicious cycle of poverty and isolation." As Crews explains it, his "own people 'were locked into social circumstances' that led to a 'kind of raging frustration that found its outlet in rank violence'" (qtd. in Carpenter xxi). And just as Carpenter argues that Rough South violence is "a means of moral reckoning" as writers go "beyond all the macho posturing" (xxii), so Rash shows deep understanding of social and psychological mechanisms leading to the inevitable violence and death and its consequences, for those involved have to live with themselves after the killing. Billy Holcombe, in *One Foot in Eden*, admits "feeling a stranger to myself. . . . It would take some while to get used to being a murderer" (127).

But characters are not the only source of violence in Rash's fiction. Violence is often rooted in the land the characters inhabit. "Place is never simply 'place' in southern writing," Patricia Yaeger writes in *Dirt and Desire: Reconstructing Southern Women's Writing 1930–1990*. It is also "always a site where trauma has been absorbed into the landscape" (13). This analysis is certainly true in Rash's fiction, where the Civil War still haunts the land, and where farmers and others living in the rural areas featured have to contend with nature every day to survive. The tradition of violence is especially clear in *The World Made Straight*. While the central narrative is set in the 1970s, occasional chapters from a Civil War doctor's journal create a link between the present and a past that continues to haunt characters—especially the 1863 Shelton Laurel Massacre, in which a Confederate force massacred thirteen Union sympathizers, including Travis's ancestors.

The past, in the form of a pair of glasses that Travis finds in the Shelton Laurel Meadow, is literally buried in the land. Believing that the glasses belonged to David Shelton, a twelve-year-old victim of the massacre, Travis puts them on and looks at Leonard.

> He squinted his left eye. "It's kind of blurry, like looking through water, but I can see you well enough." Travis opened his left eye. "David Shelton could have been looking through these glasses when they shot him. Standing right where I'm standing.". . . The [snow] flurries increased, flakes as big as the lens Travis peered through. Snow spread clean and level over the meadow. Maybe a blank page was all history could be in the end, he thought, something beyond what could be written down, articulated. (207)

This is a significant moment in the novel. Travis abandons his teenaged self-centeredness and becomes an adult who tries to connect with and learn from the past without—importantly—feeling trapped by it. The "blank page" spread out before him suggests a freedom in relation to the past—and future—that most locals do not share. Travis remembers his great-grandmother refusing to change her clocks to daylight saving time because Lincoln Republicans like her "didn't want to go along with a Democrat's idea" (84). But even Travis's father is more than happy to point out that Leonard's "momma's great-granddaddy helped kill off near every member of your family" (231), thereby making Travis question Leonard's motives and loyalty.

Leonard Shuler also feels trapped by historical and geographical circumstances. He has carried the phrase "landscape as destiny" in his head for years, unable to escape "the sense of being closed in, of human limitation." He feels as if he's living "in the passive voice," as if his life is a mere memory, "fixed and immutable" (156–57). Leonard moved from Madison County to Illinois with his wife and daughter, but his marriage has deteriorated because of his tendency of "living in the passive voice, letting others make choices so if things went wrong he didn't have to bear the blame" (54). Travis feels that *his* weakness of character, his passivity runs in his blood. He traces it back to Dr. Joshua Candler, his great-great-grandfather, whose participation in the massacre still haunts Leonard. At the end of the novel, however, he embraces his destiny and sacrifices himself to give Travis a chance to break free from the cycle of violence. Shot in the arm and captured by Carlton Toomey and his son, both tracking Travis, Leonard forces their pickup off the road, where it crashes into a gorge, and where all three die from their injuries.

Despite the focus on poor whites and their violent lives, much tension in Rash's fiction seems to emerge from his own education and the issue of education in general. In "The Natural World Is the Most Universal of Languages," he elaborated on the role of education in Appalachia: "[E]ducation's the way you get out," he said. "Any minority culture knows that" (220). Rash also explained how he wanted to challenge some of the "pervasive stereotypes about no one being able to read, no one having an education, and that's obviously not true. But you don't want to go the other way and pretend everyone has a college education. . . . So I wanted to show what, to me, was the reality, that there are people like this in the region. Not everybody is illiterate" (220–21). Those who pursue an education, however, often face obstacles in small rural communities, traditionally suspicious of education. This suspicion plays into a class division that saturates southern fiction. As Marcel Arbeit has explained in "'Send the Bloody Intellectuals to Gym': Harry Crews's Educated Super(wo)men and Victims of Both Sexes," "[I]n Southern country and small town areas, 'intellectual' is a dirty word. It implies the formal education that alienates the good country boy or girl from their roots and makes them feel superior to their former peers" (167). Part of the conflict relates to notions of masculinity. John Shelton Reed, in *Southern Folk, Plain & Fancy: Native White Social Types*, notes how the "good old boy" stereotype operates as the most masculine of positive southern social types (75). Summarizing traditional views of masculinity, Peter Schwenger, in *Phallic Critiques: Mas-*

culinity and Twentieth-Century Literature, reminds us that a real man is supposed to be one of action; a man should not jeopardize his virility by being too articulate, by showing too much comfort with and control of language, as intellectuals do. The masculine role in the twentieth century, Schwenger argues, "has become that of the 'natural' man," whose gestures are "less civilized." This particular role is built on traits traditionally associated with the working-class male (18).

This attitude explains the paradox Carpenter describes in his introduction to *Grit Lit*: "[M]any a southern writer finds himself in the peculiar position of having to defend his own Rough South pedigree, which in turn has resulted in what Hal Crowther has called a curious game of 'dueling hardships,' a 'competition for the humblest origins—who ate the most squirrels and chitlins, used the rankest outhouse, or grew up with the most lint in his hair.' Crowther says, 'Writers whose parents were solvent or—God help them—educated have been sent to the back of the bus'" (xix). What's at stake here is not merely authenticity, but masculinity itself, a paradox obvious in Rash's work, where it creates internal conflicts—both intra- and interclass tensions—as early as *One Foot in Eden*. Billy Holcombe is a former sharecropper who has become a land-owning tobacco farmer. "That had been a big doing for me," he says. "The only land Daddy and my Uncle Joel could claim was what dirt they carried under their fingernails" (121). When Billy buys his twenty acres, the seller is dubious about the purchase: "'A Holcombe owning land,' he'd said, then smiled. 'You're getting above your raising, boy'" (121). Another character who has followed this path is High Sheriff Will Alexander, who struggles morally with his profession. Upon becoming a lawman, he moved from the family's tobacco farm in the Jocassee Valley into the town of Seneca, and thereby made the significant shift from farmer to thinker, estranging himself not only from his father and brother, but also from a part of himself.

Like Rash, Will does not harbor sentimental memories of the farming life. In fact, his recollection paints a bleak picture of the farmer: "To farm a man did have to act like a mule—keep his eyes and thoughts on the ground straight in front of him. If he didn't he couldn't keep coming out to his fields day after day. . . . Don't pretend you miss such a life as this," Will tells himself (15). Yet he still doesn't feel at home in the town where he lives. Checking the weather, he feels ashamed that he doesn't need to worry about it. He gets a "certain paycheck come rain or drought" (10). When he realizes that he is "little more than a stranger" to his father, and that the family farm will "one day vanish completely as a dream," he makes a moral decision to serve out his term as high sheriff and then return to farm his family's land: "I'd farm this land until Carolina Power ran us all out and drowned these fields and creeks and the river itself. However long that was, it would give me some time to be a son and a brother again, maybe even learn how to be an uncle" (40). Will's wife, Janice, does not share her husband's longing for the country. Their different backgrounds even strain their marriage. Still playing "the wealthy doctor's daughter" (41), Janice flinches when Will uses "hillbilly talk" (7). She, too, has fallen prey to class prejudice, having been called "Mrs. White Gloves" by a town councilman, who jokes that she's probably "teaching the sheriff the proper way to unfold a napkin" (41). Will is quite aware that his decision to return to the farm will result in divorce, since his wife will not descend the social ladder to stand beside him.

Rash also highlights the role of education in *The World Made Straight*. Seventeen-year-old high school dropout Travis moves out of his parents' house, abandoning the tobacco farm and his mean-spirited father, and moves in with Leonard Shuler, the disgraced teacher-turned-drug dealer. Carlton Toomey mocks Leonard's education, derogatorily referring to him as "Professor." But Leonard's knowledge, particularly his grasp of local history—including his family's role in the Civil War massacre that still threatens to tear the community apart—fascinates Travis. Becoming educated, he thus rises above his background. The conflict that arises between Travis and his father concerns notions of masculinity as well. When Travis leaves home after his father again slaps him, his father's parting words are, "You ain't got enough man in you to go it alone" (83). Travis determines to prove his father wrong but still yearns for the man's respect. Knowing that "book-learning" will not impress him, Travis hopes his father will "admire the effort it took," since Travis not only graduated from high school, but did so "living on his own and holding down a full-time job" (216)—his employment suggesting a certain toughness associated with traditional, working-class masculinity. But after earning his GED, Travis confronts his father, and it becomes clear that to Travis, manhood means more than physical strength. "I'm a better man than you'll ever be," he tells his father, "and I've proved it by getting a GED" (234). At the same time, however, Travis cannot help feeling guilty for this breach of tradition. Driving past a tobacco field, he "smelled the plowed earth and wondered if he would ever stand in a tobacco field again or spend minutes with his hands under a spigot rubbing off tobacco resin." Travis remembers the knit bundles as "irrefutable testimony to their devotion and hard work, *their* pride, his as well as his father's" (216).

Pride in physical labor also points to part of the agrarian tradition Rash embraces. In "Introduction: A Statement of Principles," the Agrarians claim that the "first principle of a good labor is that is must be enjoyed." "The act

of labor as one of the happy functions of human life has been in effect abandoned," they lament, "and is practiced solely for its rewards" (xl–xli). We hear
echoes of this sentiment in *One Foot in Eden* when Billy Holcombe expresses
pride in the land he owns and has worked to cultivate, despite being crippled
by polio: "I'd cleared that twenty acres by myself but for [the horse] Sam, me
and that horse yanking up stumps stubborn to come out as back teeth. It
had been a man's work. You couldn't call no one a cripple who had done it"
(121). R. W. Connell, in *Masculinities*, explains how manual labor demands
"strength, endurance, a degree of insensitivity and toughness, and group solidarity" and that this performance of working-class masculinity is a means
of survival (55). This idea seems to inform Billy's pride in his work; however,
as already stated, Rash does not romanticize or sentimentalize hard labor.
The World Made Straight describes the backbreaking labor that is tobacco
farming: "Travis hanging thirty pound sticks of tobacco while balancing on a
crossbeam no wider than a railroad tie. That was the hardest work of all, not
just hanging the plants but the resin sticking to you like tar, flecks of tobacco
burning your eyes. Dangerous work" (144).

Opposed to romanticizing the proud but backbreaking labor performed by
skilled hands, Rash also depicts—again in line with the Agrarian view—the
degradation of industrial labor. Industrialization serves as a thematic background through *One Foot in Eden*, in which all characters know Carolina
Power will destroy their community with state-controlled flooding. They will
be evicted, the graves of their ancestors dug up. After describing the beauty
of the landscape and the history behind it, Rash ends the novel with a seven-
word indictment of the industrial technologies that have erased entire communities: "This was a place for the lost" (214). In *Serena*, furthermore, Rash
describes the working conditions of the lumber workers building the Pemberton empire:

> Most of the loggers were still exhausted from last week's six eleven-hour
> shifts. Some were hung over and some were injured. . . . Some used cocaine
> to keep going and stay alert, because once the cutting began a man had to
> watch for axe blades glancing off trees and saw teeth grabbing a knee and
> the tongs on the cable swinging free or the cable snapping. Most of all the
> sharded limbs called widow makers that waited minutes or hours or even
> days before falling earthward like javelins. (24)

Here Rash shows the ugly face of industrial labor, which not only degrades,
but robs and threatens to kill workers. This is an example of the evil industrial forces the Agrarians raged against. They complained that "under the

industrial regime," the modern worker's "labor is hard, its tempo fierce, and his employment . . . insecure." Under the industrial regime, they warn, "labor becomes mercenary and servile," and they regret that "many forms of modern labor are accepted without resentment though they are evidently brutalizing" (xl–xli).

In *Serena*, Rash presents several examples of the brutalizing force of the logging industry. Doctor Cheney jokes that if "you could gather up all the severed body parts and sew them together, you'd gain an extra worker every month" (26), and later, when a seventeen-year-old "chopper" accidentally cuts off Galloway's hand, it "hit . . . the ground palm down, fingers curling inward like the legs of a dying spider" (179). Rash also points out the cynical nature of the industry and the people behind it—from Cheney, who asks his employers if the maimed Galloway is worth saving, to the men who come into the camp to seek work and "wait . . . days for a maimed or killed worker to be brought from the woods in hope of being his replacement" (199). These examples from Rash's work echo the Agrarians' mistrust of the industrial order. Add to them the havoc that Pemberton's logging wreaks on the landscape: "As the crews moved forward, they left behind an ever-widening wasteland of stumps and slash, brown clogged creeks awash with dead trout. Even the more resilient knottyheads and shiners eventually succumbed, some flopping onto the banks as if even the ungillable air offered greater hope for survival" (116).

This bleak image serves as a larger metaphor for the struggle Rash's characters face. Some manage to escape their poor, violent origins—or at least take the first few steps, often through education, into another kind of life. But as Travis experiences in *The World Made Straight*, landscape can be destiny. For most of Rash's characters, that landscape is the Rough South.

Works Cited and Consulted

Arbeit, Marcel. "'Send the Bloody Intellectuals to Gym': Harry Crews's Educated Super(wo)men and Victims of Both Sexes." *The Many Souths: Class in Southern Culture.* Ed. Waldemar Zacharasiewicz. Tübingen: Stauffenburg Verlag, 2003. 167–73. Print.

"Biography: Ron Rash." *poetryfoundation.org.* Poetry Foundation, n.d. Web. 30 May 2013.

Bjerre, Thomas Ærvold. "*One Foot in Eden.*" *Still in Print: The Southern Novel Today.* Ed. Jan Nordby Gretlund. Columbia: U of South Carolina P, 2010. 233–47. Print.

Bledsoe, Erik. "The Rise of Southern Redneck and White Trash Writers." *Southern Cultures* 6.1 (2000): 68–90. Print.

Carpenter, Brian. "Introduction: Blood and Bone." *Grit Lit: A Rough South Reader.* Ed. Carpenter and Tom Franklin. Columbia: U South Carolina P, 2012. xiii–xxxii. Print.

Connell, R. W. *Masculinities*. 2nd ed. Berkeley: U of California P, 2005. Print.

Crews, Harry. "Harry Crews." Interview by William J. Walsh. *Speak So I Shall Know Thee: Interviews with Southern Writers*. Ed. Walsh. Jefferson: McFarland, 1990. 92–101. Print.

Crowther, Hal. "The Last Autochthon: Listening to the Land." *Gather at the River: Notes from the Post-Millennial South*. Baton Rouge: Louisiana State UP, 2005. 79–83. Print.

Early, Tony. "Mephisto Tennessee Waltz." *nytimes.com*. *New York Times*, 12 Nov. 1999. Web. 30 May 2013.

Franklin, Tom. "Preface: What's Grit Lit?" *Grit Lit: A Rough South Reader*. Ed. Brian Carpenter and Franklin. Columbia: U of South Carolina P, 2012. vii–viii. Print.

Gray, Richard. *Southern Aberrations: Writers of the American South and the Problems of Regionalism*. Baton Rouge: Louisiana State UP, 2000. Print.

Guinn, Matthew. "Writing in the South Now." *A Companion to the Literature and Culture of the American South*. Ed. Richard Gray and Owen Robinson. Oxford: Blackwell, 2004. 571–87. Print.

Hannah, Barry. "An Interview with Barry Hannah." Interview by Larry McCaffery and Sinda Gregory. *Alive and Writing: Interviews with American Authors of the 1980s*. Ed. McCaffery and Gregory. Chicago: U of Illinois P, 1987. 111–25. Print.

Hobson, Fred. *But Now I See: The White Southern Racial Conversion Narrative*. Baton Rouge: Louisiana State UP, 1999. Print.

Rash, Ron. "The Natural World Is the Most Universal of Languages: An Interview with Ron Rash." *Appalachian Journal* 34.2 (Winter 2007): 216–27. Print.

———. *One Foot in Eden*. Charlotte: Novello Festival P, 2002. Print.

———. *Saints at the River*. New York: Holt, 2004. Print.

———. *Serena*. 2008. New York: Canongate, 2010. Print.

———. "The Story Behind the Book: *One Foot in Eden*." *rusoffagency.com*. Marly Rusoff Literary Agency, n.d. Web. 30 May 2013.

———. *The World Made Straight*. New York: Holt, 2006. Print.

Reed, John Shelton. *Southern Folk, Plain & Fancy: Native White Social Types*. Athens: U of Georgia P, 1986. Print.

"Renegade Writers." *Writers*. Mississippi Public Broadcasting. 1 Feb. 2007. Television.

Schwenger, Peter. *Phallic Critiques: Masculinity and Twentieth-Century Literature*. Boston: Routledge & Kegan Paul, 1984. Print.

Twelve Southerners. *I'll Take My Stand: The South and the Agrarian Tradition*. 1930. Baton Rouge: Louisiana State UP, 1977. Print.

Yaeger, Patricia. *Dirt and Desire: Reconstructing Southern Women's Writing 1930–1990*. Chicago: U of Chicago P, 2000. Print.

"Everything Worth Doing
Hurts Like Hell": The Rough South
of Tim Gautreaux

L. Lamar Nisly

TIM Gautreaux's interviewers often express surprise at his knowledge of and love for machinery. "I come from a blue-collar family," Gautreaux once explained, "and everybody was always talking about machines when I was a kid because my family was made up of tugboat captains, oil rig workers, and railroad workers. They'd talk about their trades" ("An Interview with Tim Gautreaux" 26). In another interview he added ruefully, "My wife says I write fiction as an excuse to write about machinery" ("Novel Approach: Tim Gautreaux Takes 'The Next Step'" 18). Whether he's describing the intricacies of a steam engine or explaining how to tune a piano, Gautreaux's fiction clearly embodies his deep roots in the blue-collar culture of southern Louisiana.

Born in 1947, Gautreaux grew up in Morgan City, Louisiana, which during his childhood was "an oil-patch town with kind of a Wild West flavor" and a large collection of barrooms and churches ("A Conversation with Tim Gautreaux" 153). His experiences in Morgan City, along with the stories he heard from his father, a tugboat captain, and his grandfather, a steamboat engineer, led him to identify that world as his "territory as a writer" ("An Interview with Tim Gautreaux" 26). Though he moved away from it as an adult, choosing to become a college professor, his appreciation and understanding of the grittier side of his upbringing remain evident:

> When I think of the history of my family, I think of how hard it was for people to work and survive and how much my family members suffered living in a tough climate and tougher poverty. Sometimes I recall one of my father's first jobs, which was cutting down cypress trees that were five feet through the middle. He had to stand in waist-deep water, fighting snakes and leeches, and work with a crosscut saw in 95-degree heat. When a man paddled out from town in a skiff and hired him as a tugboat deckhand, he felt lucky just to be above the water for a change. Sometimes I remember that my grandfather worked under the thumb of a stingy plantation owner for sixty-five cents a day. You look back on all that history and all that misery and you almost feel like a traitor if you don't respect the people you came from and the place they made. In one way or another, you have to tell their story. ("Tim Gautreaux" 109)

Gautreaux enriches that story through his expert use of dialectical variations for characters from various backgrounds. As he has said, "There is still a rich creative metaphorical magic alive, and it's in the mouths of uneducated people. Educated people tend to speak a standard English which is not creative and which is not conducive to storytelling or bull-shitting or any verbal color at all. . . . People who are uneducated basically have to make up an idiom as they go along. These are the people I like to listen to, because they're very acrobatic with the way they use the language" ("Novel Approach: Tim Gautreaux Takes 'The Next Step'" 19).

As indicated above, Gautreaux did not remain a resident of the Rough South. He earned a bachelor's degree in English from Louisiana's Nicholls State University in 1969 and a PhD in 1972 from the University of South Carolina, where he studied poetry under James Dickey. Gautreaux's move to writing fiction came in 1977, when he took part in a writing seminar led by Walker Percy at Loyola University New Orleans. He describes the experience as deeply formative, both because of Percy's tutoring in narrative construction and because of their shared Catholic vision. Gautreaux openly embraces his Roman Catholic faith, and through Percy he learned that "you could deal with questions of value in contemporary fiction and it would work" ("A Postmodern Southern Moralist and Storyteller: Tim Gautreaux" 61). Percy further nurtured the moral foundation influenced by his Catholic upbringing and education.

This mix of influences, then, guides Gautreaux's contributions to the growing body of Rough South literature. Gautreaux portrays his blue-collar characters with sympathy and warmth, showing the world from their perspectives. They play important roles in his fiction, often as protagonists, not simply foils or stereotypes. Yet Gautreaux expects more of these characters than some other Rough South writers do. Though he unflinchingly represents his characters' pain and difficulties, he does not allow them to use these struggles as excuses for bad behavior. Throughout his fiction, Gautreaux consistently pushes his rough characters to mature and grow, to become better, more moral beings than they may have thought possible.[1]

While most of Gautreaux's fiction fits within the general Rough South designation, his first three books are most pertinent to this study: two short story collections, *Same Place, Same Things* (1996) and *Welding with Children* (1999); and his first novel, *The Next Step in the Dance* (1998). Gautreaux's more recent novels, *The Clearing* (2003) and *The Missing* (2009), are set in the 1920s and do not portray the working-class southerner's story in the same way. Set in a lumber camp, *The Clearing* certainly contains gritty figures and violent situations, but the protagonists are wealthy Pennsylvanians who come to Louisiana to run the camp. *The Missing*'s protagonist grew up on a Cajun farm, but he gets caught up in tracking down a kidnapped girl, as he tries to escape his past by living a middle-class New Orleans existence.

Though not a major theme in his fiction, tensions between the two worlds Gautreaux inhabits at times become apparent. Two stories in particular show interactions between blue-collar characters and academics. "Dancing with the One-Armed Gal," from *Welding with Children*, centers on Iry Boudreaux—just fired from his job at an ice-making plant—who picks up a hitchhiker, Claudine Glover, who just lost her position as a professor of women's studies. The story explores both characters' attitudes towards of work and purpose as they travel together. "Navigators of Thought," from *Same Place, Same Things*, portrays a crew of out-of-work professors attempting to navigate a tugboat. The story reveals their boss's pleasure in their ineptitude, as well as their own difficulty accepting their failures as academics. Gautreaux acknowledges a kind of "forked existence when you are someone raised in a blue-collar family who gets a Ph.D. in Romantic literature" ("A Postmodern Southern Moralist and Storyteller: Tim Gautreaux" 64). In part because of these dual influences, he prides himself in "writing a 'broad-spectrum' fiction, fiction that appeals to both intellectuals and blue-collar types" (65). He taught university classes for thirty years, but Gautreaux resists the "darkness and brooding" of much modern poetry. "I've become very pessimistic and cynical about pessimists and cynics," he says. "That's one reason I like blue-collar people. With all of their shortcomings and biases and pent-up angers, most of them understand the value of being good-natured and having a good time. You'd never catch a welder reading *The Waste Land*, thank God" ("Interview with Tim Gautreaux" 45).

Gautreaux's many portrayals of blue-collar characters fall into several categories. A few stories revolve around grandfathers who had been uninvolved in their children's lives, but find themselves caring for their grandchildren. Gautreaux says he encountered this pattern in conversations with his students ("Tim Gautreaux: A Conversation with Darlene Meyering" 91). "The Courtship of Merlin LeBlanc," from *Same Place, Same Things*, for instance, shows several generations of LeBlancs trying to figure out how to raise a baby. Probably the most famous of these works is the title story from *Welding with Children*, in which the protagonist Bruton, a "now-and-then welder" (2), realizes that his daughters are doing a lousy job of raising their children. Atypically in Gautreaux, Bruton provides first-person narration in this story, developing a sometimes bemused, sometimes hurt, sometimes self-critical tone that is wonderfully engaging and humorous. The story opens, "Tuesday was about typical. My four daughters, not a one of them married, you understand, brought over their kids, one each, and explained to my wife how much fun she was going to have looking after them again. But Tuesday was her day to go to the casino, so guess who got to tend the four babies?" (1). Bruton's move toward self-reflection is sparked by a comment from old Mr. Fordlyson, who calls Bruton's car a "bastardmobile" when he drives his grandchildren to the store. Bruton begins to reflect on his distant relationship with his daughters and acknowledges, "I guess a lot of what's wrong with my girls is my fault, but I don't know what I could've done different" (7). Awkwardly, with little sense of whether he is making a difference, Bruton tries to become a better influence on his grandchildren, reading Bible stories with them and challenging the foul language they use. Frequently interrupted, however, Bruton realizes that his feeble efforts cannot compete with the hours of trashy television and movies they have watched.

Bruton returns to Mr. Fordlyson, asking for advice on how to raise his grandchildren. Irascible though he is, Mr. Fordlyson offers pragmatic recommendations:

> He pulled down one finger on his right hand with the forefinger of the left. "Go join the Methodists." Another finger went down and he told me, "Every

> Sunday, bring them children to church." A third finger, and he said, "And
> keep 'em with you as much as you can."
>
> I shook my head. "I already raised my kids."
>
> Fordlyson looked at me hard and didn't have to say what he was thinking.
> . . . "And clean up your yard." (16)

Though his actions surprise his wife and others, Bruton begins to carry out Mr. Fordlyson's directives. He meets with the Methodist preacher, then has "four derelict cars, six engines, four washing machines, ten broken lawn mowers, and two and one-quarter ton of scrap iron" hauled from his yard (16). He cuts the grass and paints his house. When one daughter drops off his grandson Nu-Nu, she mentions tearfully that he just said his first word, "Da-da" (18), highlighting the absence of fathers from her life.

Yet Bruton grows through these experiences. The story ends with an Edenic image of a new beginning, as he and his grandchildren prepare to hang a tire swing from an oak tree: "Nu-Nu looked at me and yelled, 'Da-da,' and I thought how he'll be saying that in one way or another for the rest of his life and never be able to face the fact that Da-da had skipped town, whoever Da-da was. The baby brought me into focus, somebody's blue eyes looking at me hard. He blew spit over his tongue and cried out, 'Da-da,' and I put him on my knee, facing away toward the cool green branches of my biggest willow oak" (19). Though Bruton's task will not be easy as he seeks to be an encouraging[presence for his grandchildren, the story shows that change is necessary and possible. Bruton provides a model for the kind of engaged parenting valued throughout Gautreaux's fiction.

A second common theme in Gautreaux's fiction concerns people—typically blue-collar workers—who become involved in others' lives. Gautreaux identifies the source of this pattern as "being raised Catholic, where we have been taught to help people who are less fortunate than we are, not just by praying for them but by actually going out and fixing their busted air conditioners and stuff. And it also comes from my blue-collar raising." The neighbors would help each other out with repairs, leading to a "sort of a *quid pro quo* relationship among blue-collar workers" ("An Interview with Tim Gautreaux: 'Cartographer of Louisiana Back Roads'" 147). These practices are evident in Gautreaux's stories, in characters like the exterminator who tries to help a lonely widow in "The Bug Man," from *Same Place, Same Things*, and a retired maintenance worker who helps the neglected girl next door with a science fair project in "Resistance," from *Welding with Children*. In "The Piano Tuner," also from *Welding with Children*, Gautreaux draws on his own experience tuning pianos in creating the character Claude, who is called out to tune a piano for Michelle Placervent, who lives by herself in her decaying family home. Claude quickly senses that Michelle's calls for piano service have as much to do with her loneliness as her piano.

Rather than ignoring her situation or pursuing a sexual relationship, as might occur in other fiction, Claude helps Michelle get medication to treat her depression and find a job playing in a motel lounge. She decides to get a new piano, but her old upright is too heavy to remove easily, so she tries to pull it out of her house with a tractor. In a stunning turn of events, the piano catches on the back wall and pulls down the house, causing a fire. With obvious symbolism, Michelle is forced to move from her ancestral home to an apartment in town. Yet Gautreaux does not make the new beginning too tidy, for Michelle remains somewhat unstable, not quite able to find her equilibrium. Claude realizes that "Michelle could never adjust to being an entertainer. But at least she was brave" (102). Though her challenges remain, Michelle has, with Claude's encouragement, moved out from the tomb of her old home to a place where she can interact with others. Through these "helping" stories, Gautreaux explores the idea that ordinary, working-class people can take actions that transcend their average workaday lives.

Besides these more particular emphases, many of Gautreaux's stories and novels develop the broader theme of characters who need to mature and enlarge their vision. Often they are not terrible people, just people limited in their sense of what is important and incapable of sharing others' perspectives. Gautreaux's first published novel, *The Next Step in the Dance*, follows the troubled romance of Paul and Colette Thibodeaux. Married a year and a half, Colette had hoped for more from her machinist husband than he can give. Paul is committed to his wife, but he seems clueless about what will make her happy and unable to grow beyond his affection for barroom dances and fights. Frustrated, Colette quits her job as a bank teller and moves to California, hoping for a glittering life of possibility. Though he does not yet fully understand what has happened to their marriage, Paul follows Colette to Los Angeles but moves into his own apartment. Each of them quickly finds work, but they feel lost in this strange city without family or familiar customs. Even the cars they buy illustrate their different sensibilities. Colette buys a Mercedes, Paul a Ford Crown Victoria, a car Colette dismisses as "blue collar" (86). Yet in her loneliness, Colette begins to spend time with Paul, and one night they sleep together. Colette, angered by the pregnancy that follows, moves back to Louisiana and continues with divorce proceedings. But life on Tiger Island is much more difficult, for the oil bust has hit, and jobs are scarce. Paul and Colette continue to live apart with their respective parents, and both families struggle to make ends meet.

Focusing on difficult times, Gautreaux illuminates the hardscrabble nature of Tiger Island. Paul and Colette find work wherever possible: fishing in the bayou, shooting nutria, or working at a toxic waste disposal plant. Yet amidst these significant challenges, Gautreaux reveals the support that the community and their families offer Paul and Colette as each endeavors to mature. The novel explores the tension between accepting who and where one is with the need to grow beyond one's callow self. Colette complains to her father that Paul "wouldn't grow up and plan for the future." Her father scolds her, "You left him because he was happy" (150). On the other hand, Paul laments to his grandfather that Colette wants him to change. His grandfather exclaims, "Change! Hell, boy, you got to change your drawers in the town square if it means keeping your wife" (42). *The Next Step in the Dance* reveals that, though it is a long, difficult process, people can develop and mature. When Paul and others are feared dead after their shrimp boat is caught in a storm, Colette welcomes his return, hoping they can finally form a family together. The novel's end shows new hope for Paul and Colette. No longer as young and beautiful as they were at the beginning of the novel, they now share a hard-won perspective and maturity that bode well for creating a life together. The novel's final sentences capture this sense, as Colette looks over her town: "[S]he looked down at the iron roofs of Tiger Island. Some were storm-worn and bent, some eroded and rusty, porous as a ruined soul, and some were scraped clean and gleaming with new silver paint" (340).

Tim Gautreaux's fiction reveals his deep roots in the Rough South world of Morgan City. He knows these characters, tells their stories, and reveals his deep love for them. Though struggles and pain are ever present, Gautreaux always wants more from and for his characters than simply to show their working-class lives. Gautreaux's fiction reveals the possibility—indeed the necessity—of change, of growth, even though moral improvement will not be easy. Arguably, a central Gautreaux theme can be summed up in a line from "Welding with Children." As Mr. Fordlyson wraps up his advice to Bruton, he admonishes, "[E]verything worth doing hurts like hell" (16)—wisdom that Gautreaux's other blue-collar characters must claim as their own.

Notes

1. In her fine study of Gautreaux, Margaret Donovan Bauer makes a similar point: "One might therefore contrast Gautreaux's blue-collar characters with those of some of his southern contemporaries, whose darker vision of humanity seems to follow more in the tradition of Harry

Crews than of Walker Percy. . . . So even as Gautreaux adds to the body of literature being written about the blue-collar class in the South, he reminds us that no group is homogenous" (12).

Works Cited

Bauer, Margaret Donovan. *Understanding Tim Gautreaux*. Understanding Contemporary American Literature Ser. Columbia: U of South Carolina P, 2010. Print.

Gautreaux, Tim. *The Clearing*. New York: Knopf, 2003. Print.

———. "A Conversation with Tim Gautreaux." Interview by Dayne Sherman. Nisly 152–63. Print.

———. "An Interview with Tim Gautreaux." Interview by Christopher Joyal. Nisly 25–34. Print.

———. "Interview with Tim Gautreaux." Interview by Jennifer Levasseur and Kevin Rabalais. Nisly 35–53. Print.

———. "An Interview with Tim Gautreaux: 'Cartographer of Louisiana Back Roads.'" Interview by Margaret D. Bauer. Nisly 128–51. Print.

———. *The Missing*. New York: Knopf, 2009. Print.

———. *The Next Step in the Dance*. New York: Picador, 1998. Print.

———. "Novel Approach: Tim Gautreaux Takes 'The Next Step.'" Interview by Christina Masciere. Nisly 17–21. Print.

———. "A Postmodern Southern Moralist and Storyteller: Tim Gautreaux." Interview by Julie Kane. Nisly 53–68. Print.

———. *Same Place, Same Things*. 1996. New York: Picador, 1997. Print.

———. "Tim Gautreaux." Interview by Christopher Scanlan. Nisly 107–9. Print.

———. "Tim Gautreaux: A Conversation with Darlene Meyering." Interview by Meyering. Nisly 87–106. Print.

———. *Welding with Children*. New York: Picador, 1999. Print.

Nisly, L. Lamar, ed. *Conversations with Tim Gautreaux*. Literary Conversations Ser. Jackson: UP of Mississippi, 2012. Print.

Education Is Everything:
Chris Offutt's Eastern Kentucky

Peter Farris

I N late 1965, when Chris Offutt was just seven years old, Volunteers in Service to America (VISTA) entered the hollows and ridges of eastern Kentucky. At the behest of President John F. Kennedy's Appalachian Regional Commission, and as the centerpiece of President Lyndon B. Johnson's War on Poverty, VISTA volunteers descended upon Offutt's native Rowan County and encountered a stark reality there—staggering illiteracy, soaring birth rates, desperately inadequate infrastructure, steady flight of the region's best and brightest, and a coal industry gone bust, leaving in its wake an undereducated work force and a population largely dependent on government relief. Decades later, this same third-world scenario would inform much of Offutt's writing. But just as his male characters defy the popular view of hillbillies who, "at the drop of a proverbial overall strap . . . shoot, fight or fuck anything on hind legs" (*The Same River Twice* 19), Offutt's eastern Kentucky is a complicated and contradictory place—a region that from afar conveys a supernal beauty, but upon closer examination reveals slurry ponds, abandoned farms, and Walmarts where coal company stores once stood.

Similarly, one commonly held view is that Appalachia is inhabited by rugged individualists and warring clans who've chosen to live by their own law, hill people so isolated that they live as "counterpart to the aborigine or Eskimo" (*The Same River Twice* 19). To an extent this social dynamic remains, and certainly Offutt writes about the drunks, brawlers, and baby-makers who commonly populate rural fiction. But while lesser authors snag themselves on stereotypes, Offutt creates characters who emerge fully formed, characters drawn with humor, humanity, and an honesty that has over the last few decades come to constitute a departure in southern writing. Contrary to another common perception of Appalachia, Offutt's writing describes a culture ironically shackled with a lack of pride and a sense of shame, hill families haunted by their outlier status, just barely getting by, expecting little from children raised to weather a climate of subjugation and acceptance.

Close examination of Offutt's work reveals—among a multitude of creative concerns including class, group identity, cultural relativism, and father-son relationships—a theme paramount to all others, a refrain sung by author, characters (both real and imagined), and the work itself: education is everything. In a 2002 *New York Times* profile, Offutt told William L. Hamilton, "I wasn't a hillbilly who taught himself to read and write. . . . I was the smartest kid in school, who had taught himself the woods. I was the opposite of what I'd always wanted to be." The son of science fiction writer Andrew J. Offutt, Chris Offutt spent his youth roaming the woods and ridges of Haldeman, Kentucky, which he would later describe as "a zip code with a creek" (*The Same River Twice* 19). Yet while his boyhood friends were the sons of farmers and miners, Offutt lived an early life counter to theirs—with an asocial eccentric as head of the household. Perhaps these unusual (for the region) family dynamics, coupled with a life of poverty in the remoteness of eastern Kentucky, are the reasons Offutt's formative years were characterized by bouts of wanderlust and disquiet, as he bore his share of "the family darkness" (*The Same River Twice* 59), struggling with an irreconcilable affection for and discord with his Rowan County roots.

At the heart of this discord is mountain culture's deep suspicion of education, the notion that schooling serves only to "get you above your raisings," tantamount to pissing on the family tree. The narrator of Offutt's story "Sawdust," from his first short story collection, *Kentucky Straight* (1992), is a young man determined to earn his GED, though his reasons aren't immediately clear. Early in the story he explains, and with plenty of autobiographical subtext, "Not a one on this hillside finished high school. Around here a man is judged by how he acts, not how smart he's supposed to be. I don't hunt, fish, or work. Neighbors say I think too much. They say I'm like my father and Mom worries that maybe they're right" (3). Later, the narrator, ridiculed by his younger brother for pursuing the GED, gets accused of being "eat up with the smart bug," and is encouraged to "let up on that and try working" (9).

Mistrust of education peppers Offutt's work. In the opening chapters of his only novel, *The Good Brother* (1997), we meet Virgil Caudill, a maintenance worker and sometime student at a local community college. From Virgil's point-of-view, Offutt muses, "Education was like a posthole digger, a good tool, very expensive, but worthless unless you needed postholes dug" (28). The issue returns in Offutt's second memoir, *No Heroes: A Memoir of Coming Home* (2002), an account of his return to his alma mater, Morehead State University—this time not as the garbage man he was while taking classes, but as a member of the faculty. Offutt recalls the janitors' suspicions about the educated: "B.A. stood for 'Big Asshole,' B.S. stood for 'Bull Shit,' and Ph.D. stood for 'Piled High and Deep.' . . . College teachers were rich, snobby, and dumber in the head than a hog is in the ass" (25). Later Offutt details the maintenance staff's opinion of Morehead State administrators, "bigwigs who possessed more money than God and were utterly corrupt," just "further evidence that education was for fools" (25).

Whether irrational or not, this skepticism about the value of education is a principal concern of Offutt's nonfiction, and perhaps the attitude assumed by generations of hill people—one that drove Offutt at nineteen to hitchhike across the United States (recounted in his first memoir, *The Same River Twice*). Offutt elaborates on this concern in *No Heroes*, noting how severe poverty and escalating dropout rates have terminally damaged portions of Appalachia: "Eastern Kentucky offers no models for success, no paths for ambitious people to follow, no tangible life beyond the county line. Doing well is a betrayal of mountain culture. Gaining money means you have screwed somebody over and going on vacation implies you don't like living here" (43). Offutt later recalls how his son, a precocious boy languishing in the Rowan County school system, suddenly exhibited an uncharacteristic lack of interest in learning. Meetings with his son's teacher and the school principal yielded little, only reminding Offutt that nothing had changed in eastern Kentucky, that educators still used outmoded methods, failing to challenge students or to conform to higher academic standards. Distilling the region's social, economic, and cultural deficiencies, Offutt succinctly observes, "It was not the children who were ignorant, but the teachers" (*No Heroes* 196).

Offutt also uses illiteracy to great effect in his characterizations, accomplishing more with nuance and implication than with fancy wordplay. Examples abound in Offutt's fiction. In the opening chapter of *The Good Brother*, he renders the lush beauty of Blizzard, Kentucky, in great detail, the "dips and folds of the wooded hills" reminding Virgil Caudill of "a rumpled quilt that needed smoothing out" (16). But geography and isolation insulate the community—and not just physically, a notion subtly expressed when an unidentified regular purchases a money order at Blizzard's most vital building, the post office. The postmaster, Zephaniah, understanding that his customer can neither read nor write, patiently fills out the form for the man. As Virgil acknowledges, "Zephaniah would stand there all day rather than insult the man by asking him to write his name on the money order" (17). Later in *The Good Brother*, Virgil and garbage crew boss Rundell explain to a coworker named Dewey, who'd never "heard of no Mexican Ocean" (53), that the Mississippi River feeds into the *Gulf* of Mexico, and that Mexico itself is a country. It's a humorous scene, the exchange both light-hearted and telling, with Dewey portrayed not as a rube or imbecile, but a representative of an underclass culture. It is a culture in which meeting the demands of everyday life via labor takes precedence over knowledge that may seem trivial—like knowing what lies beyond the county borders, borders that many of Offutt's characters rarely cross. Similarly, in Offutt's second short story collection, *Out of the Woods* (1999), "Melungeons" (which draws its title from the name of an isolated racial group unique to central Appalachia) tells the story of a woman named Beulah Mullins, who leaves her home in the mountains to settle— and perhaps perpetuate—a decades-old feud with another Melungeon family. Beulah is as feral as any character in Offutt's fiction, a woman who during her descent into town sees asphalt for the first time. She's never voted or paid taxes, and she can't read, but she's so tuned to the natural world that, upon sighting a flock of vireos, she knows "winter would arrive early" (49).

In one of Offutt's most humorous and heartbreaking stories, *Kentucky Straight*'s "Blue Lick," we enter the impoverished life of a young boy. In just a few pages we learn of our narrator's feeble-minded brother, an alcoholic jailbird father, a mother who has run off with another man, and a VISTA volunteer grappling with guilt and pity while trying to "save" the promising boy from his destitute surroundings. Providing a compelling contrast to the book-smart, "funny-talked" VISTA lady (115), the narrator's father, through the fog of a hangover, takes a moment to pass on to his boys some common sense of the more local variety. "Useful stuff," the narrator states, "that we were supposed to never let go of": "Always throw the first punch," "Shoot to kill. . . . never wound," "fold a three-flush after five," and "Don't give women gifts" (122). The father's advice presents a clear dichotomy for the young narrator to contend with, but by story's end, his fate is still uncertain. Offutt paints his characters with no clear sympathies or antipathies, leaving readers to wonder whether the boy will join the "civilized" world of the VISTA volunteer, or succumb to the familiar rhythms and patterns of his own people.

Perhaps it's fair to suggest that Offutt's path to publication and career trajectory have amplified the aforementioned themes in his work. Earning an MFA in fiction from the prestigious writing program at the University of Iowa, and teaching creative writing at the college level for most of his adult life, Offutt has no doubt seen his share of students benefit from higher education. Curiously, his "other" successful career, writing for and producing popular cable television series like *Weeds* and *True Blood*, has probably brought more attention to his memoirs, novel, and short story collections than his academic career, book tours, prestige grants, and magazine profiles ever could. For new readers, these popular offerings assert what many admirers already knew: that Offutt's work belongs comfortably in the same sandbox that other Rough South authors have been playing in since Harry Crews emerged in the late 1960s. In 2012, Tom Franklin told the Associated Press's Chris Talbott that Offutt "somehow hasn't ever been embraced by the southern institution," but then added, "I sort of feel like the southern world is embracing him now in the way it hasn't before." Franklin's observation is poignant, for despite certain readers' and reviewers' perceptions of Offutt, his sensibilities as an artist are attuned to the same concern that preoccupies his peers from the Rough South: the plight of the undereducated, the underemployed, the ostracized, and the outlawed.

By way of comparison, when Offutt's *Kentucky Straight* was published in 1992, Mississippi firefighter-turned-literary sensation Larry Brown had already published two novels and two collections; Tar Heel Tim McLaurin had published two books; and South Carolinian Dorothy Allison had published her first short story collection and the seminal novel *Bastard out of Carolina* (1992). Interestingly, western North Carolina's Ron Rash was two years away from publishing his first short story collection, and fellow Kentuckian Silas House's *Clay's Quilt* (2001) would not see bookstore shelves until almost a decade later. At the very least, this sampling demonstrates Offutt's place in the timeline of this new wave of underclass writers. More importantly, this sampling reaffirms Offutt not only as a vital contributor to the new southern literary movement, but as an artist who has captured, chronicled, and humanized his people like few others have done before.

Works Cited

Hamilton, William L. "At Home with Chris Offutt: Learning Not to Trespass on the Gently Rolling Past." *nytimes.com. New York Times*, 18 Apr. 2002. Web. 25 Aug. 2013.

Offutt, Chris. *The Good Brother*. New York: Simon & Schuster, 1997. Print.

———. *Kentucky Straight*. New York: Vintage, 1992. Print.

———. *No Heroes: A Memoir of Coming Home*. 2002. New York: Simon & Schuster, 2002. Print.

———. *Out of the Woods*. 1999. New York: Simon & Schuster, 2000. Print.

———. *The Same River Twice: A Memoir*. 1993. New York: Simon & Schuster, 2003. Print.

Talbott, Chris. "Offutt Scores TV success, Ready to Abandon It." *knoxnews.com. Knoxville News Sentinel*. Web. 26 Oct. 2012. 2 Sept. 2013.

Daniel Woodrell, Ozarker

Shawn E. Miller

THE Daniel Woodrell brand has always been rough. In the black and white photo on the dust jacket of his first novel, the expressionless author gazes coolly upon readers, while slouching against a weathered brick wall. He wears a rumpled denim jacket with a carelessly unmoored collar and pocket flaps. The accompanying copy identifies him as a "Hot-tar-roofer, loading dock laborer, former U.S. Marine" before supplying his name and more conventional credentials. Both photograph and text assuredly gesture toward what Doyle Redmond, Woodrell's alter ego from his fifth novel, *Give Us a Kiss* (1996), will call a hook: "Something that'll get some key profiles written. Something that'll get the public imagination keen on me" (69). Yet they're also not entirely studied fabrications of Woodrell's publisher's marketing division. Woodrell never hailed from a world exactly like his fictional Venus Holler, a place Sammy Barlach, from his sixth novel, *Tomato Red* (1998), calls "the most low-life part of town" (39), but his neighborhood was never very far away from it, either. In the Missouri Ozarks, where Woodrell lives two blocks from the graves of his ancestors, no neighborhood ever is.

Born in 1953, Woodrell spent his first year in West Plains, Missouri, the Ozark town where his family had lived since the first half of the nineteenth century. His father, the son of a maid abandoned by her alcoholic husband, was Robert Lee Woodrell, whose pursuit of work led the family to St. Charles, the scene of Woodrell's childhood and the model for his Bayou Trilogy's fictional St. Bruno. Woodrell credits his mother, Jeanneanne, and a childhood illness that periodically left him bedridden, with fostering in him a passion for reading. Among his early favorites were Mark Twain and Nelson Algren. Among his early ambitions was writing, a goal he announced as a third-grader. In 1968, when Woodrell was fifteen, his father's work again precipitated a move, this time to Kansas City, a place his son once described as "the worst possible place for me" (Tibbetts 192). Woodrell dropped out of school and enlisted with the marines the week he turned seventeen, preferring "slopping around in the [Vietnamese] jungle on foot" ("An Interview with Daniel Woodrell" 102) to spending "another week in this fucking suburb" (Williams). Instead, the marines sent him to Guam to work on his GED.

Eighteen months into his enlistment, Woodrell was discharged for drug use and spent the rest of the '70s figuring out what to do with himself. He attended college off and on. He knocked about the country hitchhiking. He married in 1974. He worked odd jobs. He claims to have quit college for two years "just to read the reading list that Hemingway recommended in his 'Notes to a Young Writer' or whatever it was called" ("An Interview with Daniel Woodrell" 83–84). At twenty-three, Woodrell decided that writing seemed something it had never been before: a reasonable possibility.

A new decade saw the end of Woodrell's six-year marriage, his graduation from the University of Kansas with a bachelor of general studies degree, and his matriculation at the Iowa Writer's Workshop, where the Michener Fellow met fellow novelist Katie Estill. They were married in 1984 and lived briefly in Arkansas, Ohio, Missouri, and California before the advance for *Give Us a Kiss* enabled them to buy a house in Woodrell's native West Plains, in the same neighborhood where his mother had been born and where the couple now lives.

Like his life, Woodrell's work features a time of knocking about before a homecoming. Readers who came to him through his eighth novel, *Winter's Bone* (2006)—and nearly all of them have—will have a hard time believing that the same author wrote his first four books. Three of them, now known as the "Bayou Trilogy"—*Under the Bright Lights* (1986), *Muscle for the Wing* (1988), and *The Ones You Do* (1992)—bear all the window-dressing of urban pulp crime fiction, with content that arguably matches. The first two were published under Henry Holt's Rinehart Suspense imprint, known for its skeleton-key logo and Sue Grafton's early alphabet mysteries. *The Ones You Do* was spared only because the imprint had been retired. All three feature semi-lurid, cartoonish dust jackets and teasers like that for *Under the*

Bright Lights: "Jewel Cobb had come to Saint Bruno to dip his spoon into the fabled gravy train of the big city, and as he tucked the .32 Beretta into the waistband of his trousers, he just knew he was about to turn midnight fantasies into the stuff of legend." The sentence doesn't come from the novel, but the spoon-and-fabled-gravy train metaphor does. Woodrell's setting is fictional St. Bruno, located just north of New Orleans and modeled partly on St. Charles, Missouri—only bigger. His hero is police detective Rene Shade, a hard-bitten loner who doesn't hesitate to dirty his hands, but—a master of every situation that doesn't require emotional honesty—won't be corrupted by the rot around him. Woodrell has said that in this series, "The crime aspect was more or less an excuse to link things together as I really dealt with family issues" ("An Interview with Daniel Woodrell" 94). This claim rings especially true vis-à-vis the final installment, as Shade's deadbeat dad, John X., absent since his son's youth, returns to town with his ten-year-old punk daughter—pursued by Woodrell's homage to William Faulkner's corncob-wielding gangster, Popeye—at roughly the same time Shade's main squeeze announces that he's knocked her up. Domestic drama ensues.

Woodrell's second novel, written when he worried that *Under the Bright Lights* would not sell, is likewise unlike his more recent fiction, unlike the Bayou Trilogy, and perhaps unlike just about any other novel, though it has often been called a western and compared to the novels of Cormac McCarthy. *Woe to Live On* (1987) is a reworking of Woodrell's first published short story, "Woe to Live On," which appeared in the *Missouri Review* in 1983 and is now part of the short story collection *The Outlaw Album* (2011). The novel was reissued as *Ride with the Devil* in 1999 to coincide with the release of Ang Lee's film adaptation, and again in 2012 with the original title restored. It's the first-person account of nineteen-year-old Jake Roedel, who rides with the First Kansas Irregulars in the Missouri-Kansas Border Wars of 1861–63.

The novel is notable for its frank treatment of a little understood and often misrepresented piece of Civil War history— one including William Clarke Quantrill's notorious raid on Lawrence, Kansas, in August 1863—as well as for its language, which is at once simple, historically inflected, and beautiful. The book is also exceptionally violent, a characteristic announced in the first scene as Jake's company, disguised in Federal uniforms, comes upon an immigrant family and sports with them before hanging the father from a cottonwood tree. When the grief-stricken son, about thirteen, moves to loosen the rope, Jake shoots him in the back. More unsettling are the characters' jaded postures as perpetrators and witnesses. "Pups make hounds," Jake announces after shooting the boy. "And there are hounds enough" (8). But Jake needs to believe "that aloneness would not be [his] fate" (43). "It was for this that I searched," Jake decides, "communion and levelness with people who were not mine by birth, but mine for the taking" (18). The book's core concern, then, is love; war is important only insofar as it enables or prevents love. Unlike many westerns, McCarthy novels, and most war books, *Woe to Live On* progresses toward marriage and the promise of a domestic future, although getting there "is a hot, hard ride by road" (226).

While these early novels seem the product of a different vein than Woodrell has mined more recently, and while they lack the contemporary social realism we associate with Rough South writing, they have thematic ties to both. At the core of much Rough South fiction is a form of orphanhood, often expressed through a son (and occasionally a daughter) estranged from the father and therefore adrift and unanchored in the world. Both Rene Shade and Jake Roedel enact this trope. While Shade's father, John X., figures prominently only at the end of the Bayou Trilogy, his absence is a key feature of his son's development from the beginning. Shade drifts in an uncomfortable limbo between his disreputable Frogtown roots (personified by his older brother, Tip, who slings suds at a seedy bar), and the gilded legitimacy of the St. Bruno power structure (the orbit of his younger brother, Francois, of the district attorney's office).

The trilogy resolves with John X.'s death, his daughter Etta's acceptance into the Shade circle, and the tableau of the three brothers coming together to toast John X., absent yet again. Jake Roedel's estrangement from his father points to broader cultural conflicts. Emblematic of his own limbo, Jake was born during his family's migration to the United States, "on a cold dark wave, pitched high to be dropped low, somewhere between Hamburg and Baltimore" (71). Raised by his father's employer, when war comes, he fights for secession alongside his foster brother, while his father, like most German immigrants, is a loyal unionist. Indirectly, Jake is responsible for his father's murder during the war. Throughout, he struggles to be seen as an American—he shoots the boy, in part (perhaps mostly) because in the scene with the German family his comrades watch him for signs of divided loyalty—and to feel at one with his fellows. This is a subject Woodrell often revisits: the recognition that human beings are utterly alone, and that our conditions are terrible. When we try to transcend life's difficulties, we create only half measures whose effects are fleeting when we're lucky, and still more terrible when we're not.

Woodrell's homecoming novel, *Give Us a Kiss*, written in San Francisco, presaged and financially enabled his return to West Plains. Here, he abandons St. Bruno for West Table, Missouri, which has served as the setting for his fiction ever since. Woodrell provided the generic subtitle, *A Country Noir*, and stylistically the book evokes the cheesy noir qualities of the Bayou Trilogy, but the language comes from a narrator-protagonist who's also a writer with a graduate degree, suggesting that the style is affectation and perhaps indicative of Doyle Redmond's other masks.

That Doyle's biography so often parallels Woodrell's lends the book the playful quality of a literary hoax. Like his creator, Doyle has parents in Kansas City, entered the marines instead of finishing high school, earned a GED in Guam, attended Fort Hays State College, graduated from the Universities of Kansas and Iowa, and wrote "four published novels nobody much [has] read" (110). Unlike Doyle, Woodrell didn't marry an aspiring poet whose Volvo he stole when she tried to sleep her way into the quarterlies, but about other details we can be less certain. (Was he ever into past-life regression therapy? Did he once get a magnificent blowjob from a sergeant on Guam while tripping on acid?) To this mix, add the screenplay by Doyle's romantic interest, Niagra (daughter of Big Annie), about a girl named Falls (daughter of Large Lucy)—a piece of thinly disguised autobiography Doyle derides as the work of "a total fuckin' amateur" (73)—and the distance between Woodrell and Doyle is still more negligible.

Give Us a Kiss is about identity. Like Rene Shade and Jake Roedel, Doyle occupies the interstice between his heritage and his present and future. Recently, he was a not-so-successful, MFA-carrying novelist in touch with his past lives and living in northern California with his wife Lizbeth, a poet at fictional Hichens College. Doyle says he "plain ol' did not belong" in the academic world (105). While wanting to kick the ass of the Big Name poet Lizbeth is sleeping with, he reflects, "My mammy dropped me in the Ozarks and I'm an Ozarker wherever life takes me" (105). But that assertion is not altogether certain, either. Soon after Doyle arrives in West Table at the beginning of the novel, it becomes clear that he's a queer Ozarker, perhaps an even queerer Redmond—at least as far as his grandfather, Panda— the family patriarch known for murdering a sworn enemy named Dolly—is concerned.

Before long, Doyle is involved in his brother Smoke's dope-growing operation, along with Smoke's girlfriend Big Annie and her daughter Niagra, lured by Smoke's promise of "a hillbilly endowment toward the support of artsy bullshit," the means to "whip out any book you want and not give a fuck if the public buys it" (48)—and lured, too, by Niagra's virgin hotness. Doyle murders two Dollys along the way, besting Panda's tally by one and earning the approval of the dead Redmonds, whose portraits line the walls of the family homeplace. He also earns prison time, enough publicity to rekindle his writing career, and the conviction that if ever released from prison, "I'll be who I always dreamed of being" (237).

Who that is is a writer people will talk about after he's dead. Doyle believes he lacks only a hook, and his burgeoning notoriety at the end of the book suggests he has found it—or, as he says, his hook has found him. But Doyle's word choice here—not *what* but *who* he dreams of being—resonates with the book's near-constant series of statements about who Doyle Redmond is. He's a Redmond, an Ozarker, "a somewhat educated hillbilly who keeps his diction stunted down out of crippling allegiance to his roots" (39), *and* he is a Nobel Prize aspirant. His past selves call him Imaru, a self over or outside the lesser selves, a personage Doyle speaks of in the third-person and claims not to "know . . . real well yet" (168).

When Doyle meets Niagra, it's difficult to say which attracts him more: her too-short shorts, or her first words, "I know who you are" (30). The book's other major focus is a series of embraces and other physical intimacies, underscored by the one between Doyle's parents when they're brought into the brothers' business venture. It's a hug preceded by his father's words, "Give us a kiss" (203). During an impromptu family reunion at the Redmond homeplace and just after Doyle reflects upon learning to assert rather than suppress his Redmond Ozarker identity, the embrace clearly suggests something larger.

For Doyle, acts of physical intimacy mean that somebody else accepts his queer self, that he belongs. His quest to possess Niagra sexually—she is coy at first, making Doyle work for it—parallels his enactment of shitkicker Redmond identity; he succeeds with Niagra only after he's murdered the first Dolly and knocked out the second. The book ends happily, then, with a giant hug from the world—or so Doyle would have us believe. Of course, we can also see that he's been driven here—against his will—by his need to belong, or by the genes he believes have him "cornered" (58), and that *here* is, in fact, prison.

Alienated narrator-protagonists seeking transcendence through physical intimacy also appear in Woodrell's next two books. Unlike Doyle Redmond, Sammy Barlach of *Tomato Red* thinks he knows exactly who he is, and that belief is best expressed when, finding himself inside a mansion, he sees how the quality lives: "*I ain't shit! I ain't shit!* shouts your brain, and this place proves the point" (11). Before *Tomato Red*, characters like Sammy played only bit parts in Woodrell's work, standing in as the idiot tool of the St. Bruno criminal element, Jewel Cobb; pursued by Rene Shade in *Under the Bright Lights*; or as the caricatured antagonist Dollys in *Give Us a Kiss*.

In Sammy, we meet a fully realized, fully credentialed native of the southern underclass. He's a twenty-four-year-old drifter from Blue Knee, Arkansas, with a sketchy history and a bad work ethic, despite his new job at the

West Table dog food factory. He's served time. He can't sleep well unless he knows there's food nearby. He drives a crappy black Pinto that holds most of his belongings—most importantly his tape collection and a stained blue shirt with a "history of supplying good luck, pussy-wise" (32). Until recently, it also held a pistol he's since sold to "a pretty temperamental Indian" outside a Tunica, Mississippi, casino because he knew he'd eventually shoot somebody with it (33). Woodrell gives the book to Sammy; it's his story. We see it through his eyes and hear it in his words since he narrates it, but the more remarkable feature of the narrative is who it requires us to be, the way it constructs hearers for Sammy's tale. In what Megan Abbott, in her foreword to the novel, calls a "down-the-rabbit-hole first sentence" (xi), Sammy begins, "You're no angel, you know how this stuff comes to happen" (3). He caps off the twenty-five or so lines that follow (which constitute one sentence) with, "Can't none of this be new to you" (4), and returns to periodic direct address for the rest of the novel, ending with "Now you've heard it" (225). Who is this *you*? Woodrell is asking us to play a part: We're Sammy's cell-mate, maybe, since he's soon to be pinched, or we're who we really are, none of us angels, knowing plenty more about the world than we'd willingly admit. Whichever explanation we prefer, we wind up closer to Sammy than expected and on the verge of concluding that his story is somehow our own.

The axis of Sammy's story is a longing for human fellowship redolent of Jake Roedel's in *Woe to Live On*, his pursuit of "the bunch that would have [him]" (49). Sammy is a stranger in town, drawn to an East Main trailer park by "the coed circle of bums gathered there" to drink from the communal tequila jug and snort the communal crank (3). Companionship is also what drives him to break into a mansion to steal drugs, even after his recently acquired acquaintances abandon him. "I could yet maybe find what we looked for [and] return to the trailer park on foot as both a hero and the sudden life of the party," he thinks (7).

Sadly, this is but the first of many abandonments he'll suffer. The job and home offered him by two people he meets in the mansion turn out to be a joke, he loses his real job, and his landlady locks him out for not paying the rent. Subsequently, Sammy finds what he believes to be a real place in the lives of the three other intruders he met in the mansion, siblings Jamalee and Jason Merridew of Venus Holler, and their mother Bev, a well-known whore. By degrees, Sammy works his way in and consolidates his role in the family, sharing their food and drink, sharing a bedroom with Jason, accepting the role of protector assigned him by Jamalee, learning to smoke Bev's cigarettes (thus mastering the one vice that had eluded him), taking their troubles on his shoulders, and eventually having regular sex with Bev and scoring with Jamalee. The novel comes to crisis with Jason's murder and the hush money offered as compensation. Jamalee flees with the money, a final abandonment Sammy finds he can't abide when in a blind rage he murders an innocent man with a crowbar.

Jamalee (Sammy calls her Tomato Red, after her dyed hair) shares a motive with many of Woodrell's recent female characters: Niagra of *Give Us a Kiss*, who dreams of acting in Hollywood; Glenda Akins of *The Death of Sweet Mister* (2001), who arranges to run away with a cruise ship cook to live on the high seas; and Ree Dolly of *Winter's Bone*, who wants to join the army. The compass of all four women points anywhere but here toward reinvented lives, though Jamalee's plan is the most ambitious: She means to put Jason, the prettiest boy in the Ozarks, to work sleeping with rich women for money before blackmailing them for more, thereby growing rich with all the trappings somewhere in Florida. She is an avatar of an old American archetype, close kin to Jay Gatsby and Thomas Sutpen. All four women must leave the men in their lives to get what they want, and both Niagra and Jamalee succeed in the leaving— though Niagra's removal is innocuous compared to Jamalee's, which destroys Sammy.

In *The Death of Sweet Mister*, thirteen-year-old fat boy Shuggie Akins turns out to be more determined than Sammy not to be left alone. Like Sammy, Shug tells us the story. He is the son of Glenda and, nominally, of her violent husband, Red, whose appearances consist largely of demeaning Shug as a stupid "tub of shit" (57) or Glenda as a witch. He slaps them both around, getting high, screwing, and using Shug to lift drugs from recently discharged cancer patients and the like. He's an irredeemable sort. Even so, Glenda seems resigned to life with him and seeks, from her son, the emotional support and tenderness Red won't give her. The lonely teenager has readily accepted the role long before we first meet him. From the beginning of the novel, we see that for Shug emotional tenderness seldom fails to mix with the erotic. Glenda is naturally flirty, and a hot dish besides, one given to treating Shug to ice cream, cake, and other sweets and to calling him her sweet mister. As the story progresses, so does the erotic tension between the two, culminating in a rather serious scene of dishwashing-turned-groping that Glenda resists only mildly, and only with her shorts and panties around her ankles.

Glenda's resignation to life with Red transforms with the appearance of Jimmy Vin Pearce, a cook. Glenda and Jimmy begin an affair and end up killing and burying Red. Consistent with the book's focus on food, the murder scene appears to be the kitchen, the murder weapon a skillet. Soon after, with a job for Jimmy nearly lined up in New Orleans and the suspicions of Red's brother and best friend turning toward them, the three plan their escape. Shug, who initially resists the idea, finds himself persuaded by the prospect of beignets, "shrimp big as chicken drumsticks" (177), and sandwiches the size of pies. But Jimmy's job falls through, and it's not long before he's lined up another on a cruise ship where Glenda can join him, but Shug can't.

When Glenda—who's already stopped calling him "hon" and hugging him—gives Shug he bad news, he reacts: "The bottle where I hid my life-long screams busted wide" (191). He makes sure Red's brother, Carl, and best friend, Basil, know Jimmy Vin killed Red. And, much to Glenda's distress, Jimmy fails to appear at the appointed hour—or ever—to take her away. But Shug is there to console her, to convince her that she's been dumped, and to assure her that he, at least, will never leave her. The conclusion clearly suggests that, in a bid against abandonment, Shug becomes the one man Glenda could never leave—and that man looks less like sweet mister than he looks like Red. The sun rises along with Shug's hand on Glenda's thigh, as the narrator reflects, "I'd say no dawns ever did break right over her and me again" (196).

Winter's Bone brought Woodrell the readership that had always eluded him. According to the author, none of his earlier books had sold more than five thousand copies, a total *Winter's Bone* tripled in hardback even before the 2010 Debra Granik film adaptation that won at Sundance and received four Academy Award nominations. After the film, the paperback sold "in the six figure range" ("A Conversation with Daniel Woodrell"). Like what happened after Doyle Redmond found his hook, all of Woodrell's earlier fiction was soon reissued by his new publisher, Little, Brown and Company.

Winter's Bone is in some ways a continuation of Woodrell's turn to the Ozarks. We find ourselves immersed in the Dolly family we met in *Give Us a Kiss*, and in the violent, hard-living, drug-centered subculture that is Sammy's universe in *Tomato Red*. In other ways, *Winter's Bone* is something new for Woodrell. Ree Dolly is his first attempt at a female protagonist, and unlike Doyle, Sammy, and Shug, she doesn't get to tell her own story. Woodrell returns to a third-person omniscient point of view he hadn't practiced since the Bayou Trilogy. This narrative voice, however, tends more toward earnestness than the trilogy's playful irony. Unlike its predecessors, the book is seldom funny. One reason, perhaps, has to do with the rarified kind of story Woodrell tells. Ree Dolly is a monomythic heroine, one face of the hero Joseph Campbell said has a thousand; this reading perhaps explains the somber but basically happy ending, too.

Still, Woodrell adapts many of his characteristic themes to this mythic heroine's journey. Ree's estrangement from her father is quite literal: Jessup Dolly is missing as the novel begins, not an altogether unusual occurrence, as he's often off cooking crank or in jail. This time, however, his absence is threatening. He's out on bail, has used the family house and land as bond, and his court date is approaching. If Ree doesn't find him, her family will lose everything, and their helplessness, she believes, will trap her forever.

Ree faces trials of all kinds: the unmet needs of her younger brothers; her mother's inert mental state; stern warnings from her menacing Uncle Teardrop; the deception of Blond Milton; the stony silence of Thump Milton; and a brutal beating from Thump's women. The heroine is steadfast, however, and assisted by many: her best friend Gail; the Hawkfall stranger, Megan, who points the way to Thump's house; Jessup's mistress, April Dunahew; and finally Uncle Teardrop, who becomes Ree's savior and guide. After witnessing her courage (and the ire of a community initially set against her), the women who beat her take her to Jessup's body and help her remove his hands, an act that brings both "sorrow and a blessing" (187): proof of Jessup's death, consequent annulment of his bond, and a sack of cash more valuable than Ree's family's house and land.

Speaking of the book's title, Woodrell has said that *bone* carries the sense of "throwing a sop to someone, 'Oh, give him a bone.' In this case, it is winter itself giving a gift, a bone, to Ree Dolly" ("Reading Group Guide" 3). The bag of money is clearly such a gift, but perhaps not the only or the most important one. The fact that Ree dreams of joining the army and escaping her life in the Ozarks, and that this is, at first, her primary motivation, links her to Woodrell's other women, dreaming of escape and reinvented lives. Unlike those women, though, Ree voluntarily rejects escape after achieving its means, telling her brother Harold on the book's final page that she isn't leaving, that she'd "get lost without the weight of [the boys] on [her] back" (193). Since getting lost, of course, was the point of the dream in the first place, the statement doesn't begin to explain why Ree has changed her mind. Perhaps Harry Crews offers some insight when he describes the homeplace as "vital and necessary as the beating of your own heart" and "your anchor in the world" (16). Ree's quest has taken her deep into the Ozarks of her people, a world she masters. Maybe that's the reason she prefers an anchor to getting lost, a preference that can't possibly be foreign to Daniel Woodrell of West Plains, Missouri.

In any case, Woodrell's work since *Winter's Bone* has given no hint of departure from his Ozarks domain. *The Outlaw Album* is a collection of twelve stories, nine of them previously published, and all set in the Ozarks. With his next novel, *The Maid's Version* (2013), Woodrell returns to historical fiction and to West Table. Based on the 1928 dance hall explosion in West Plains that killed more than thirty people and was never fully explained, the story, according to Woodrell, is "a semi-autobiographical account that starts off with a character who resembles myself spending the summer with his grandmother and she spends all their time together telling him these things she knows about the explosion" ("A Conversation with Daniel Woodrell"). The grandmother is based on Woodrell's paternal grandmother, a maid who worked for a wealthy family rumored to be involved in the explosion. As Doyle Redmond might point out, Daniel Woodrell now seems to have found his hook somewhere in the Ozarks.

Works Cited and Consulted

Abbott, Megan. Foreword. 2010. *Tomato Red*. 1998. By Daniel Woodrell. New York: Back Bay, 2012. ix–xiii. Print.

Crews, Harry. *A Childhood: The Biography of a Place*. 1978. Athens: U of Georgia P, 1995. Print.

"Daniel Woodrell." *Contemporary Authors Online*. Detroit: Gale, 2012. *Literature Resource Center*. Web. 5 Feb. 2013.

"Reading Group Guide." *Winter's Bone*, by Daniel Woodrell. 1–11. Print.

Tibbetts, John C. "The Hard Ride: Jayhawkers and Bushwhackers in the Kansas-Missouri Border Wars—*Ride with the Devil*." *Literature/Film Quarterly* 27.3 (1999): 189–95. Print.

Williams, John. "Daniel Woodrell: The Ozark Daredevil." *independent.co.uk*. *Independent*, 16 June 2006. Web. 05 Feb. 2013.

Woodrell, Daniel. "A Conversation with Daniel Woodrell." Interview by Keith Rawson. *litreactor.com*. *LitReactor Magazine*, 5 Oct. 2011. Web. 5 Feb. 2013.

———. "Daniel Woodrell." Interview by Dustin Atkinson. *southeastreview.org*. *Southeast Review*, 1 April 2009. Web. 5 Feb. 2013.

———. *The Death of Sweet Mister*. 2001. New York: Plume, 2002. Print.

———. *Give Us a Kiss*. New York: Holt, 1996. Print.

———. "An Interview with Daniel Woodrell." Interview by Kay Bonetti. *Missouri Review* 22.3 (1999): 79–104. Print.

———. "Live Fast, Learn Slow." Interview by Matt Baker. *oxfordamerican.org*. *Oxford American*, 10 June 2011. Web. 12 Feb. 2013.

———. *Muscle for the Wing*. New York: Holt, 1988. Print.

———. *The Ones You Do*. New York: Holt, 1992. Print.

———. *The Outlaw Album*. New York: Little, Brown, 2011. Print.

———. "'Riddles across the Sky': Daniel Woodrell Talks about *Winter's Bone*." Interview by John C. Tibbetts. *Literature/Film Quarterly* 39.1 (2011): 30–38. Print.

———. *Tomato Red*. New York: Holt, 1998. Print.

———. *Under the Bright Lights*. New York: Holt, 1986. Print.

———. *Winter's Bone*. 2006. New York: Back Bay, 2007. Print.

———. *Woe to Live On*. 1987. New York: Back Bay, 2012. Print.

Kaye Gibbons:
Tough Women in a Rough South

Rebecca Godwin

BORN Bertha Kaye Batts on May 5, 1960, Kaye Gibbons grew up in a four-room, tin-roofed farmhouse in a Nash County, North Carolina, farming community named Bend of the River. The house lacked electricity and running water and was often the scene of abuse and turmoil. Her mother suffered manic depression but held the family together, getting the tobacco crop to market when her alcoholic husband was incapacitated. When Gibbons was ten, her mother committed suicide by overdosing on sleeping pills; her father drank himself to death soon thereafter. Orphaned at age twelve, Gibbons lived briefly with an aunt and then in a foster home, before moving in with her married older brother.

Gibbons learned early to love the written word, a key to her survival. She writes in *How I Became a Writer: My Mother, Literature, and A Life Split Neatly into Two Halves* (1988), that "I read myself out of my community, my past" (4). After graduating from Rocky Mount High School in 1978, she attended North Carolina State University on a Veterans Administration scholarship, and later transferred to the University of North Carolina at Chapel Hill. There, she took one of Louis D. Rubin's southern literature courses and, emboldened by the familiar, colloquial language she found in the assigned reading, showed him the manuscript-in-progress that, with his encouragement, became *Ellen Foster*, her first novel. It was published in 1987 by Rubin's fledgling Algonquin Books of Chapel Hill. Gibbons and husband Michael Gibbons had three daughters before divorcing in the early 1990s. She married Raleigh attorney Frank Ward in 1993, but that union ended in divorce as well (Snodgrass 13–29).

While at NC State, Gibbons was diagnosed with manic depression, an illness often transmitted through the maternal line. She explains in *Frost and Flower: My Life with Manic Depression So Far* (1995) that periods of hypomania, with their intense combinations of words and images, inspire her greatest creativity, as with the largely autobiographical *Ellen Foster*, which she wrote in six weeks, turning memories into art. In *Frost and Flower* she also admits that, during down periods, she fears a return of the poverty of her childhood. And yet, as Gibbons mines and moves beyond the hardships of her lower-class upbringing, she speaks authentically of domestic violence and turmoil, as well as class and racial tensions, creating strong female characters who learn to survive difficult times.

Gibbons's debut novel features a plucky eleven-year-old narrator already conscious of her status as "trash" (16). The term connotes ignorance and laziness, implying that those in this lowest of white social classes bear at least some responsibility for their poverty, an indictment Gibbons does not wholly deny. Abused and rejected not just by her lower-class father, but by her dead mother's middle-class family, young Ellen recounts in plain vernacular reminiscent of Huckleberry Finn's the story of how she escaped her family's shabbiness through intelligence and resolve. Gibbons draws on her own childhood to critique both the classism and racism deeply rooted in the working-class South, partially destabilizing the "white trash" stereotype through her narrator's efforts to find a home.

Ellen's poignant first line, "When I was little I would think of ways to kill my daddy" (1), elicits immediate sympathy from readers envisioning a child living a life of deprivation and pain. Indeed, Ellen's father fits the "white trash" stereotype. He's a shiftless alcoholic who does not provide for his family, but dominates the household through verbal abuse and intimidation. Young Ellen stands up to her pathetic father as best she can—at one point telling him to get up off the bathroom floor and lie in his truck so others can use the toilet. She tries to protect her ailing mother, even lying beside her as she dies from an intentional overdose of heart pills after Ellen's father forbids the girl to phone for help. He later threatens incest, grabbing Ellen and calling her by his dead wife's name and acting on an inebriated friend's suggestion that

Ellen is "just about ripe. You gots to git em when they is still soff when you mashum" (44). She learns to lock herself up when her drunken father talks about her "girl ninnies" (52), and she thinks her bruises her own concern, not that of the teacher who asks about them. Her experiences teach her self-reliance and discretion. She refuses to be victimized by a dysfunctional family or a community that looks down on her tattered clothes.

One can hardly imagine a life rougher than the one young Ellen endures, even as she moves from her no-account father to her mother's higher-class family. After her mother dies, Ellen lives alone except during her drunken father's sporadic visits. She once asks to stay with her mother's sister, but does not beg when Aunt Betsy keeps her only one weekend. When the courts decide that Ellen should live with her mother's mother, Ellen suffers the full brunt of her grandmother's hatred of the man who convinced her daughter to marry beneath her class. The epithets "nigger" and "trash" (23), which the grandmother hurls at him at her daughter's funeral, foreshadow the hostility she visits upon Ellen for having "that bastard's eyes" and (88), in her mind, precipitating her daughter's suicide. Her grandmother makes Ellen work the fields and wait on her like a servant. When the old woman dies, the orphan is subjected to haughty snubs from her aunt Nadine and her spoiled cousin Dora. Their rejection of her homemade Christmas presents leads Ellen to insult Dora's intellect, an affront prompting Nadine's plan to "call the damn judge at home and get [Ellen] out of her house" (132). Seeking less to improve her social status than to find a nurturing home, Ellen approaches a woman she's seen taking foster children to church and offers her all the money she's saved, $166, to be her new mother.

Thus, while Ellen's father reifies the worst "white trash" stereotypes, and her mother's middle-class family embodies the small-mindedness that sometimes accompanies financial security, Ellen's good sense counters the dissipation and callousness of these so-called adults. With her father, she plays the role of adult, using cash that his brothers leave in the mailbox to pay bills and buy food. She learns later that her mother's mother provides the money, but has also secured from her father's brothers what had been his land. Ellen surmises that her grandmother sends the cash because, though spiteful, "she did not have it in her to starve a girl" (89). But after county officials move Ellen in briefly with her art teacher, her grandmother begins sending less money. Through Ellen's reflections on her grandmother's motivations, Gibbons indicts the middle class for an inability to sympathize with the despair of the lower classes. Her uncle Rudolph "would waste that little bit of money so in the middle of the wasting he might forget his life had always been bad and was getting worse all the time. . . . He was fresh out of hope," Ellen recognizes, even if she can't forgive him for being "weak enough to be beat to death by a little old lady no matter how mean she is" (88). Ellen's observation that her grandmother could "take all the feeling she needed from somebody and then stir it up with some money" to scare people from her "big" house paints a picture of class-based intimidation (80). While we can agree with Ellen that her father might be "a mistake for a person" (58), Gibbons builds at least some sympathy for his social class by creating an equally revolting representative of the middle class.

Negotiating the clash between these two white social groups, Ellen finds sanctuary in African American culture, to which her relationship is also marginal. When she needs to escape her drunken father, the parents of her best friend, Starletta, open their home, pretending not to know why she hesitates to eat their "colored biscuit" and giving her for Christmas a sweater that a shocked Ellen says "does not look colored at all" (38). Working with blacks in her grandmother's cotton field, Ellen again finds the moral sensibility lacking in her own family. She basks in their kindness and spies on their warm, cheerful home life, seeing in their example the kind of family she seeks. Beginning to lose her ingrained racial prejudice, Ellen is pleased that she can "pass for colored" after the sun tans her skin (78). As Matthew Guinn asserts in *After Southern Modernism: Fiction of the Contemporary South*, fieldwork "blurs the racial demarcations by which all the whites of her acquaintance, regardless of social standing, measure themselves" (76). Even "white trash" feel sure that their skin makes them superior to African Americans. Ellen acknowledges participating in this white ideology as she hopes that Starletta, when older, will forgive her for "all the ways I slighted her oh not by selling her down a river or making her wash my clothes but by all the varieties of ways I felt God chose me over her" (116). Gibbons explained in an interview that Ellen's evolving racial views mirror her own: "I can remember as a child my father parroted to me all the bigotry that he'd grown up with. . . . And I can remember having those feelings, but Martin Luther King and black friends intervened into my life before they were burned into the front of my head" ("Kaye Gibbons" 78). African Americans in Ellen's life likewise show her the senselessness of racial divisions and the absurdity of linking race to class.

Gibbons ascribes to Ellen not only her experiences with racism, but also the desire for education that propelled her own upward mobility, a propensity also driving the novel's sequel, *The Life All Around Me by Ellen Foster* (2006). In the first book, Ellen asks the school librarian to recommend "everything of some count" (10), and from her father's house, she walks to a nearby crossroads to meet the bookmobile. Her sophisticated reading life shows in her allusions to Hemingway's Nick Adams and Chaucer's Wife of Bath, among others. The sequel begins with fifteen-year-old Ellen writing the president of Harvard University, proposing that she begin studies there immediately, having educated herself beyond her small-town high school by reading her way through the home library that her foster mother, Laura, has set up. But the letter's self-congratulatory tone belies Ellen's lingering feelings of insecurity. Still bound by a sense of poverty, she feels unworthy of the debt Laura will incur by sending her to a Johns Hopkins humanities program. Selling her own poems to help fund the trip, Ellen encounters in Baltimore the stigma associated with being a southerner of any class. Other students ask "what it was like being a curiosity in a world of nonreaders and racists" (76–77). She does not even try to make them understand that "they could be the ignorant ones" (77) for judging groups they do not know—a strong critique of patronizing attitudes from a writer born into the working-class South.

Yet *The Life All Around Me* presents traces of the "white trash" stereotype that fuels the mostly northern students' question. Winter brings a "plague of cloakroom lice" to the school back home (62). Water sometimes flows through the door of a classmate's house, which is often on the verge of falling into the river. The family of Ellen's friend Stuart, whose writing proves him barely literate, eats off records; the father makes his living by trading used rubber he gets from burning old tires in his backyard. Two girls living with Ellen in the foster home, with "hordes of imprisoned people in their genealogy" (45), sneak foul-mouthed, diseased-looking boys into the house when Laura is away. And Gibbons portrays in this novel, as in others, the hard lives of women whose men treat them badly. Many of these women rest at Laura's on Sunday afternoons, finding comfort in tea and biscuits that mark the civilized life they do not enjoy at home.

Gibbons's second novel, *A Virtuous Woman* (1989), features narrators of a slightly higher social class. The novel is told from alternating points-of-view, moving back and forth between Ruby Stokes and her husband Jack, blue-collar tenant farmers who possess Ellen's work ethic and the family values she craves. Their story allows Gibbons to reveal much about the South's class configuration, including its ties to land and the animosity of its lower classes towards those who are socially superior.

Ruby Pitt, born, like Ellen's mother, into a land-owning family, buys into the kind of moonlit romance perpetuated by Elizabeth Taylor and Spencer Tracy movies. When she runs off with John Woodrow, a migrant worker from her father's farm, she throws herself into the itinerant world of the Rough South, toiling in fields even when her husband refuses to, and living in "one falling-down place right after the other, migrant houses, trailers, places he scrounged up for them to rent" (18). Ruby lives the lesson of class conflict her mother discerns when she invites the migrants to eat on her good dishes: They trash the place, putting cigarette ashes in her African violets and butter in the tea. From then on, the migrant workers eat outside, a fact that John later throws in Ruby's face, calling her parents "uppity" even though Ruby knows her father worked hard to acquire what he owns (33). Her quick recognition of her childish mistake—solidified when she finds John in bed with another woman, makes Ruby too ashamed, after he dies of wounds incurred in a knife fight, to go home to her parents, kind and reliable working-class people who raised her lovingly yet protected her too much from life's ugliness, among them frauds like good-looking John Woodrow.

Ruby's inner conflict highlights the tension between the Rough South and the more refined working-class South her family represents. She learns too late that John's siblings did not cheat him out of his birthright, as he claims, but that he became an itinerant laborer after serving a three-year prison term for burning down his father's tobacco barns after failing to stab him with a butcher knife. After John's release, he steals and wrecks his sister's car. When John expects Ruby to ask for her inheritance early, so the couple can discontinue migrant work, he shows the crude laziness that Ruby, the product of a working family that values honest self-sufficiency, cannot abide. In daydreams of returning to her home, Ruby thinks, "What would I have said? 'Daddy, did you ever hear of *Tobacco Road*?'" (34). Her allusion to Erskine Caldwell's tale of violence and sex among a family of shiftless whites captures Ruby's own miserable life. Gibbons does not romanticize the underclass Woodrow represents, but focuses instead on the hard life of an underclass woman, called "bitch" but expected to stand by her cheating man.

Gibbons continues her focus on working-class interactions by having Ruby marry a tenant farmer twenty years her senior after Woodrow dies. Jack Stokes, the son of a part-Cherokee mother who dies of food poisoning and a Holiness father who has to borrow money to bury her, grows up in poverty. Jack labors diligently on the land of Lonnie Hoover, staying on even after a tractor turns over and kills his father. He expects that Hoover might leave him a piece of land to reward his hard work and compensate for his father's death, but Hoover doesn't, affirming Jack's understanding that the landed class often selfishly sidesteps simple human compassion. Hoover knows how important owning land is to a man who works it, however, for he offers forty-eight acres to Burr (whose family has rented for four generations) if he will marry his shrewish daughter, pregnant by another man. Jack agrees that Burr has no choice but to take the offer, and when Burr gives him a section of the land after Ruby dies of cancer, the grieving sixty-five-year-old finally decides to "try to live" without her (158). Land of his own gives Jack pride and a reason to strive, a reality that a writer growing up in the rural working class knows firsthand.

Ruby shares Jack's resentment of unfair treatment from upper-class whites, her wider range of experience lending credibility to her views. Before she meets Jack, she works as a maid for Hoover's wife, knowing that the woman wants to "show off white help" at her daughter's wedding reception. Ruby wants to stick her fingers in the wedding cake, identifying with black Whistle Dick, who once dared to taste food off her parents' anniversary buffet. Her family's black maid, Sudie Bee, reminds the child of his place and white people's judgment: "You aint got to be no nigger just 'cause you black" (49). This conflation of "nigger" and bad behavior, the same blurring that Ellen's grandmother commits in *Ellen Foster*, reflects the race/class correlation Gibbons observed growing up, and Ruby's experience in three levels of the working class—"white trash," tenant, and small farm owner—makes her a credible voice for the injustice experienced by the working class.

Another significant aspect of Gibbons's realistic portrayal of the working class in *A Virtuous Woman* relates to voice, particularly the vernacular Jack Stokes speaks. As she lets the child speak for herself in *Ellen Foster*, Gibbons lets the language of this poorly educated southerner speak for those who traditionally have not had a voice in either literature or history. Jack uses such idioms as "might could" (2), "would could've" (58), and "used to I used to" (1), dialect straight from southern fields and small towns, used to emphasize possibility and references to time. The cadence of this regional folk speech rings true, demonstrating Gibbons's ear for dialect as well as her intent to honor the country people who speak it without shame.

Moving beyond her own experience for her third novel, *A Cure for Dreams* (1991), Gibbons researched Great Depression Federal Writers Project papers in the Southern Historical Collection at Chapel Hill. These manuscripts transcribing the vernacular of mill hands, small farmers, housewives, and unemployed plain folk intensified Gibbons's commitment to the artistic power of everyday speech (Snodgrass 18). *A Cure for Dreams* creates a matriarchal family lineage, a community of talking women making do, but enjoying life in a society dominated by working-class men. Betty Randolph recounts tales of family poverty and persistence. Her Irish Catholic grandmother, Bridget, left Galway, Ireland, for destitution in Kentucky, and her mother, Lottie, escaped that extreme poverty by marrying a work-obsessed North Carolina Quaker farmer who kills himself when the Depression stymies his efforts to get ahead. The Depression pushes the poor working class to its limits, of course, but also gives people a chance to show their mettle—or lack thereof. When people on Milk Farm Road feel "destined never to have anything," the men go wild and spend what little money they have on "mill tarts" (37). Sade Duplin, "already on the verge of losing the farm her father had passed to her" (38), gets away with murdering her philandering husband when Lottie chooses to overlook household details pointing to her guilt, just as a community of women covers for the murderess in Susan Glaspell's play "Trifles" (1916). Lottie refuses to "let herself wallow in the times" but keeps her spirits high (50), helping those poorer than she, such as Trudy Woodlief, denied store credit after her shiftless, thieving husband leaves her pregnant with twins to add to her dirty brood. Betty learns from her strong mother to make do and live cheerfully despite hardships. Understanding that people sometimes have to cure themselves of dreams, Betty marries a dull local boy before he leaves for World War II, remaining with her mother on Milk Farm Road and enjoying life in a community of spunky women, a harbinger of Gibbons's later work.

Charms for the Easy Life (1993) portrays another family of wise and hard-working women whose gumption improves the lot of the suffering lower class. A granddaughter narrates the story of Charlie Kate Birch, a self-proclaimed doctor who works the white, male-dominated political system of the early twentieth-century South, exposing upper-class ineptitude and arrogant discrimination. When her illiterate husband leaves after moving Charlie Kate from coastal Pasquotank to Wake County, North Carolina, she thrives as a public health activist, shaming the textile mill owner into installing sidewalks so children need not wade "through mud and gore from the meat-packing house up the hill," and bringing city sewage lines to the Hooverville mill district by reminding councilmen that residents are "all white" (21). She is disgusted by their racism, but takes advantage of it where she can. She secretly forces the retirement of a bigoted doctor, whose inattention to African Americans' maladies results in deaths. Reading medical textbooks, the *New England Journal of Medicine*, the *New Yorker*, and literary fiction to educate herself, Charlie Kate pays a poor boy's way through medical school and trains her daughter and granddaughter as health caregivers and readers. This vigorous can-do woman cannot sit through a showing of *Gone with the Wind* (1939), knowing its hideous portrayal of old South, upper-class nostalgia will make viewers "walk out retarded" (89). While Charlie Kate herself is not poor, having inherited stock from a wealthy former patient and investing wisely, her disregard for class status argues for egalitarianism. The well-born wife of the man whose education she funds follows her lead, moving to impoverished Pasquotank County during the Great Depression to teach "riff-raff, trash, [and] white niggers," even when her family disowns her for doing so (142). Although the novel's narrator, Margaret, will marry into a socially prominent family as this fourth novel ends, she is solidly grounded in her grandmother's humanism, aware of the damage wrought by class conceit.

Guinn writes in *After Southern Modernism* that, "Considered sequentially, Gibbons's work moves upward through the social hierarchy with each novel, from the 'trash' perspective of *Ellen Foster* to the blue-collar milieu of *A Virtuous Woman*, from the vague middle class of *A Cure for Dreams* and *Charms for the Easy Life* to the landed bourgeoisie of *Sights Unseen*" (84), a novel exploring the effects of a mother's manic depression on herself and her family. Through daughter Hattie Barnes's narration of her nurturing by black cook and housekeeper Pearl, Gibbons continues her critique of the South's relegation of blacks to the margins of the social order. Again, in *On the Occasion of My Last Afternoon* (1998), Gibbons's Civil War novel, black cook and housekeeper Clarice appears as a resilient, intelligent woman who captures Gibbons's thesis on race and class when she forces her upper-class owner to recognize as a human being the slave whose throat he has slit: "He had a name and it was Jacob" (8). To her fellow slaves, she gives this advice: "Be proud to what you is worth" (15). That Clarice's "worth" here refers, perhaps sarcastically, to the slaves' price on the auction block only enhances Gibbons's advice for the black woman: Individuals must value themselves enough to value others.

Writing in the *Christian Century*, Ralph C. Wood inadvertently refers to Gibbons's upbringing when he commends her characters' rural ties: "Gibbons's work shows what is wrong with the old canard that the cultured discuss ideas while rustics tell stories. Though meant to disparage the countrified, this saying unintentionally exalts them: narratives strike deeper than concepts because they reveal how character and motive prompt action . . . prompt lives" (846). Gibbons learned from her own hardscrabble beginnings in a household beset by mental illness and alcoholism that the important ideas about being human are not restricted by such external conditions as race or class. Her Rough South characters are as complex as humans anywhere, a fact that she often shows with humor, like other writers who have arisen from the wrong side of the tracks to show the South as it really is. In *Ellen Foster*, when Ellen imagines her Aunt Nadine telling Dora that her father is not dead, but "up in heaven strumming on a harp with the angels . . . looking down at how pretty" his baby girl is, she offers this assessment of her aunt's refusal to face the truth: "Chickenshit is what I would say" (112). Writing honestly from the perspective of one confronted early with the less than pretty South, Kaye Gibbons would likely say the same.

Works Cited

Gibbons, Kaye. *Charms for the Easy Life*. New York: Putnam, 1993. Print.

———. *A Cure for Dreams*. Chapel Hill: Algonquin, 1991. Print.

———. *Ellen Foster*. Chapel Hill: Algonquin, 1987. Print.

———. *Frost and Flower: My Life with Manic Depression So Far*. Decatur: Wisteria P, 1995. Print.

———. *How I Became a Writer: My Mother, Literature, and a Life Split Neatly into Two Halves*. Chapel Hill: Algonquin, 1988. Print.

———. "Kaye Gibbons." Interview by Bernard Thomas. *Broken Silences: Interviews with Black and White Women Writers*. Ed. Shirley M. Jordan. New Brunswick: Rutgers UP, 1993. 65–82. Print.

———. *The Life All Around Me by Ellen Foster*. Orlando: Harcourt, 2006. Print.

———. *On the Occasion of My Last Afternoon*. New York: Putnam, 1998. Print.

———. *A Virtuous Woman*. Chapel Hill: Algonquin, 1989. Print.

Guinn, Matthew. *After Southern Modernism: Fiction of the Contemporary South*. Jackson: UP of Mississippi, 2000. Print.

Snodgrass, Mary Ellen. *Kaye Gibbons: A Literary Companion*. Jefferson: McFarland, 2007. Print.

Wood, Ralph C. "Gumption and Grace in the Novels of Kaye Gibbons." *Christian Century*. 109.27 (1992): 842–46. Print.

Lee Smith: A Diamond from the Rough

Linda Byrd Cook

ORN November 1, 1944, in the southwestern Virginia coal-mining town of Grundy, Lee Smith was an only child and a voracious reader. Her father, Ernest Lee Smith, came from so-called mountain people who had lived in the area for generations. Her mother, Virginia Marshall Smith, came from coastal Virginia and, college-educated, worked as a teacher. Smith recalls that growing up in Grundy, she consciously tried to conform to the image of an aspiring southern "lady." Though she considered writing a practice she should keep secret—it wasn't considered proper for a girl—she published several pieces in a children's magazine. After graduating from St. Catherine's School in Richmond, she went to Roanoke's Hollins College to take part in their writing program. There she studied under Louis D. Rubin Jr. and R. H. W. Dillard, both of whom strongly influenced her writing. Initially Smith wrote about romantic and foreign subjects, believing no one would be interested in reading about her home, but after encountering Eudora Welty's work in a southern literature course, she realized the importance of writing from one's experience.

From the humorous and outrageous to the serious and epiphanic, Smith's eleven novels and four short story collections consistently probe the crises of identity that plague so many contemporary Americans, particularly women.

In virtually all of her works, a female protagonist struggles to find her identity. Her female characters reflect the complexity and contradictions inherent in southern heritage and demonstrate Smith's vision of hope for the future. Like their creator, they long for something to believe in, a divine power that neither patronizes nor silences women. Smith's primary characters are lower-middle-class women who, amid a limiting and restrictive culture, seek wholeness during a time of "radical dislocation and social change" (Ketchin 4). Hairdressers, boardinghouse proprietresses, orphans, unwed mothers, and mentally challenged misfits, they often tell their own stories, as Smith forces readers to reexamine long-held beliefs and stereotypes about the lower classes. As Erik Bledsoe notes of other recent southern authors in "The Rise of Southern Redneck and White Trash Writers," Smith "challeng[es] the literary roles traditionally assigned poor whites" (68). These characters may simultaneously serve as comic figures, victims, and villains, but they are also in some way heroic. Many of them yearn to escape the Rough South, but most either remain or return there, coming full circle in their quest for wholeness. Like other members of her generation of southern writers, Smith creates a full, complex world of characters who confirm some stereotypes and transcend others. Bledsoe notes that this new writing demands that "we make room" (88) for all types of people, broadening our vision and understanding to encompass the entire South—not just the South as viewed from the plantation porch or the ruins thereof.

From her earliest works through her most recent, Smith introduces transgressive females; her earliest characters, however, seem unable to nourish others *and* satisfy their own sexual needs. In her first novel, *The Last Day the Dogbushes Bloomed* (1968), nine-year-old Susan Tobey remains at odds with her surroundings as she seeks to understand and articulate her experiences. Susan's older sister, Betty, tells her that "girls get to spend all the money and they don't have to shave and they can look beautiful all day long and make all the men fall in love with them" (39), but Susan "c[an't] think of anything worse" than kissing boys and growing breasts, "big blobby things flopping around all the time in front of [her] chest" (41). Left motherless after the so-called Queen departs with her lover, Susan refuses to conform to the passive, silent role society prescribes for her. *Family Linen* (1985), however, introduces Candy, whom Katherine Kearns, in "From Shadow to Substance: The Empowerment of the Artist Figure in Lee Smith's Fiction," calls the "impossible reconciliation of the mother and the whore as she nurtures and satisfies every need, the figure of the happily sensual woman" (180). Candy becomes the prototype that Smith has repeatedly gravitated toward in her later fiction: a sexual woman who enjoys fulfilling others' needs while also gratifying her own. To this category belong Justine Poole, from *Oral History* (1983), Geneva Hunt, from *Fair and Tender Ladies* (1988), and Martha Fickling, from *On Agate Hill* (2006).

Smith populates her fiction with rebellious females who struggle to find their identities. In the three novels that follow *The Last Day the Dogbushes Bloomed*—*Something in the Wind* (1971), *Fancy Strut* (1973), and *Black Mountain Breakdown* (1980)—teenage girls and young women display sexual aggression and experience pleasure from sexual intercourse. Because society openly condemns such behavior in females, the respective protagonists of these novels—Brooke Kincaid, Monica Neighbors, and Crystal Spangler—all suffer to varying degrees. Smith, however, refuses to judge them.

Brooke Kincaid of *Something in the Wind* receives advice similar to that Susan receives from her sister in *The Last Day the Dogbushes Bloomed*. Before Brooke leaves for college, her mother advises her, "You ought to go out every weekend but you shouldn't go out two nights in a row with the same boy." She tells Brooke that "boys don't like pale little egghead girls," and that a "smart man is one thing but a smart woman is something else" (33–34). While at college, Brooke, not quite the southern belle her mother had envisioned, explains that she had "slept with just about everybody" (127), telling them all she's a virgin, but only with Bentley T. Hooks does she experience the transformative power of erotic ecstasy. Brooke moves in with Bentley, completely breaking the code of behavior imposed upon southern girls. The relationship is short-lived, however, since Brooke is ultimately unable or unwilling to complete the painful process of integration and regeneration begun with Bentley.

Monica Neighbors, of *Fancy Strut*, experiences a similar opportunity for transformation in her extramarital affair with Buck Fire, an out-of-work actor. Monica, married three years, is already restless, at first trying to use her overflowing energy in a socially acceptable way by repeatedly redecorating a new house. Monica is in effect a grown-up Brooke, seen after after a few years of marriage with her identity even more divided. For three years, Monica has been a model wife, or so it seems, but suddenly she feels on the verge of madness; everything seems artificial. Like Brooke, Monica has split herself into public and private selves, refusing even to attempt to integrate the two. Her divided identity frightens her, and she presents the outward appearance of a happy housewife while secretly harboring fantasies of sexual degradation. She imagines driving to a sleazy motel to meet a lover with whom her sexuality is unrestrained, even secretly entertaining a "wild hope" that her husband Manly will "burst through that door . . . and rip off her Tanner dress so violently that the buttons would sound like bullets as they hit the wall, and throw her down upon the floor. . . . [S]he wished he would strip her and set her up on the coffee table and make her do terrible things" (177–78). Monica's sexuality heightens owing to her affair with Buck, and he calls her "wild," admitting "she can wear him out" (243), a confession that illustrates society's fascination with and even fear of the sexually aggressive adult female. As Monica lives out her fantasy of an illicit love affair and performs sexual acts she's never thought of committing with her husband, Buck satisfies in Monica a need that the ironically named Manly leaves unfulfilled. Monica thinks with satisfaction that she'll go straight to hell, having given in to desires of the flesh, but she decides she doesn't believe in hell anyway. At the end of the novel, however, Monica, like Brooke, returns to the safe world of conventional southern society.

Crystal Spangler of *Black Mountain Breakdown* epitomizes the passive female torn between society's conflicting values. At the end of the novel she is permanently silenced, paralyzed in her inability to achieve integration. Like protagonists in earlier Smith novels, Crystal initially follows the conventional path assigned southern women, the one validated by those around her, but her emerging sexuality, a source of confusion and fascination, prevents her from finding contentment. Crystal decides to fall in love with Roger Lee, the football star and high school hero, at first ignoring Mack Stiltner, the "mean country boy" who keeps staring at her (51). Although Roger promises Crystal a lifetime of happiness, she senses a void in their relationship. A sexual being like Brooke and Monica, Crystal then pursues Mack, the high school dropout with a bad reputation. For her protagonists, Smith consistently imagines nonconformist male counterparts, often shocking and unusual in appearance and manners, to suggest the necessary disturbance of the status quo in awakening a female's sacred sexuality. Crystal says she would rather be with Mack than anyone else, as only with him can she be her true self. Considering the sexual freedom her relationship with Mack offers, Crystal decides "it means she can fuck him if she wants to, which she does" (97). After her breakup with Mack, she experiences religious salvation at a local revival, but she admits that her relationship with Mack seems to have more connection to real life than her salvation does.

Crystal's communion with Mack, in fact, serves as a type of salvation for her, since she says she can be herself with him; he houses the potential to "save" her from her own passivity. The divine nature of their mutual sexuality is more real to Crystal than salvation amid the religious patriarchy that denies women both physical pleasure and a voice. Crystal likes to visualize near-rape scenes, much as Monica does. When she imagines the ideal life, married to a man for whom she feels "a magnetic attraction," she envisions being in Nashville with Mack. Her fantasy continues: Mack "pulls her toward him and rips off the top of her cowboy suit, scattering sequins all over the white shag carpet. They make love on the carpet, in the red sequins, and it is wonderful" (131). This imagined scene of male sexual dominance, with the scattered sequins, is reminiscent of Monica's fantasies of Manly coming home and tearing off her clothes. Both women crave the intensity of sexual and spiritual passion often associated with violence, and both fantasize about male aggression. The end of *Black Mountain Breakdown*, however, finds Crystal married to Roger Lee, somewhat aware of the loss of selfhood but unable to find the strength or words to assert herself.

For her 1985 novel *Family Linen*, Smith researched her subject matter by working as a shampoo girl in a beauty salon in Chapel Hill, North Carolina. Of all the characters in the novel, only the illegitimate daughter Candy, a beautician, seems satisfied with herself and her life. Her perception of and appreciation for the beauty of each individual stems from deep self-knowledge and acceptance of others. In an interview with Michelle Lodge, Smith described Candy as the heroine of the novel, the most important character and the most successful, well-integrated person (310). Since Candy is a love child, she possesses a certain freedom from conformity that allows her to lead a life different from those of her brother and sisters. She explores her sexuality while successfully fulfilling the role of mother.

Her sisters Sybill and Myrtle consider Candy their inferior because of her occupation and her promiscuity as a teenager and young adult. Although Candy has given her children the freedom to grow and become successful adults, Myrtle labels Candy a "terrible mother" (58), and both sisters express amazement that one of Candy's children attends law school and the other teaches art. Smith not only emphasizes Candy's sexuality but elevates her to a spiritual level through the imagery associated with her and her home. She uses such terms as "magical," "rose-pink," and "sweet" to describe her (118), creating images that Smith consistently associates with feminine divinity. Candy, a complex woman, is the only female in the novel linked to both life and death. Even her beauty shop—with its mixture perfume, shampoo, formaldehyde, and pine Lysol in the air—smells inviting.

Candy's warm, life-affirming nature manifests itself throughout the novel in her response to and treatment of family members. After her mother's stroke, when Candy visits her in the hospital and holds the dying woman's hand, Myrtle, although shocked, acknowledges Candy's "good intentions" and "big heart" (59). Unlike her sisters, Candy accepts and enters human suffering. She responds to life. As the entire family stands gathered at the hospital, awaiting the news of Elizabeth's imminent death, Candy's brother

Arthur thinks, "Candy's a toucher," she "always makes you feel better" (106). Despite her own anguish at losing her mother, Candy manages to pat, stroke, or touch each of her siblings in order to comfort them.

Candy's willingness and desire to touch others, especially those she loves, is perhaps most obvious in her decision to prepare Elizabeth's body for the funeral by shampooing and setting her hair and applying her makeup to make sure she looks her best. After the funeral, as the family sorts through Elizabeth's belongings and lays claim to various household articles, Candy again consoles her siblings. She continues to comfort her family after the shocking discovery of the remains of Jewell Rife and the news of Fay's death, when the family members are overwhelmed with their own pain. Offering comfort to Clinus, the mentally handicapped son of Nettie's late husband, with whom only Arthur has contact, Candy takes his arm and leads him into the house, later driving him home. In *Lee Smith*, Dorothy Combs Hill describes Candy as the "mythic ennoblement of what society would see as sweet, transitory, and pleasurable, the very way in which women are so often labeled, marginalized, and trivialized" (99). With her name and profession, Candy runs the risk of being so labeled, but Smith's treatment of her precludes such categorizing.

Like female characters in Smith's previous novels, Candy is consistently linked to wildness as opposed to domesticity, further emphasizing the writer's insistence on the necessity of abandonment in achieving total integration. From the beginning of the novel, when Sybill visits the hypnotist, Candy's liminal position in the family is reflected in Sybill's comments to Dr. Diamond that Candy didn't go to school like the other children because she was "too busy dating the boys" and eventually "ran away and got married" (37). Candy herself admits that she and her mother were "natural strangers" (123). No other statement could better describe their relationship. The words resonate with irony, since Candy is the biological daughter of Jewell and Fay, not Elizabeth, but Candy never learns this fact.

Candy comforts not only her sisters, brother, aunts, and customers, but her twenty-year affair with Don Dotson, Myrtle's husband, marked by generosity and acceptance, also foreshadows the union of future couples in Smith's works. In this relationship, Smith transgresses boundaries and disturbs society's prescribed code of acceptable behavior, since Candy and Don ostensibly betray her sister, who is also his wife. Candy and Don, deeply committed to their relationship, harbor mutual respect and a generosity of spirit. Here Smith subverts the usual moral code to assert a new set of ethics and values. She neither judges nor condemns Candy and Don; in fact, they function as the novel's divine couple, compassionately depicted and strongly associated with divinity. Complete on her own—unlike females in Smith's earlier novels, who require the presence of a man or men to feel a sense of wholeness—Candy enjoys her occasional passionate union with Don.

Possessing an understanding of humans as interdependent beings, Candy accepts life's paradoxes and complexities and consistently maintains a sense of equilibrium. After her mother's death, Candy reflects on life's mysteries, deciding, "If you're not crazy sooner, you'll be later." She concludes her reverie with profound simplicity, observing, "Life is long and wild and there is usually a point where it makes you crazy. That's natural" (113). In Candy's understanding and acceptance of life's mysteries and death, Smith emphasizes that this female character, perhaps easily misunderstood as a simple beautician from a lower social class, possesses extraordinary depth and understanding.

With her 1988 masterpiece, *Fair and Tender Ladies*, and the introduction of Geneva Hunt (one of Ivy's female friends, former schoolmate of Ivy's mother, and proprietress of the boardinghouse in Majestic), Smith offers an alternative for females as she continues to explore the expanding possibilities for ordinary women's lives. An epistolary novel, *Fair and Tender Ladies* spans the life of a strong mountain woman who can conquer any obstacle. The novel is generally recognized as one of Smith's greatest works, winning her the Appalachian Writers Award and the W. D. Weatherford Award for American Literature.

In the novel, Ivy meets Geneva when her family moves to Majestic after the death of Ivy's little brother Danny, and because of the generosity, acceptance, and love of this "soft" woman (83), Ivy, her mother, and her two little brothers find a home and supportive environment. Associated with nature and sexuality, Geneva first appears emerging from the boardinghouse, where "buttercups was blooming early," like "she was blowed by the wind" (81), an image reminiscent of other sexual females. Even though Geneva has been married three times and announces that she is finished with men, Ivy's intuition about Geneva's sexual appetite proves accurate. Ivy spots one of the male boarders "sneaking outen Genevas room, carrying his shoes" (90–91), then later notices that Sam Russell Sage, a famous preacher holding a revival in town, has become "Geneva's sweetie" (97). This affair between a sexually accommodating boardinghouse proprietress and a preacher recalls the relationship between Justine Poole and Aldous Rife in *Oral History*.

With her portrayal of Geneva as openly sexual, nurturing, and deeply caring, Smith transgresses boundaries by depicting these qualities as coexistent, desirable, and even admirable. Serving as a mentor for Ivy, Geneva offers many words of wisdom through the years of their friendship, early on telling the seventeen-year-old Ivy, confused about God, sexuality, and her future, that sometimes "a girl has just got to let down her hair" (96–97). Geneva is not only sexually accommodating with her male guests but loves to cook, preparing and serving elaborate meals to patrons and townspeople alike. Smith thus connects nurturing through sexual contact and nurturing through food, suggesting that both appetites must be satisfied in order to achieve integration and wholeness. Right after Ivy returns to Sugar Fork from her interlude with Honey Breeding and sinks into grief and depression, seventy-year-old Geneva visits in order to reassure her that what she has done will soon be forgiven and forgotten. When Ivy worries about being such a "scandal," Geneva offers Ivy the same advice she gave her younger sister Ethel years earlier, then openly admits, winking at Ivy, "*I used to be a scandal myself. . . . Now I'm an institution.*" Geneva accepts her sexuality as part of her selfhood and encourages Ivy to do the same, but Ivy, still uncomfortable with her own behavior, writes to Silvaney that she greatly admires Geneva's way of life but lacks "gumption and pluck" (236–37) herself. Ivy's words in describing Geneva's lifestyle, "rid[ing] hell for leather," echo Granny Younger's interpretation of Red Emmy's sexual aggressiveness with Almarine in *Oral History*. But Smith presents Geneva in a much gentler way—through Ivy's perspective—than Granny depicts Emmy. The sexually expressive Geneva survives and flourishes in a society that accepts and needs her; as she admits, she's become "an institution."

In *Saving Grace* (1995), Smith tells her story through the voice of a young, lower-class girl. Florida Grace's sensuality is revealed early. Then, when she is fourteen and has her first sexual encounter, like Ivy Rowe, she does not feel guilty, even though her father is a preacher. After years of a marriage that has produced two daughters, Grace also engages in an extramarital relationship. The affair is reminiscent of the brief relationship between Ivy and Honey in *Fair and Tender Ladies*, and Smith describes both affairs in religious terms. Other characters call both Ivy and Grace "whore of Babylon" (*Ladies* 251, *Grace* 227), but Smith clearly depicts them as sexual beings who are also loving mothers. While Ivy leaves her children temporarily to spend time with Honey, Grace abandons her two daughters permanently to run away with her lover. Interestingly, neither woman is condemned, nor is either desertion sentimentalized as completely justified. After decades of searching for the salvation that has continuously evaded her, Grace eventually completes her circular journey toward integration and self-knowledge at Scrabble Creek, ending where she began.

Molly Petree, the protagonist of Smith's 2006 novel *On Agate Hill*, early identifies herself as an "orphan girl," an "unfortunate child," and proclaims herself a "spitfire and a burden"—but then adds, "I don't care" (7). Throughout Smith's many novels and a writing career that spans five decades, she has constructed female characters who refuse to remain within the boundaries of what their respective societies demand. Molly Petree is only the latest of a host of females who declare their liminality. Writing to dispel the myth of the southern belle, Smith enlarges the possibilities for females lives and allows for a variety of life-paths.

Smith demands of her readers a broader sense of empathy, a new kind of understanding, particularly in her sympathetic portrayals of damaged females or those victimized by society. One of the most poignant examples occurs in *Fair and Tender Ladies* with the representation of Silvaney, Ivy's brain-damaged older sister. In her first letter to Hanneke, Ivy, in writing about her family, explains, "I love Silvaney the bestest, you see. Silvaney is so pretty, she is the sweetest, all silverhaired like she was fotched up on the moon" (8–9). Ivy perceives Silvaney as the other side of herself, a part necessary for her to fully function, and in continuing to write to her absent, then dead, sister, she preserves the divine, wild, fiery part of her own spirit. In her depiction of the symbiotic relationship between the sisters, Smith expands women's relationships beyond the man-woman combinations that in earlier novels are required to make female characters feel complete. In her first letter to Hanneke, Ivy says that even though Silvaney is five years older and much bigger than she, "[I]t is like we are the same sometimes it is like we are one" (9). In her letters Ivy addresses Silvaney as "my love and my hart" (94), "my lost one, my heart" (111), salient reminders of the indispensability of one to the other. Ivy writes her most private thoughts to Silvaney, almost talking to herself in an effort to write herself into being, to validate herself and her experiences. She says, "I can talk to you for you do not understand, I can write you this letter too and tell you all the deepest things, the things in my hart" (94). Until Ivy learns from her brother Victor that Silvaney died in the 1918 flu epidemic, she plans to take her sister back to the mountain one day, for, as she explains in a letter to Victor, "I have felt like I was split off from a part of myself all these years, and now it is like that part of me has died, since I know she will never come" (173–74).

Smith emphasizes Silvaney's mysterious nature by having Ivy describe her sister "gliding" across a creek, with the full moon large and low, on the night that Babe, Silvaney's twin brother, is murdered (60). And once Silvaney is taken away, Ivy writes to her sister Beulah, "I keep thinking I see Silvaney but it is never her, it is only ligt in the trees, and so often I think I hear her talking but no one is ther, it is only the wind" (69). Wandering the mountains aimlessly, Silvaney eludes domestication or containment. Ivy's mother explains Silvaney's mental problems as the result of her having "brain fever," which "burned out a part of her brain" when she was a baby (9), and Silvaney is continually linked to fire, which in Smith's works consistently suggests both the passion and the potential danger of female sexuality. Silvaney is considered abnormal, since she behaves "like a wild animal" with "a ligt in her eye . . . like a reglar fire, it is like her whole face is lit up from inside, like they is a fire in her head shining throgh, and its not long I think before this fire is going to burn her up" (56). Ivy seems the only one who understands her sister, writing to Mrs. Brown after Silvaney has been taken to the asylum, "Silvaney is diffrent from all, she needs to wander the woods, and she needs some woods to wander" (63–64). Ivy senses that being enclosed in the Elizabeth Masters Home in Roanoke will destroy Silvaney. In a letter to her dead father, Ivy describes Silvaney's blue eyes as being like lakes with "flames, flames" right under the surface. Then Ivy asks her father, "Were you ther when she walked in the fire?" (56–57). This vague reference to Silvaney walking in fire, coupled with the earlier mention of her gliding across water, links Silvaney to biblical references to Christ walking on water and appearing in flames.

In her depiction of Fay in *Family Linen*, Smith traces the damage done to a female society neither accepts nor understands. Family members and circumstances not only deny Fay the right to sanity, but prevent her from raising or acknowledging her own child and deprive her of a life of her own. With Fay, Smith continues to explore female victims. As with *Black Mountain Breakdown*'s Crystal, the physical abuse Fay suffers leads to her complete passivity. She seems simply a crazy recluse who lives on television and magazines until close to the end of the novel, when Nettie explains the source of her sister's insanity. In her journal, Elizabeth described the teenaged Fay as a "sweet presence" with a tendency to wander (184), like so many damaged sexual females in Smith. With her heavy yellow hair, which eventually turns completely white, and her love of flowers—family members give her flowers throughout the novel—Fay is aligned with divinity and female sexuality.

Nettie's description of the scene during which Jewell rapes Fay illustrates Fay's ultimate violation. As she stands at the kitchen sink washing dishes and singing, "with her yellow hair falling in curls down her back" (231), Jewell suddenly slams his fist down onto the table and calls to her. Nettie notices that a terrible expression replaces Fay's blank look, and suddenly she appears completely changed, with wet, red lips, shining eyes, and pink cheeks, her whole face taking on "a *waiting* look." With a "loose, sweet smile," Fay sings jumbled, indecipherable words in a voice "high and thin." As Fay is sexually violated, Nettie says she looked like "the end of the world," and indeed, Fay suffers permanent damage. Fay's garbled speech symbolizes her regression from the cultural order represented by the male-dominated patriarchy. After the rape,

Fay's voice can no longer be heard or understood; she is silenced, robbed of a will of her own. Nettie describes Fay sitting on the countertop, bereft of panties, her legs spread apart, and Jewell, his pants around his ankles, "fucking her," without holding or kissing her (232–33). Deprived of love, Fay is denied the source of sensuous pleasure—the cuddling, kissing, and holding. Fay's face remains indelible in Nettie's mind, how it changed from "that waiting, knowing look into something terrible where wanting and hating went back and forth . . . faster and faster, ending up as something awful which you've not got the words to say." Even Nettie, equipped with the power of language, is silenced by the horror she witnesses. As Nettie continues to watch, spellbound with shock, another look comes over Fay's face, one that seems to say, "*I know what I'm up to. I know.*" Nettie interprets the look as "pain so pure it was like a real thing twisting and yelling in the air between her and me." Then the look vanishes, and Fay regains the same "sweet blank expression" she had before and has had ever since (233–34). A more graphic picture of male violation and female submission could not be drawn. This paradoxical description of the rape, with Fay's "sweet, awful smile" and her look of simultaneous "wanting and hating," emphasizes Fay's helplessness and victimization. She has a look that suggests her complete knowledge of and consent to the violent assault. She willingly sacrifices herself to Jewell despite her agony, personified as a writhing, wriggling, hissing snake.

After the discovery of Fay's pregnancy and the sisters' seclusion in Lynchburg, Nettie describes Fay as sweeter and quieter, a "smile spread out all over her face" (244), often sitting on the porch swing with her hands on her stomach to feel the movement of the baby. After Candy's birth, Nettie observes that "having a baby came natural to her, like having a cold, and didn't hurt her the way it does most" (250), again aligning Fay with nature and natural processes. But Fay is disallowed any role in the child's life, one of society's ways of punishing the damaged. First stripped of her sexuality by Jewell, next robbed of her right to be mother to her child, Fay becomes quieter, sadder, more confused, eventually sinking into permanent passivity and what society labels "insanity."

Lee Smith's fictional world, populated with a wide variety of female characters, demonstrates the author's vision for the possibilities in women's lives. Choosing as her subject matter characters drawn from the lower middle classes, Smith forces readers to see the Rough South as populated by real people with valid disappointments and joys. They may exist in what Bledsoe calls a "world of excess—excessive alcohol, excessive sex, excessive violence" (68), but they are humans whose voices deserve to be heard and understood.

Works Cited

Bledsoe, Erik. "The Rise of Southern Redneck and White Trash Writers." *Southern Cultures* 6.1 (2000): 68–90. Print.

Hill, Dorothy Combs. *Lee Smith*. New York: Twayne, 1992. Print.

Kearns, Katherine. "From Shadow to Substance: The Empowerment of the Artist Figure in Lee Smith's Fiction." *Writing the Woman Artist*. Ed. Suzanne W. Jones. Philadelphia: U of Pennsylvania P, 1991. 175–95. Print.

Ketchin, Susan. *The Christ-Haunted Landscape: Faith and Doubt in Southern Fiction*. Jackson: UP of Mississippi, 1994. Print.

Lodge, Michelle. "Lee Smith." *Publishers Weekly* 20 Sept. 1985: 110–11. Print.

Smith, Lee. *Black Mountain Breakdown*. New York: Putnam, 1980. Print.

———. *Fair and Tender Ladies*. New York: Putnam, 1988. Print.

———. *Family Linen*. New York: Putnam, 1985. Print.

———. *Fancy Strut*. New York: Harper & Row, 1973. Print.

———. *The Last Day the Dogbushes Bloomed*. New York: Harper & Row, 1968. Print.

———. *On Agate Hill*. Chapel Hill: Algonquin, 2006. Print.

———. *Saving Grace*. New York: Putnam, 1995. Print.

———. *Something in the Wind*. New York: Harper & Row, 1971. Print.

A Country for Old Men: The South of

Clyde Edgerton's Early Novels

Robert Donahoo

I F we accept Erik Bledsoe's description of the Rough South as "a world of excess—excessive alcohol, excessive sex, excessive violence" (68), the works of Clyde Edgerton hardly seem to qualify. Indeed, Yvonne Mason, in *Reading, Learning, Teaching Clyde Edgerton,* declares his work "infinitely suitable" for "young readers in the English Language Arts classroom" (81)—an appraisal difficult to imagine for the fiction of Harry Crews or Larry Brown. Born in Durham, North Carolina, in 1944, Edgerton boasts a far less colorful, much less traumatic family history than many of his peers. His childhood in Bethesda, just outside Durham, centered on family: a father who taught him to hunt, a mother who encouraged him to study piano, and an extended family of storytelling women. "I grew up in a house filled with women who talked a lot and with men who didn't," he told one interviewer (Stephenson 76). His home was also a religious one: His family, he said, was "regular" in attendance at what he characterized as "a 1950s fundamentalist Baptist church" (Brown 120; "Conversation" 68).

In *Contemporary Fiction Writers of the South,* R. Sterling Hennis Jr. reports that after high school, Edgerton left Bethesda for the University of North

Carolina at Chapel Hill, where he majored in English and joined the Air Force ROTC to fulfill an early dream of becoming a pilot. Graduation in 1966 led to an air force commission and four years of active duty as a fighter pilot during the Vietnam War. Leaving the air force, he returned to Chapel Hill for a master of arts degree in teaching and, after a stint teaching high school in Durham, a PhD in English education. After marrying Susan Ketchin in 1975, Edgerton joined the faculty of Campbell University in Buies Creek, North Carolina, where he taught until 1985, leaving after he published his first novel, *Raney* (1985), which in the opinion of university administrators "did not further the goals and purposes" of the conservative Baptist institution (114–16). Edgerton continued to teach, but his focus increasingly turned toward writing, and he quickly completed his second and third novels, *Walking Across Egypt* (1987) and *The Floatplane Notebooks* (1988). Today, he lives with his second wife and three young children in Wilmington, North Carolina, where he is professor of creative writing at UNC-Wilmington. He has published seven more novels—most recently *The Night Train* (2011)—as well as a memoir, *Solo: My Adventure in the Air* (2005), and a work of nonfiction, *Papadaddy's Book for New Fathers: Advice to Dads of All Ages* (2013).

Reflecting on his upbringing, Edgerton once said that he might as well have been raised "two or three hundred years ago." His parents, he explained,

> were so much like their great-grandparents they could've changed places with them because they grew up knowing nothing except raising what you eat and living off the land. I was raised comfortably, but my parents weren't, and I was raised by them, so [even though] I'm a little bit removed from it, I've felt their life [story]. . . . My parents were in almost every way—educationally, religiously, politically—exactly like their grandparents, great-grandparents. So in many ways I feel like [I am] really more connected to the past. (Cornett 164–65)

In examining Edgerton's first three novels, the works that established his reputation and remain some of his best-known, these links to a fading or lost past offer a way to understand Edgerton's South, a world that increasingly belongs to and is defined by aging and death. It is a world that individuals inhabit less in space than in time, a world that, for all its vitality, bears a sense of loss and doom. It is in learning to cope with this sense that Edgerton's characters define themselves and the essential nature of contemporary life in the South.

Edgerton clearly places change at the center of *Raney*, which opens with a marriage that necessitates an unequal migration. After the wedding, Raney moves only a few miles, to a nearby North Carolina town, but her new husband, Charles, moves not only the hundreds of miles from Atlanta, but from an urban metropolis to a rural backwater. And this is more than a migration in space; it also involves a return to a past when southern communities had general stores, when Free Will Baptists were not uncommon. Raney's values are her family's values, and much of the humor in the opening chapters arises from cultural clashes: Raney's shock upon learning that her new mother-in-law is a vegetarian; her anger that Charles drank alcohol at their wedding rehearsal; her insistence on having "my marriage consumed [*sic*] *after* I was married" (17); and her outrage at Charles's "different idea which I do not have the nerve to explain" about sex on their wedding night (18). Raney's first-person narration reports her husband's failure to adopt her family's habits. "He has no appreciation for just setting and talking" after Sunday dinners, she says. "And I don't mean going on and on about politics or something like that; I mean just talking—talking about normal things" (24). Her narration also links such attitudes to the South through her views on race. When she overhears Charles phoning his army buddy Johnny Dobbs and realizes he's likely an African American, her old southern racial values ring out: "[I]f he *is* a nigger, he can't stay here. It won't work. The Ramada, maybe, but not here" (29). Given that the novel is set in 1975, a decade after passage of the Civil Rights Act, Raney clearly holds to a way of life that belongs to the past—a past that Charles resists, thus creating tension in the new marriage.

Charles's sense of unease is underscored by his lack of connection to traditional southern masculinity. With his narrow shoulders and job as an assistant librarian, he does not embody traditional manliness. He proves an unsuccessful fisherman during a family beach trip, and he refuses to go hunting with his father-in-law because, as Raney explains, "Charles don't like to shoot things that are alive" (207). His past as a soldier remains at the novel's margins, while Edgerton foregrounds Charles's assumption of the couple's cooking duties. As the novel winds to a close, Raney observes, "Sometimes he thinks he's Julia Child" (215). The reference to a female chef further carves out a cultural space for Charles that's less than traditionally southern. In one early argument, moreover, Raney objects to his desire to associate with colleagues from the college where he works, rather than with her local friends:

> "It has to do with who I want to be friends with," says Charles. "Madora and—what's his name?—Larry are not interested in anything outside their kitchen, living room, and bedroom."
>
> "I'll have you know," I said, "that Madora and Larry go to Bethel Free Will

Baptist Church. Don't tell me that Jesus Christ is only in their kitchen, living room, and bedroom."

"The problem," says Charles, "the whole problem is just that: Jesus wouldn't have a kitchen, living room, and bedroom."

"He would if he lived in Bethel." I tried to let that sink in. (70)

As time passes, the couple adopts more non-southern ways, including sessions with a marriage counselor—a "psychiatric" (151), as Raney puts it—and, at the novel's close, their decision to baptize their baby at an Episcopal church. At the comic climax of the novel, there is also Raney's decision to have sex with Charles on feed sacks in the back room of her father's store. "'Hand me a warm-up of Southern Comfort, Charles—my fanny's getting cold,'" the former teetotaler tells her husband. "And after that it was me, Charles, and the feedbags. And I'd just had my hair done that afternoon. But I didn't pay a bit of mind to that. I was happy and it was wonderful" (212). Not only is the act of sex outside the traditional bedroom important here, so is Raney's distinctly non-southern devaluation of the ministrations of the beauty parlor.

That a 1980s novel shows the traditional South declining is, by itself, not particularly surprising, but in *Raney* there is also a fortress of stasis strongly linked to the aged. The novel's second section, as if to contrast Raney's desire to live in an unchanging South, focuses on the realities of such an attempt. The section's initial action focuses on organizing a Golden Agers' Day, featuring the firing of a Civil War cannon. The cannon's owner, Mr. Earls, not only flies a Confederate flag, but tries to live a nineteenth-century lifestyle. "I don't have a phone," he tells Raney and Charles. "Don't have a television. I wouldn't have lights if they hadn't already been hooked up when we bought the place" (100). He brags that his children avoided a college education, and he treats his wife Birdie as if, in Raney's words, "[s]he's a slave" (104). Earls proudly proclaims his old southern values: "I model my life after Stonewall Jackson, one of the greatest generals in the history of war. Birdie knows I do, and abides it. . . . He was a great general, a great man, a Christian" (102). So linked is he to the old South that he declares at one point, "I been in the Civil War business over forty year [*sic*]" (101). Though Raney offers some defense of Mr. Earls, Edgerton makes him a target of humor, having him captured on video for the local news but cut off before he can finish barking a command at his wife: "Birdie, go get the—" (115). Edgerton underscores the irony of the man's limited realm of authority as Raney observes, "We thought it was funny it got on television. We said maybe it would be preserved forever" (116).

If Mr. Earls provides a humorous critique of attempts to keep the old South alive, the experience of Raney's aging male relatives in the novel's second section captures the inevitable failure of similar aims. Her Uncle Newton dies of natural causes, and while the family tries to respond with a traditional southern visitation and funeral, Charles refuses to look at the body, then argues with the funeral director about his industry's exploitation of grief. Raney's Uncle Nate soon commits suicide, telling his sister just before he dies, "I shot myself. To get it over with" (133). Because of Nate's inability to return to normal life after serving in World War II, the minister at his funeral pronounces him "one of the last casualties" of the war (140). But Charles argues that Nate was also a victim of his family's traditional beliefs, their attempt help him through religion rather than mental health treatment: "It was a whole family's refusal to look for alternatives to . . . a way of life. To read—to become educated about a problem staring you in the face. Given the self-righteousness . . . of fundamental Christianity in this family, your Uncle Nate didn't have a chance" (143). The fates of these two characters link the traditional South to death. No matter how much Raney and her family try to maintain the old ways, biology will not be denied.

Indeed, the only true hope for the traditional South is conversion, drawing outsiders like Charles into its ideological fold. Instead of conversion, however, the novel reveals a reliance on the kind of gradualist change that mirrors the expectations and practices of many southerners prior to the Civil Rights movement (see Chafe 89–91 and Sokol 4, 10–11). Charles learns to eat fried okra, thereby adapting to the fare of his new in-laws, but such an accommodation pales beside Raney's moves away from traditional southern views. Though she continues to reject the sexual perspectives of *Playboy* and *Penthouse,* she reconciles herself to sex outside the bedroom, and if her racial views send Johnny Dobbs to the Ramada Inn instead of her house, she accepts him as the godfather of her child at the end of the novel. By muting the inevitable outcome of such change in a fading South, the novel—even as it refuses to deny that inevitability—maintains its comic direction and demeanor and softens the rough future that awaits the South in a balancing act that Edgerton's second novel also struggles to maintain.

Walking Across Egypt can be casually read as a southern farce, a novel that juxtaposes incongruous characters for comic effect. Yet the story of Mattie Rigsbee, a seventy-eight-year-old woman who begins the novel thinking she is "too old to look after a dog" that shows up on her doorstep (2), reveals a South that is intent on slipping Mattie into her grave—or at least a grave-like stasis that self-destructively denies her true self and what makes the South what it is.

Both her age and stereotypical habits characterize Mattie as an avatar of the traditional South. From the novel's opening pages, she is intent on feeding everyone she meets, even the dog she declares she is too old to keep. Later, she also feeds the dogcatcher, her neighbors, the upholsterer, her grown children, the law officers who come to her house, and Wesley, a juvenile delinquent in lockup to whom she takes both cake and pie. Cooking, in short, is "the core of Mattie Rigsbee's world" (Dvorak 91). Mattie is also highly concerned about family heritage, worrying that she has not convinced her childless adult children, Robert and Elaine, that "having a family was more important than anything in the world. . . . After all, through the blood is the only way you really can give of your *true* self—the self that is in your blood and that has been there since Adam, that stream of blood flowing unbroken since Adam and Eve" (151). She is also deeply religious. In *Of Fiction and Faith: Twelve American Writers Talk About Their Vision and Work*, W. Dale Brown calls Mattie "a Bible-reading literalist" (117), but if this label implies a narrowness in her vision, it would be more accurate to say that she is an active churchgoer who lives by biblical ideals that she sees as clear, particularly trying to help "the least of these," for "doing unto the least [is] the same as doing for Jesus" (87–88). The novel humorously echoes this worldview through the soap opera Mattie religiously watches, *All My Children*.

Though everyone in the novel is more than willing to eat at Mattie's table, none share her values. Robert, who runs a convenience store, derides his mother's cooking and chastises her for feeding the stray dog. Elaine is a schoolteacher Mattie imagines as the end point for a button collection Mattie's great-grandmother began. Despite music lessons, neither continues to play the piano upon which Mattie nightly entertains herself, playing and singing hymns. Her neighbors, Alora and Finner, put their trust in guns and at one point almost shoot the dogcatcher. More central to the novel is the fact that Mattie's church turns against her for trying to help Wesley. When she takes him to Sunday school, a class member concludes, "She was going to *have* to do something. Call the authorities" (156). The head deacon decides that in the wake of Mattie's involvement with Wesley, she is no longer fit to lead the missions offering: "He liked Mattie. . . . But his duty was not to Mattie Rigsbee, it was to higher offices: Duty, Church, God" (214).

For Cynthia Huggins, author of "Witnessing by Example: Southern Baptists in Clyde Edgerton's *Walking Across Egypt* and *Killer Diller*," the point of the contrast between Mattie and her fellow Baptists is "that Mattie's Christianity is of a different, more genuine sort" (92), but it more aptly works to define the nature of the South in which she lives. The community's assault on her religious practice assails Mattie physically. A 2012 study in the journal *The Gerontologist* argues that attendance at religious events, rather than private religious practices, positively impacts the health of the elderly (Hybels

683), and it is just such attendance that the church tries to curtail in Mattie's case. By relieving her of her work for the missions fund and asking her to resign her leadership role in the Sunday school class, her community encourages her decline—a decline imaged in Pearl, Mattie's older sister, who "had stopped going to Listre Baptist the month the church carpeted the backs of the pews, hung microphones over the choir, and started busing," and who takes Mattie to "pick out a casket" (38).

Mattie is a force against such a complacent view of death—a trait that moves her beyond the merely comic and moral. Edgerton emphasizes this extra dimension by juxtaposing his usual straightforward prose with passages that tend toward the lyrical. At one point, after a discussion of bowel regularity and hemorrhoids, the novel offers this passage:

> She walked into the kitchen, turned on the light and saw through the window that the eastern sky was dark red. It was her favorite time of day. . . . It was cool. She also liked it when it was cold and she could stand there taking in the cold morning while the sky was red, and time stopped, stood still, and rested for a minute. People thought that time never stood still, except in Joshua when the sun stood still; but she knew that for a minute before sunrise when the sky began to lighten, showing dark, early clouds there was often a pause when nothing moved, not even time, and she was always happy to be up and in that moment; sometimes she tried to stand perfectly still, to not move with time not moving, and it seemed that if she were not careful she might slip out of this world and into another. That made the moment risky, bright shining, and very still at the same time. (82)

It would take a dull ear to miss the tonal shift from the discussion of digestion to a moment of motionless time, and that shift signals a deeper level in Mattie, one that identifies her as resistant to change and as committed to maintaining her resistance—no matter how futile—to the last. This resistance, as much as her thin but pragmatic theology, explains her taking in the sixteen-year-old Wesley, whom southern society has relegated to the dust bin that is the Young Men's Rehabilitation Center. Essentially, she converts Wesley to her traditional southern values of food, family, and church—the only means she has of keeping them alive. The novel underscores the evangelistic nature of her decision through the use of Christian symbols: the communion of her table, the baptism of her bathtub, the adoption/marriage into her family. For a society defined as much by values as geography, such motherly nurturing is essential for survival. Not surprisingly, Edgerton in one interview linked Mattie to his own mother, adding, "I was not taught how to put on a condom, but I was taught how to look people in the eyes and shake their hands" (Brown 132).

The larger South around Mattie rejects such an attempt at continuation. Mattie's Sunday school classmates have no use for Wesley and summon the law to remove him. Robert worries that senility has set in, and Elaine is sure "[s]he's lost her mind" (221). Edgerton never claims that Mattie will succeed, and he maintains a sense of comedy by suspending the novel's ending: Mattie considers rescuing the dog that appeared on her porch at the beginning of the novel, but delays her decision until she sees how her rescue of Wesley works out. Given Mattie's age and the challenges Wesley presents, realism predicts a rough road ahead for her. Even the reliable *Reader's Digest* can't be counted on to avoid discussions of sperm, and allusions to Hawthorne's *The Scarlet Letter* remind readers of that novel's final image of a tombstone. Though the novel ends with Mattie risking and "bright shining" (82), Edgerton makes it clear that hers is a shrinking South of old people, who keep the region alive only by resisting the pressures of modern southern culture.

The Floatplane Notebooks, Edgerton's third novel, is his most technically complex, using five narrators—Noralee, Bliss, Thatcher, Mark, and Meredith—as well as the voice of a wisteria vine in the family graveyard to tell the story of the Copelands, but the novel remains consistent with his first two works in viewing the South as a place consigned, or being consigned to the past. For the most part, it does so by threading through the family story metaphors of air flight and written records that arise out of efforts by Thatcher and Meredith's father to build a floatplane. The novel's epigraph, from a 1920s hymn, points to flight as an escape: "When I die hallelujah by and by / I'll fly away." Moreover, the plane functions as Albert's escape from his ordinary existence and, ultimately, Meredith's escape from disabling war wounds. Yet for most of the novel, the plane does not fly, and it exists most vividly in Albert's notebooks, which in the words of George Hovis, in *Vale of Humility: Plain Folk in Contemporary North Carolina Fiction*, "serve as a metafictional device" and "a means of preserving his family's history" (215). The books are a hodge-podge of entries about test flights that seldom resemble actual events, family events, and newspaper clippings—essentially an image of the novel itself. The books become a fictional past in which the novel's characters breathe; indeed, by the novel's end, that past is the only place the characters continue to live—a reading Edgerton's original ending for the novel strongly encouraged. As he himself explained in an interview,

There used to be a last page, really, a newspaper clipping, and it was dated 2088. It was about a graveyard being discovered covered all over with vines.

They had found a woman's grave with the date 1988. They had taken what they called a sonogram, a photograph from above, so they could see the bones and stuff, and they couldn't understand why her leg had been buried in another part of the graveyard. I took that last page out. . . . So I was left with Meredith talking from the graveyard. The fact that it was italicized demonstrated that. (Brown 138)

Edgerton suggests that the novel's imagined future is one in which the graveyard has been neglected and forgotten, where "Meredith" is assumed female, where a leg buried in the nineteenth century is confused with the one Meredith lost in Vietnam. In short, it is a future in which the novel's present South is lost in the past.

Edgerton also stresses the static nature and/or death of the South through the lives of each human narrator. Noralee, the youngest, opens the novel in 1956 as a toddler, her passage almost pure sensation: "The dogs breathe in my face. They come to me and breathe in my face and turn around and run, then another one comes up and does it" (5). Her final passages, both from 1970, when she is in high school, point to her rejection of her family's values. In the first, she reveals that she is dating Barry, an East Carolina senior whom her father writes off as "a hippie" (190), and in the second, after learning of Meredith's war injuries, she notes that her oldest brother "is terrible to Barry" and, more importantly, acknowledges, "I wish Meredith had [gone to Canada]" (199). After that, she is silent, reduced to taking care of Meredith and Rhonda's baby—a job Meredith notes she does well, "except when she sulks" (236). Rejecting the traditional southern values of her family, she remains silently buried in her region—hardly a sign of a hopeful future.

If Noralee is thinly developed but likeable, Thatcher's similarly slight development is more plainly negative. His first narration suggests he is merely exasperated by the eccentricities of his family: "This floatplane thing Papa's working on. I swear" (17) are his first words. Bliss, however, who will soon become his wife, views him positively: "The words I like to say about Thatcher are these: 'Thatcher stands tall.' He is slightly over six feet and I think he stands tall not only in stature but in spirit. He has a firmament about him. A steadiness" (8). By the time of his 1959 entry, however, Thatcher's only apparent steadiness is a steady increase in his anger and immaturity: "Why the hell do I have to get the damn truck out of the damn trash pile? Why me? . . . If I had drove the damn truck over the damn left field bank of the ball field you think *Meredith* would be helping get it out? Hell no" (81). Worse still, in his 1967 entries, he focuses only on revealing Meredith's flaws, as if tattling on his younger brother. When the family learns of Meredith's wounding, Bliss reports Thatcher's response, which is, at best, unfeeling: "Well, at least he ain't dead. . . . He's too hard-headed for that" (195). When Thatcher himself narrates Meredith's injuries, his brother gets little mention. Instead, Thatcher complains about Noralee—"She's dating a hippie and word was, a couple of years ago, that she had the hots for a nigger" (215)—and fails to understand his wife's reaction to Meredith's condition. His final narrative segment is reportorial in tone, flat. He reports being the one who noticed Meredith's wheelchair careening toward a lake, but he cannot say that he acted heroically. The chair simply stops when "Meredith reaches sand or something at the end of the boat ramp" (262). The final image he leaves of himself is almost a copy of the one with which he began: begrudgingly accepting his father's orders, caught in a role he should long since have outgrown.

In contrast, Mark, a cousin of the Copeland boys and a childhood friend of Meredith, undergoes major changes in viewpoint that carry him away from the traditional South as he follows his one consistent trait: a desire for acceptance. Early in the novel, he is clearly led by Meredith, adopting traditional southern views on race in blaming a non-existent black man after the two boys play with a mechanical well digger, and he bows to pressure to adopt traditional southern religious values, telling Meredith, "Last night I rededicated my life to Christ. . . . I had to. Jesus called me" (60). But as his circle of peers moves beyond the Copelands and Listre, he adopts other values, drinking beer when invited to play with a band and later justifying drinking and whoring in Vietnam, claiming, "It's not like home, but I'm not home now" (183). In his most powerful narrative section, Mark describes a bombing run over Vietnam and momentarily recognizes the landscape below him as North Carolina, recognizes a human target as "someone I know" (185). He quickly buries those thoughts beneath the technical details of the bombing, only to have the nagging sense of identification return in the section's closing sentence: "The vane assembly is ivory-colored, walking along the dirt road myself walking to the store in North Carolina myself along Lumley road to get a loaf of Merita bread and a quart of Long Meadow milk in a brown paper sack" (186). Mark's last two appearances in the novel show him walking away from Meredith's hospital bed in Vietnam without waiting to find out his friend's fate, and planning to have sex with Rhonda, Meredith's wife, who has abandoned her disabled husband and their child. Mark thinks, "Why the hell deprive myself, and in this case, nobody gets hurt. That's the real situation. Nobody is getting hurt" (246). For Hovis, this development earns Mark the label of "the clear Judas of *Floatplane*" (219), but such a negative designation ignores the fact that Mark is the one true pilot in the novel, that he is— to echo the epigraph—flying away from the traditional South. And his actions, even if judged as flawed, are the actions of a randy *young* man and keep him in motion.

Mark's moves to reject the traditional South, moreover, are echoed by a far more positive narrator, Bliss. Michael McFee, in "'Reading a Small History in a Universal Light,'" argues that Bliss "best embodies . . . true regionalism," focusing on her "almost embarrassing" eagerness to join the Copeland family that she idealizes (66). Indeed, it is through Bliss's narratives that many of the details of Copeland family rituals—a Christmas hunting trip to Florida, a spring graveyard cleaning, and the storytelling these events entail—are related to readers. But Bliss is not a static character. After her initial embrace of the Copelands, she sees a need for other ties, declaring, "I am overcome with the black valley between my family and the family of my husband-to-be. . . . Oh, but for a bridge" (38). Also, on first seeing the wisteria vine in the family graveyard, she describes it as "a horrific splendor" that generates "a mixture of splendor and dread" (40)—apt terms for a beautiful plant later revealed to have been used as rope in a lynching. In addition, Bliss comes to view the Copelands more critically. As Mark and Meredith prepare to head to Vietnam, she lays out the difference in the family's reaction and her own: "I wanted to explode with my concern so that this family would somehow register what was about to happen. . . . They'll talk far more about Old Ross, Tyree, bird dogs and cooking, than they will about these young men going away to war" (122). In her concern for Mark and Meredith she enunciates her sense that the Copelands have allowed themselves to be overshadowed by the past—and to the detriment of the present—"pretending," as she once observes of Uncle Hawk, "he's Old Ross, his granddaddy, and singing while he cooks breakfast like Old Ross used to" (24). In contrast, Bliss rejects merely re-creating the past; she alters it, as when she insists on being the first female to go on the annual bird hunt—a change that leads to her "mortified" discovery that "we were hunting on posted land" (133). Bliss's greatest variance from the Copelands' traditional southern values, however, occurs after Meredith returns from Vietnam. While other family members see to his feeding and cleaning, Bliss alone sees the sexual dimension of his suffering—and responds to it, giving Meredith his greatest pleasure since returning home. In his words, "It was like heaven" (249). Yet Bliss does not, like Mark, fly away from the Copelands. Her final narration begins, "The splendor of the wisteria has not abated one iota" (253). She comes to admire them and all they represent—not idealistically, but with open eyes. Nevertheless, by locating her final narration in the family graveyard, the novel links her to death and to the past, to a country for the old and dying.

In that same narration, Edgerton presents a startling image of Meredith, the character he has called "the core, the center of the book" (Brown 140), and makes plain the connection of the South with aging. Bliss describes Meredith at a 1971 graveyard cleaning as he moves about "by leaning over in the walker, putting his weight on his right elbow, steadying the walker with his short left arm and skipping forward with his right leg, then lifting the walker with his stub and moving it forward" (253). Having begun the novel as a thirteen-year-old, "a-sparkle-in-his-eye type, as cute as a button" (8), Meredith resembles at the end an aged and struggling resident of a nursing home, a physical fragment of his former self. It is literally this debilitative transformation that returns him to his old home in the South. Viewed objectively, this prematurely old man should be a symbol of despair and ruin—a version of Poe's crumbling mansion in "The Fall of the House of Usher" (1839), or the unpainted Compson house in Faulkner's *The Sound and the Fury* (1929).

However, Edgerton uses the symbolic Meredith ironically. For if the war robs Meredith of his youthful body, it gives him a voice. His narration begins only after his wounding, and his voice dominates the novel's final pages. Hovis reads the appearance of Meredith's voice as a "force[d] . . . awareness of life he had previously chosen to avoid" (216), but it can also be seen as compensation for or even a saving grace because of being thrust into the dying country of old men. It empowers storytelling. Certainly, one of his narrations images his mind as something similar to the floatplane notebook, with its collage of materials and personal information:

> Every morning when I wake up I try to remember the day it happened and I can't, so I try to remember one day in my life at home. I get a piece of it, like me and Mark frog-gigging, or hunting at Uncle Hawk's, or playing ball, and I try to remember everything in that piece of day. I put it all together, little piece by little piece. I hold it there and get the pieces together like a puzzle, then I run my fingers smooth over the pieces four or five times and by then breakfast is over—a nigger feeds me—and Miss Clairmont is on the way with a big smile and letters and she takes her time with me, like she's got all day. I want her to take her hair down so bad I don't know what to do. I could eat every inch of her with the half of my mouth that works. Yankee Doodle. (213)

Meredith's narrations are not entirely flattering to the traditional South. He questions his culture's and his family's failure to think through the war, he questions God, and he records Rhonda's inability to stand by her man. Yet he is hardly all-condemning, either. In other—and sometimes the same—passages, he sees another side, recognizing his own failure to envision the war realistically, acknowledging the kindness of church women, illustrating his awareness of the difficulty of Rhonda's position.

Meredith's fate is to become one with the vine, his speech literally claiming the vine's italics in the novel's closing passage. As such, he is one with the past, one with the graveyard and all who are there. From a purely realistic perspective, he becomes one with death—perhaps the roughest South one can imagine. Yet, having created both a floatplane notebook and *The Floatplane Notebooks*, there is a nagging sense of continuance. Edgerton told one interviewer, "The most I can say about Meredith and the whole family is that for me they had a kind of lovely stubbornness" (Brown 140). His first three novels, then, suggest that a stubbornness of the old develops, and as many of us over the age of fifty will attest, that's a rough world indeed.

Works Cited

Bledsoe, Erik. "The Rise of Southern Redneck and White Trash Writers." *Southern Cultures* 6.1 (2000): 68–90. Print.

Brown, W. Dale. *Of Fiction and Faith: Twelve American Writers Talk about Their Vision and Work.* Grand Rapids: Eerdmans, 1997. Print.

Chafe, William H. *The Unfinished Journey: America Since World War II.* New York: Oxford UP, 1986. Print.

Cornett, Sheryl. "Like a Brother: Profile of a Literary Friendship." *North Carolina Literary Review* 12 (2003): 160–73. Print.

Dvorak, Angeline Godwin. "Cooking as Mission in Southern Culture: The Nurturers of Clyde Edgerton's *Walking Across Egypt*, Fannie Flagg's *Fried Green Tomatoes at the Whistle Stop Café*, and Anne Tyler's *Dinner at the Homesick Restaurant*." *Southern Quarterly* 30 (1992): 90–98. Print.

Edgerton, Clyde. "A Conversation with Clyde Edgerton." Interview by Daren Dean. *Image: Art, Faith, Mystery.* 50 (2006): 67–78. Print.

———. *The Floatplane Notebooks.* Chapel Hill: Algonquin, 1988. Print.

———. *Raney.* New York: Ballantine, 1985. Print.

———. *Walking Across Egypt.* New York: Random House, 1987. Print.

Hennis, R. Sterling, Jr. "Clyde Edgerton." *Contemporary Fiction Writers of the South: A Bio-Bio-graphical Sourcebook.* Ed. Joseph M. Flora and Robert Bain. Westport: Greenwood P, 1993. 112–22. Print.

Hovis, George. *Vale of Humility: Plain Folk in Contemporary North Carolina Fiction.* Columbia: U of South Carolina P, 2007. Print.

Huggins, Cynthia E. "Witnessing by Example: Southern Baptists in Clyde Edgerton's *Walking Across Egypt* and *Killer Diller*." *Southern Quarterly* 35 (1997): 91–96. Print.

Hybels, Celia F., et al. "The Complex Association between Religious Activities and Functional Limitations in Older Adults." *Gerontologist* 52 (2012): 676–85. Print.

Mason, Yvonne. *Reading, Learning, Teaching Clyde Edgerton*. New York: Peter Lang, 2009. Print.

McFee, Michael. "'Reading a Small History in a Universal Light': Doris Betts, Clyde Edgerton, and the Triumph of True Regionalism." *Pembroke Magazine* 23 (1991): 59–67. Print.

Sokol, Jason. *There Goes My Everything: White Southerners in the Age of Civil Rights, 1945–1975.* New York: Knopf, 2006. Print.

Stephenson, Shelby. "Clyde Edgerton: Singing This Song." *Carolina Quarterly* 48 (1996): 75–81. Print.

Jill McCorkle: The Rough South
from One Remove

Barbara Bennett

U NLIKE authors at the center of Erik Bledsoe's essay "The Rise of South-ern Redneck and White Trash Writers," Jill McCorkle did not grow up amid poverty, and in fact calls her upbringing in 1960s Lumberton, North Carolina, "very much middle-class"—even upper class by the standards of her elementary school classmates. McCorkle's father was a postal worker, her mother a secretary, and at work they encountered people of all types. More progressive than their neighbors, perhaps, they introduced their daughter to every kind of person along the local social spectrum (personal interview), and as a result McCorkle's fiction reflects the whole South, rather than just its middle class. Her latest novel, *Life After Life* (2013), provides a clear case in point. Set in a retirement home that, like the doctor's office in Flannery O'Connor's "Revelation" (1965), is full of varied people who might rarely in-teract otherwise, it implies that despite their differences, they have more in common than not. So even though she isn't one of Bledsoe's "Southern Red-neck and White Trash Writers," who "write from *within* the [lower] class, not by observing it from without" (68), when McCorkle writes about the lower class, she does so with sensitivity and sympathy. She may not *be* Rough

South, but she often writes about the Rough South from a perspective none-theless authentic, even if at one remove.

More so than *Life After Life*, however, an earlier novel better illustrates the continuum of class in a small southern town. *Ferris Beach* (1990) is the com-ing-of-age story of Kitty Burns, a middle-class girl whose father teaches math and whose mother is a homemaker. Kitty encounters people of all classes, from the aristocratic Mrs. Poole to the poverty-stricken Perry Loomis. All offer Kitty a look at their South, teaching her something about her own in the process. By the end of the novel, she has seen all sides and, as a result, has developed a progressive attitude about class, positioning herself squarely as a resident of the new South, where birth does not necessarily determine fate.

At the top of the local social hierarchy is Mrs. Theresa Poole, rarely re-ferred to by her first name—a clear indicator of position in the small south-ern town of Fulton. She represents the old ways, in which classes and races segregate distinctly by geography and conduct. She is the "busybody neigh-bor" who "attempted to maintain aristocracy in a primarily blue-collar town." She could "see no merit in *any* changes," including "black children walking the halls" of local schools (35). She is the arbiter of proper comportment and a believer in noblesse oblige.

Mrs. Poole follows strict but arbitrary rules of decorum for southern women, such as "smoking only while seated, with a roof over her head" (44). Part of her role, as she sees it, is to impress upon other women the virtues of tradition and stasis. She holds afternoon teas, and "women were expected to dress for the occasion," but she invites only those she deems important— "our community's finest citizens," she calls them (46). Being excluded clearly relegates a woman to a lower class. For Kitty, as often for readers, this kind of behavior is primarily comic, so exaggerated are Mrs. Poole's rules of de-portment. Throughout the novel, McCorkle uses Mrs. Poole's opinions as a foil for Kitty's more progressive ideas. She represents the old standard; Kitty comes to stand for the new.

So extreme is Mrs. Poole's nonsense that when Kitty's mother forces her to join the Children of the Confederacy, she lapses into a giggling fit in the mid-dle of a meeting and finds herself banished to the kitchen until she can regain control of herself. The point of the group—tradition, heritage, elitism—is lost on Kitty. McCorkle, as a child pressured by her grandmother to join the same group, likewise claims to have missed the real purpose of the organization, remembering only attending a club slumber party and delivering a report on cotton. She never took it seriously—beyond making her grandmother happy (personal interview).

Besides rewriting history, as she attempts with her dead husband's reputation, Mrs. Poole's main job is frustrating change. The new South is nowhere she wants to live. When construction is set to start on land across from her home, she "mourned the loss of the farmland and the barns and sheds dating back to the 1800s" (1). It's not just the loss of what she considers historical sites: She mostly fears what will replace them. At a meeting of the historical society she tries to stop the sale of the land, dramatically parodying Paul Revere: "The split-levels are coming! The split-levels are coming" (1). The architecture of the houses, however, is not the problem; the problem is the type of people she fears will move into them. "It happens slowly at the beginning, one house here, another there," she explains, "and then before you know it, the decent people stop coming and more and more riffraff come in, prices drop and so others can afford to come in." She tilts her head surreptitiously in one direction and whispers, "A colored family lives down there. . . . It *can* happen" (9).

To Kitty, the past is just the past, and Mrs. Poole's ideas hold little influence over her own. She's more concerned with the present and future, like many inhabitants of the new South. The cemetery near her house, for example, is not a site to ruminate upon history and those who played a part in it, but a private place where she can meet her boyfriend. History, for Kitty, extends only to her own life and that of her parents.

Kitty's mother, Cleva, is a mostly willing disciple of Mrs. Poole, who generally approves of her. The Burnses live in an old-enough house, built in the early 1800s, and have ancestors who qualify Kitty for Children of the Confederacy. But while her mother has "composure and reserve" (3), Kitty's father, Fred, is less concerned with genealogy, representing a more indifferent and modern take on history. Kitty's childhood home therefore becomes a battleground. In her attempt to win Kitty over, her mother denigrates and disparages her husband's less-than-respectable relatives, most notably Kitty's cousin Angela. Angela, who has a bad track record with men, lives in Ferris Beach, the embodiment of lower-class living, with its "pier and lots of bait-and-tackle shops, no motel or tall buildings . . . just a trailer park and rows of small pastel houses" (19). Despite their Confederate ancestors, Fred's more recent relatives are less than aristocratic. His father had operated a shrimping boat, and his grandmother lived a "palmetto-spangled life" (4). Cleva impresses upon her daughter the importance of heritage, but Fred tells Kitty, "You're half Scotch and half soda" (2). Is it any wonder that Kitty leans toward her father's perspective? While her mother asks Kitty to dress up and attend teas in celebration of dead ancestors, her father, preparing to write a murder mystery, encourages Kitty to roll him up in a carpet and see if she can drag him down the hall.

Cleva's efforts, therefore, fail to claim Kitty for her side. Kitty is simply less attracted to her dead relatives than to her living ones. Instead of imagining an aristocratic life, she envisions a poor, tragic, romantic one, picturing herself as the Little Match Girl. In fact, she occasionally wishes she were an orphan, a meaningful impulse for a southern girl. Joan Schultz, in "Orphaning as Resistance," observes that by rejecting family names and identities—a sort of self-orphaning—young southern girls "signal themselves as resisting, refusing, or rejecting the kind of family identity, family roles, and family ties with the past or the present considered so vital to the Southern way of life" (92). Kitty rejects both Mrs. Poole and her mother, as well as her heritage and its attendant rules and traditions. Carol Pearson and Katherine Pope point out in *The Female Hero in American Literature* that female heroes, like male heroes, must reject the status quo and traditionally held beliefs before they can discover truth, recognize potential, and reconcile with the dominant culture. As a young adult coming of age in the 1970s, then, Kitty must reject the class system advocated by her mother—and, by extension, Mrs. Poole.

As she turns from her mother, Kitty embraces Angela, her father's niece. Kitty knows little about Angela's lifestyle. Her opinions about her cousin, idealized and mostly inaccurate, formed the first time they met, on the sands of Ferris Beach. It was a romantic and heady experience for Kitty, first because she knew her mother disapproved of Angela (her father asked her to keep the meeting a secret), and second because Angela seemed young and free from the responsibilities and structure of home, the epitome of a free spirit. In response to seeing her young cousin's birthmark—a purple stain on her cheek, about which Kitty was sensitive—Angela "pressed her lips to that same cheek" (5), metaphorically accepting and loving Kitty's flaw. Kitty is smitten by the gesture and, from that day on, attaches to her cousin "everything beautiful and lively and good; she was the easy flow of words and music, the waves crashing on Ferris Beach" (7).

Years later, teenaged Kitty falls out with her mother and seeks refuge at Angela's apartment in Ferris Beach, and only then does she realize why her mother and Mrs. Poole insinuate that Angela is "trash" and that her marriage was "founded on the floor of a bar and grill and/or bowling alley" (87). In Angela's apartment Kitty finds "dishes in her sink, sparse furnishings with sandy, threadbare upholstery," and a bed with "a bird dog print sheet dragging the gritty linoleum" (330). The setting might mark Angela as lower class, but McCorkle is careful not to associate class with ignorance. Angela shows her hard-won wisdom by giving Kitty the most honest advice she's ever heard about love, accepting one's limitations, and getting along with her mother. Class plays no part in Kitty's feelings for Angela—as it does in Mrs. Poole's opinion of Kitty. She accepts Angela in the same way Angela accepted her so many years before.

Angela is not the only female role model Kitty discovers. Another woman who influences her understanding of the class structure in her little town enters Kitty's life. Mo Rhodes, the mother of Kitty's friend Misty, moves in across the street from the Burnses. The Rhodes family occupies one of the previously slandered split-levels, and their arrival in the neighborhood draws the attention of Mrs. Poole and Cleva Burns, who take notice of each item the new family carries in from the moving truck. At one point Mrs. Poole comments derisively, "I saw what looked like it might be a bar, you know to house liquor" (8–9). Mrs. Poole associates Mo's class not only with drunkenness but also with tastelessness, and she holds the Rhodes family personally responsible for the fact that their house is painted "electric blue" (17). Mo only increases Mrs. Poole's ire when she digs up her grass and builds a Japanese rock garden, complete with goldfish pond, pussy willows, and a mailbox shaped like a pagoda.

In contrast to Mrs. Poole's ideas of decorum, Mo laughs too loudly, prefers store-bought cookies to homemade, and names her children after pop-culture icons rather than dead relatives. She installs purple shag carpeting and at Christmas decorates her house with colored lights, placing a plastic reindeer with a blinking red nose on the roof. Mrs. Poole attributes this parade of poor taste to Mo's upbringing. She remembers Mo riding horses as a young girl in Ferris Beach, but "they were not *her* horses" (16). Kitty, in contrast to her rejection of Mrs. Poole and her sharp class judgments, falls in love with the whole Rhodes household, especially Mo. She finds color and energy in the Rhodes home, dismissing her mother and Mrs. Poole as "plain and somber," their houses as "sparse and bare" (14).

Mo Rhodes and her family are really only middle-class—financially much the same as Kitty's family. But families of the lower class, of the true Rough South, live in a row of houses separated from Kitty's house by a field of kudzu, "junky" car parts, and the cemetery. In contrast with the Burnses' house, these houses are cheaply made, with tarpaper roofs and a "bare bulb swinging on a chain." Cleva claims she'd be "surprised if their walls are made of anything stronger than cardboard," calling the houses "an eyesore." Kitty remarks, "She and Mrs. Poole often talked about all the families who lived there and how ours was the last 'nice' street before the town *fell*" (32). And while Kitty's involvement with the Rhodeses is less forbidden than countenanced with inevitable resignation, she is warned never to go near the other houses. The Rhodeses are merely tasteless, but it is implied that the houses on the other side of the cemetery might be downright dangerous.

Kitty does go near those houses, though, and one of their inhabitants significantly influences her understanding of class. Merle Hucks, whose name is reminiscent of that of Mark Twain's poor white hero, at first seems to fit the "poor white trash" stereotype, smoking and beating up other kids. His family encompasses all the Rough South stereotypes: One brother is in jail; another rides a motorcycle and is perpetually in trouble at school; and their mother, tired and feckless, has named a young daughter Maybelline. Kitty, who is initially frightened of Merle and his buddy R. W., notices that "every morning they came to school smelling of bowling-alley food, the hot-dog relish and onion rings they had had for breakfast" (138).

McCorkle based Merle (and others like him) on her childhood classmates. She admits that when she was young, she wasn't exposed to the real poverty in her county, even though it was all around her. But she was at least conscious of class differences:

> My friend and I have talked about this a lot—how when you're a kid, you have no idea what other kids are living through. And as you get older you look back and remember the kid—we thought it was cool—the kid who was over at the donut shop getting a hot dog for breakfast or the kid who reeked of onions. And you realize that they were boys who were pretty much on their own. . . . I remember being very aware of a girl in my elementary class who wore the same dress every day. And I remember telling my mother about it and feeling so sad. My mother was always the kind of person who would say, "That person needs extra kindness. You go out of your way to do nice things for that person." (personal interview)

Merle, however, transcends the Rough South stereotype and distinguishes himself from his family and friends. Kitty first notices his difference when she meets him in the kitchen during a Children of the Confederacy meeting. Finding him on a break from work in Mrs. Poole's yard, she overhears Mrs. Poole's housekeeper ask him about his sick mother. Suddenly she feels empathy for him, and from then on he "seemed like a different person" to her (162). This is the effect—the transition in opinion—that Rough South writers strive for in their works. As Brian Carpenter reminds us in his introduction to *Grit Lit: A Rough South Reader*, Rough South writing is not about "exchanging one set of clichés for another," but about "getting beyond the caricature and introducing a little compassion and complication into the conversation" (xxvi). Merle's humanizing begins to change Kitty's opinion of others like him.

McCorkle argues that offering a job to Merle redeems Mrs. Poole, "by helping him out and giving him work so he can have an income and an influence for good. It gives him hope" (interview). Certainly, Mrs. Poole's actions complicate our judgment of her, making her, too, less of a cliché. Without hope for a better life, Merle has little chance of transcending his family, although when Mrs. Poole admits that Merle is a "nice boy," she does temper the compliment with "they say the apple doesn't fall far" and her hope that "he doesn't take a turn" (253, 254).

Mrs. Poole takes seriously her responsibilities for the collective behavior of Fulton. When she finds Merle's father on the streets, drunk in his Santa suit, she dismisses him "on behalf of the town of Fulton," and adds, "You are a filthy, lying man who cannot even support his family" (44). Yet she is also the first to step in and rescue the families in his neighborhood when a fire destroys their houses. Her sense of noblesse oblige forces her to care for those she denigrates at every opportunity, as she does when one family puts up "string after string" of Christmas lights, which she calls "*Carnival*" (210–11). As soon as the fire dies down, she says, "We better start right now gathering up some clothes and food. I wonder if we might be able to rent out Brown's Econo Lodge again" to house the displaced. Her explanation hints at the complicated life she must lead as a member of what she considers the ruling class. "It's all part of being who I am" (257), she explains.

Kitty, though, has fewer reservations about Merle and his neighbors, and her attitudes eclipse both Mrs. Poole's charity and her mother's sheepish collusion. Kitty, deciding she likes the colored Christmas lights, says the house is "the one that did not leave me feeling empty" (211). She begins changing her attitude toward Merle through empathy, by imagining "what it must feel like to be a member of that family" (65). Eventually she concludes, "All of a sudden I realized that Merle had changed, slowly, occasionally lapsing into his old ways, but nevertheless changed; I couldn't help but wonder when the softness had begun." She comes to find in him "hopes of a future other than that of his father" (206). The change, though, is not Merle's alone, but a combination of his changing behavior and Kitty's changing perspective.

Merle, in fact, crosses class lines and becomes Kitty's first boyfriend, cementing for her the belief that class doesn't dictate character. Their social differences rarely disturb their relationship, and Kitty learns to respect his hard-working attempts to move beyond his family's station. He, more than Kitty, is critical of his family, complaining, "Sometimes I hate all of them just because they're who they are and because they'll be that way forever" (277). When they have to move from Fulton, and he considers a fresh start, Merle finds wonder in the possibilities: "I've never been anywhere else, never been where people don't say, 'Oh yeah, you're a Hucks'" (270). In fact, one of Mc-

Corkle's themes in this novel is "a whole world of possibilities" for her characters (343), a fresh start without the restraints of class or family.

Bledsoe writes that characters like Merle and his family "often drink too much, fight too much, 'fuck' too much, get in trouble with the law and have trouble keeping jobs, but nevertheless many of the characters are able at the same time to transcend such stereotypes, to reveal the humanity behind the people who populate the poolrooms and bars" (88). Merle is one such transcendent character. He's that "good-hearted poor white" in contemporary literature, one of those characters who, according to Bledsoe, often show a "moral fortitude" that "distinguishes them from the rest of their family, which they inevitably must renounce" (76).

So as not to leave readers with this ultimately optimistic account of poor whites—and thereby color Kitty's impressions too rosily—McCorkle includes one additional lower-class character to temper the optimism and teach Kitty that class can, indeed, equal fate. Perry Loomis enters Kitty's consciousness in the same way, perhaps, that Angela does—through illusion and misinterpretation based on mere appearance. Perry is a beautiful country girl with "thick blonde hair that hung past her shoulders" and "dark brown eyes" (137). Boys "focused more on her body than her face" (138), and Kitty dreams of being friends with Perry, of even being noticed by her, never realizing that Perry won't speak to her because, seeing Kitty as "one of the enemy" (148), she feels sharply the division of their classes.

Other girls of Kitty's class detest Perry Loomis because of her beauty and popularity with boys. Kitty, on the other hand, "couldn't help but envy her" (141). She looks beyond the poor white image and its attendant assumptions: that Perry "puts out" and, as one woman comments, is just plain "bad." "All these children from out in the country," she complains, "I hear they are so bad. The filthy language. Filth" (145). Despite prevailing opinion, Kitty feels drawn to Perry, wants to know and understand her, wants to make friends with her as she has with Merle—perhaps because Kitty, with her birthmark, knows how it feels to be treated unfairly because of circumstances she can't control. Their similar experiences, she senses, are more significant than their different backgrounds.

Unlike Kitty, though, Perry is a girl with few options, including where to find love and a secure future. As the boys who fantasize about her eventually find more suitable long-term girlfriends, she ends up with Merle's delinquent brother, Dexter, a despicable boy who ultimately incites a gang rape of Perry. Afterwards, she has no recourse but to pretend that she was in on the act. Her other options are to risk injury from a knife-wielding Dexter, or risk permanently tarnishing her reputation by going public with the hard-to-prove crime. By choosing to submit to the lie, she "earns" the "pre-engagement" ring Dexter gives her for Christmas (228). For Perry, it's worth the trade-off. It's all she wants: the security of a powerful male to get her out of the life she's leading, even if rape and humiliation are the price she has to pay.

Merle tells Kitty that "She's not that kind of girl any more than *you* are" (185), but the truth is that it doesn't matter. Perry's Rough South beginnings have set her on a course she cannot change. Merle can better himself, perhaps, because he's willing to work hard, and because the fire and subsequent move to another town offer him a new beginning. Possibly also because he is a male and can stand on his own, he has a chance. But Perry is stuck in Fulton, unable to outrun her upbringing, dependent and desperate and female.

In *Life After Life*, McCorkle introduces C. J., Perry's daughter, revealing that Perry was, indeed, destined for a short, tragic life. Perry once told her daughter about trying to move up in the world, but warns C. J. that "it was impossible to cross lines, to have people see you and accept you in a whole new light" (23). In the end, Perry commits suicide, leaving a note saying simply, "Please forgive me. I can't take it anymore" (22). The novel summarizes her story as follows: "Once upon a time she was beautiful and the pictures of her as a young girl would have surpassed anyone in this town, but it doesn't take long to age when you're poor and abuse your body. You can go from young and beautiful to looking like shit . . . and by killing herself she made sure C. J. wouldn't have it any better or would have to work like hell to even get a chance" (16).

C. J. does "work like hell," but the legacy of poverty and shame Perry bequeaths her is more powerful than any effort she can make, even though Perry had told her, "I was ashamed. But I have always been ashamed so what's the difference. *I don't want that to be your story*" (23; emphasis added). In *Life After Life* C. J. also meets a tragic and violent end, murdered by her married lover when she starts expecting too much and lacks bargaining power.

Such violence is common in Rough South literature, where it is "an ever-present threat" (Carpenter xxi). In *Ferris Beach*, which at first appears to be a southern girl's heartwarming coming-of-age tale, there are numerous incidents of extreme violence. Mo abandons her family and runs off with her lover and baby, only to be killed tragically in a car wreck when supposedly on her way home. Perry Loomis is gang-raped at knifepoint. Her boyfriend Dexter has his throat cut and is left to burn on his motorcycle along with a whole row of houses. Domestic abuse is hinted at in one of Angela's relationships, and Kitty's father, Fred, dies from a heart attack. These incidents alone might mark McCorkle as a Rough South writer, despite her education and gender. Women, after all, rarely earn the designation. *Grit Lit: A Rough South*

Reader, edited by Carpenter and Tom Franklin, includes only three women and is unrepentant about doing so, arguing that, "[w]ith the notable exception of Dorothy Allison and a few others, the Rough South genre remains by and large a boys club . . . with a taste for violence and the hypermasculine" (Carpenter xxix).

In *Ferris Beach*, Kitty meets characters from all different classes, each of whom has different potential. Clearly she rejects the notion of class as an automatic advantage when she rejects Mrs. Poole and her conservative opinions. By doing so, she also rejects her mother's ideas, slightly more progressive but stifling nonetheless. (Cleva was generally fine with Kitty's dating Merle, for example, but is outraged when she finds the couple having sex—and would have been utterly enraged, I'd imagine, had Kitty decided to marry him.)

In the end, Kitty's ideas about class evolve and line up with those of her generation, those raised in the '70s. She sees class as inevitable but not determinate. Equality is still a long way away for Kitty and her friends, though, despite what they want to believe. McCorkle is fair and honest about the inequalities of class. While we don't know what happens to Merle Hucks, we do learn in *Life After Life* what happens to Perry Loomis, her daughter C. J., and Kitty herself. McCorkle has written, though, that she believes Merle would have made it to "solid middle to upper middle class" because of his "strong work ethic" (personal email). While Perry and C. J. suffer the worst their class can offer, we learn that despite her birthmark, her shyness, and the early death of her father, Kitty succeeds. She leaves Fulton, earns a higher degree, and ends up teaching at Harvard. For Perry, C. J. and Kitty, therefore, class does seem to be destiny. With only the random advantage of birth, Kitty succeeds at the highest level, while Perry and C. J. find nothing but violence and tragedy.

Kitty is a transition figure between the old South, with its clear divisions of class, and the new, where what a person does is more important than where that person came from. The characters Kitty encounters—Mrs. Poole, her mother, Angela, Mo, Merle, and Perry—not only teach her about class structures in her town, but lead her to a more progressive attitude toward others. Like McCorkle, Kitty sees past stereotypes and develops empathy for people unlike herself. Like other writers of this generation, McCorkle "demands that [her] readers reexamine their views of class in the South, demands that we make room" (Bledsoe 88).

Works Cited

Bledsoe, Erik. "The Rise of Southern Redneck and White Trash Writers." *Southern Cultures* 6.1
   (Spring 2000): 68–90. Print.

Carpenter, Brian. "Introduction: Blood and Bone." *Grit Lit: A Rough South Reader*. Ed. Carpenter
   and Tom Franklin. Columbia: U of South Carolina P, 2012. xiii–xxxii. Print.

McCorkle, Jill. *Ferris Beach*. 1990. Chapel Hill: Algonquin, 2009. Print.

———. *Life After Life*. Chapel Hill: Algonquin, 2013. Print.

———. Personal interview. 26 Apr. 2013.

———. "Re: Merle Hucks." Message to the author. 17 May 2013. E-mail.

Pearson, Carol and Katherine Pope. *The Female Hero in American Literature*. New York: Bowker,
   1981. Print.

Schultz, Joan. "Orphaning as Resistance." *The Female Tradition in Southern Literature: Essays on
   Southern Women Writers*. Ed. Carol S. Manning. Champaign: U of Illinois P, 1993.

"The Spiritual Energy of the Trees":
Nature, Place, and Religion in Silas
House's Crow County Trilogy

Scott Hamilton Suter

"I am a writer because I grew up in a family of storytellers, of working people," declares Silas House, born in Lily, Kentucky, in 1971. "I lived on a one-mile stretch of road where I was either kin to everyone or knew them so well that we might as well have been kin" ("A Conscious Heart" 11). House supplemented the storytelling skills he inherited from these kin with formal education, earning a bachelor of arts from Eastern Kentucky University and a master of fine arts from Spalding University, but his rural Appalachian upbringing exercises a far more pervasive influence on his fiction. He finds in the closely woven communities and hard-working families of eastern Kentucky's coal country many of his most representative characters and themes. His first three novels demonstrate binding connections to both family and place. *Clay's Quilt* (2001), *A Parchment of Leaves* (2002), and *The Coal Tattoo* (2004) trace four generations of several families in fictional Crow County, Kentucky, portraying their struggles and triumphs in one of the northwesternmost extremities of the mountain South.

Set in the 1980s, *Clay's Quilt* introduces Clay Sizemore, an orphaned teen raised by his aunt, uncle, and extended Crow County family. Looking back several decades, *A Parchment of Leaves* describes life in Crow County in the early 1900s, when Vine, a young Cherokee woman, marries a local worker of Irish heritage and establishes the family line that will carry through to *Clay's Quilt*'s Sizemore, their great-grandson. Set in the 1950s and '60s, *The Coal Tattoo* centers on Anneth and Easter, sisters who struggle to cope with their father's death in a coal mine and their mother's subsequent suicide. Like its predecessors, the novel emphasizes the significance of family and considers further the role of land and place in the lives of both family and community. Anneth and Easter also introduce another prominent aspect of regional identification, religion. Taken together, the three novels explore the evolving social and economic structure of a region peopled by coal miners and their traditions, as well as by coal barons and their physically and psychically destructive approaches to business. A closer examination of the trilogy, moreover, reveals the ties and disparities between Pentecostal Christianity and meaningful spiritual links to land.

Raised in the Pentecostal Church, House places important metaphysical emphasis on spiritual relationships with nature and one's native land. He often links a devotion to the land with a spiritual element that transcends conventional religious experience. Describing himself as "very interested in spiritual and religious ideas" ("A Conversation," *Coal* 333), House also says, "the land is simply a very important part of my being" ("A Conversation," *Parchment* 288). His outlook leads him to combine two elements that appear as leitmotifs in his fiction. The most memorable characters in his fictional Crow County demonstrate the correlation between the rigid expectations of Pentecostalism and the individual spiritual experiences one may encounter in nature. In *The Coal Tattoo*, for instance, Easter recalls that her grandmother Vine Sullivan, the protagonist of *A Parchment of Leaves* and matriarch of House's fictional family, "didn't go to church anyway. She couldn't stand being inside for that long and [said] she liked camp meetings, tent revivals, and brush arbors because they were at least out of doors, where God could see you without obstruction" (*The Coal Tattoo* 102). Church in these novels is the Pentecostal Church, and it features, as Edith L. Blumhofer writes in *The New Encyclopedia of Southern Culture*, a "precise understanding not only of valid spiritual experience but also of appropriate Christian general behavior. Prohibitions against pork, coffee, colas, chewing gum, tobacco, alcohol, dancing, 'spectator sports,' and mixed bathing were common, as were directives regarding jewelry, short hair for women, and many types of clothing" (108). Easter, the most devout character in the trilogy, struggles realistically with her need to uphold these strict tenets. At one point in *The Coal Tattoo* she backslides, beginning a career as a honky-tonk singer, and starts finding spiritual satisfaction elsewhere, including in nature. Having skipped a church service to fish with her husband El McIntosh, she has a kind of religious experience: "When they came to a place of slick, moss-covered rocks, El had taken her hand and guided her through. He had run his thumb across her palm and it had stirred up a feeling in her that felt very much like a kind of salvation" (86). Easter's continual guilt over her "sins . . . piling up" (97), however, culminates in the stillbirth of her child, leading her to lose faith in God and in life. "I want to die" (187), she eventually confesses. House, drawing on the land and nature to offer her the salvation she thought she felt earlier as a churchgoer, has her sister Anneth, who has never felt the tug of organized religion, take her to the nearby mountaintop: "When they got to the summit, Anneth paused for a minute in the shade of the woods before stepping out into the field of wildflowers, her favorite place in the world. . . . This was her church, the one place she prayed" (188). Feeling the spiritual power of the spot, Anneth works to restore Easter's faith. In response to Easter's declaring "I don't believe in God anymore," Anneth asks, "How can you doubt there's some kind of God when there's a morning like this?" (189). The field of wildflowers was the same place the sisters' grandmothers had communed, and it plays a significant role in the natural world of each of the novels.

Anneth's action is significant, for though she has never been a churchgoer, she has frequently experienced spiritual renewal in nature. Her beliefs are often juxtaposed with Easter's, as in the passage above, and House frequently places the sisters together in nature to highlight their divergent responses to spirituality. A flashback in *Clay's Quilt* describes an exhilarated, inebriated Anneth as Easter attempts to quiet her:

> "Look at it, Easter. I love a little slice of a moon, don't you? They way better than a full one."
> "Let's go in, Anneth. You've woke the whole holler up."
> Anneth laughed. "We ought to stay out here all night and study that," she said, staring at the sliver of moon. "That's church to me." (18)

House contrasts the sisters' perspectives in *The Coal Tattoo* as well. As Easter, after repenting for her backsliding, is baptized, she realizes that "[s]he had never been so happy in her life." Anneth, on the other hand, "stood amidst the trees, watching. . . . It filled her with a great sadness" (198).

Prone to bouts of depression and floundering in a second unsatisfying marriage, Anneth frequents the mountains around her home, seeking succor:

[S]he went for long walks up onto the ridge that Vine had explored as a girl. She sat down in the woods and listened to the world. Mostly all she could hear was the drone of the coal tipple down there in the valley, but sometimes she could find a cove between two mountains where the noise of the coal camp was not able to enter. Here she could hear the growth of fern and the licking of the earth beneath her back and the music of falling water. She studied the sky through the bobbing leaves and ran her hands down the trunks of trees (*The Coal Tattoo* 229).

Anneth passes this connection to the natural world to her son Clay, even though he is only three years old when she is murdered. Like Anneth, Clay finds in the forest a cómfort and salvation that the Pentecostal Church does not provide. As an adolescent, he begins to experience something of his mother's adoration of the natural world:

Clay never had felt really close to God inside the church, not the way he did when he could see the creek running over the rocks and the mist coming down off the mountain. By the time he was about thirteen, he began to realize that God didn't just live inside this old church house, even though the preacher called it God's house every chance he got. . . . He closed his eyes and felt God floating all around him. He felt his presence burning into the trees, popping on the air. . . . He kept going to church with Easter. He felt the fire of the Holy Ghost run up and down the back of his neck, he clapped and sang along to songs . . . but it wasn't the same feeling that came to him when he was on the mountain, alone. That was where he prayed. On the mountain, he was able to recognize the Lord hanging in the trees, blowing against his face. (*Clay's Quilt* 47–48)

Created as a character three years before Anneth, however (*Clay's Quilt*'s late twentieth century precedes *The Coal Tattoo*'s early twentieth century), Clay is more tentative in his response to the established church, perhaps reflecting House's own still-evolving thoughts on organized religion. Reflecting on his portrayal of religion, House has said, "Although I really didn't have an agenda about Pentecostals when I started the book, I knew I had to portray the religion in such a way that readers understand how it works in the lives of the characters. Clay, for instance, has learned how to be a good person by going to the Pentecostal church, but he knows that he can't be true to himself and keep attending the church because of some of the very strict doctrines of the church" (*Clay's Quilt*, "A Conversation" n.p.). In this first novel, House acknowledges the role religion can play in one's life; in *The Coal Tattoo*, which followed three years later, Anneth completely disavows any tie to Pentecostalism, asserting that nature provides the salvation she craves.

Given this devotion to land and the recognition of its spiritual value, it is no surprise that House's characters often fight to save the land from the destructive and dishonest maneuvers of businessmen and coal companies. Represented in *A Parchment of Leaves* by Tate Masters and in *The Coal Tattoo* by Liam Trosper and the Altamont Mining Company, these outsiders see nature only as a commodity, not as a source of spirituality. Masters, a wealthy business owner from the nearby city of Black Banks, finagles the land at Redbud Camp away from Vine and her Cherokee family and neighbors. While none of the parties can produce a deed, bigoted local magistrates award him the land, which he promptly clears to build a mountaintop mansion, displacing the Cherokees at the same time.

Years later, Vine returns to show her daughter the place of her origins, describing her emotions "as the remains of Redbud Camp was slowly revealed to me. It existed no more. . . . It was the worst feeling, to look upon the place of my childhood and realize that it had been swept away like sand at the swing of broomstraw" (*A Parchment of Leaves* 240). Vine's reaction indicates the significance of the land to her descendants, as revealed in House's other Crow County novels. Like her descendants, Vine has a spiritual connection to the land and nature. At one point she reflects, "I wondered if the trees were God. They were like God in many respects: they stood silent, and most people only noticed them when the need arose. Maybe all the secrets to life were written on the surface of leaves, waiting to be translated" (70). House confirmed the significance of this passage in an interview with Lee Smith, recalling, "I really did try to live more simply while I was working on this book. I spent a whole lot of time studying the woods, soaking up the spiritual energy of the trees. My favorite line in the book is 'Maybe the trees were God'" (*A Parchment of Leaves*, "A Conversation" 283).

Granddaughters Easter and Anneth, although of different minds religiously, both feel the power of nature and place. Easter notes that "their land was the most important thing they had besides one another. That loving the land was a given, not something one could choose, the same way you love your sister or brother even when you don't want to" (245). The sisters have chosen different paths, however. Easter, the caretaker of the family's mountain property, lives in her parents' house with husband El McIntosh. Anneth, after a youthful marriage and brief sojourn in Nashville, returns to Crow County a young divorcee. Eventually she marries the mine foreman of the Altamont Coal Company, Liam Trosper, and the two move into the former Masters mansion. While she enjoys the lifestyle her husband's wealth affords them,

Anneth eventually cannot reconcile her husband's materialistic disregard for the land with her own spiritual and familial ties.

Relying on a broad form deed¹ signed by the women's great-uncle, the Altamont Coal Company claims Easter and Anneth's undeveloped land, leading to a culminating battle on the mountain. The year is 1966, and coal companies have begun to struggle. As Liam explains, "[T]he coal business is in bad shape now, Easter. The boom is over. So they're all turning to strip mining. It's cheaper. They'll cut down all the trees and then they'll come in and doze the mountain down until they get to the coal. There won't be a mine entrance. The whole mountain will be dozed" (238). Easter's response, "Once you strip that land, it'll be changed forever. All those trees, the field of wildflowers up there," emphasizes her fervent attachment to place and nature. Anneth's reaction portends the end of her marriage: "She couldn't believe she had married a man who was going to tear up the land she had loved all her life, a man too stupid to see that she loved that land more than him. He couldn't even fathom the idea of loving a place, and she couldn't comprehend the idea of someone's not understanding how that felt, to love a place so much that you could cry for it, that you could hurt for it" (242).

As the bulldozers appear unexpectedly on the mountain, the crisis reaches its climax. With the community's men all away, the company plans to begin stripping the mountain. Left alone to protect their spiritual home, Easter, Anneth—seven months pregnant—and their aunt Sophie defy the company by locking arms and lying down in front of a bulldozer's scoop. As deputies struggle to remove them from the machine's destructive path, news photographers appear, shooting images of the women being forcibly carried from the site. Jailed for striking an officer, Easter learns the next day that photographs of the event have been carried nationwide and the story has become a landmark moment in landowners' struggles against strip mining. House acknowledges the personal significance of that section of the novel, commenting, "[I]t's a very emotional scene for me, that sense of unity and love for the land" (*The Coal Tattoo*, "A Conversation" 333).

Told from Easter's point of view, the narrative here emphasizes the incongruity between church-inspired morality and obedience and her personal, moral position that the land, too, is sacred. Faced with breaking the law or accepting "legal" destruction of her land, Easter chooses the former, jeopardizing her standing in the church community that she prizes so highly. House makes clear, however, that her decision is not viewed negatively. She awakens in a jail cell to the sound of singing from the street outside. As she peers out the cell's small window, she realizes that "there must have been a hundred people out there, all their voices rising up into one. . . . She could see people that she went to church with—everyone in the congregation must have been out there" (302–3). With this scene of unity, House emphasizes his belief that the life of a place is manifested in loyalty to the land, illustrating his conviction that nature is as influential as religion.

Since the publication of these novels, House has become increasingly active in protests against mountaintop removal or strip mining. His fiction is clearly a reflection of his own moral and spiritual beliefs, as well as his devotion, like that of his characters, to the land from which he hails. Arguing that mountaintop removal is a cultural as well as an environmental issue, House argues, "We talk a lot these days about 'a sustainable economy.' But what about being a sustainable people, a sustainable culture?" Believing that mountaintop removal "threatens our storytelling tradition" ("A Conscious Heart" 7), House understands, as he demonstrates in his fiction, that land, nature, and place all form the basis for his South. He argues that without the mountains and their significance to Appalachian culture, the region could produce no distinctive literature. And that literature, as he creates it, stems from the people and their relationships to the land. After witnessing a town meeting focused on modern coal mining techniques, House describes a "standing-room-only crowd of people who had come to share their stories of their experiences with mountaintop removal. These people are a part of the land, and they live with mountaintop removal every day. *It is their stories that matter*" (Burns 6; emphasis added). And these are the stories that he recreates in his fiction: not stories about mountaintop removal specifically, but about the people who have struggled and survived in the midst of coal mining and mountain culture and continue to do so.

Recalling Brian Carpenter's assertion in *Grit Lit: A Rough South Reader*, that the Rough South is "mostly poor, white, rural, and unquestionably violent" (xxvii), it is easy to see that House's Crow County, Kentucky, is both Rough and South. House writes of it, however, in a manner that emphasizes the land and its effect on the people. Certainly there are poverty and a rural setting, but he connects those aspects with the positive role that setting plays. Emphasizing the spiritual and religious beliefs of his characters, House demonstrates the significant role the natural environment plays in Appalachian culture. While he explores the importance of traditional religion, he juxtaposes those customary expressions with the spiritual significance of the natural surroundings.

House's fiction demonstrates his own gradually clearing focus on this revelation. As he has stated in interviews, he finds religion an important part of the fictional world he created. *Clay's Quilt* introduces Crow County and explores the effects of Pentecostalism on characters' lives. Nature, too, appears as an alternative source of salvation. In *A Parchment of Leaves* he moves back in time, recounting the beginnings in his fictional families of what Emerson terms "an original relation to the universe" (7). *The Coal Tattoo* then demonstrates House's personal recognition that the surrounding natural world is a source of goodness and salvation. The process of creatively describing his region has led the author to believe that nature and the land define his culture in many ways: "The mountains dictate everything: our economy and our traditions and the way we talk" (Scanlan). There is a "spiritual energy" in the trees, mountains, and hollows. Active in the struggle against mountaintop removal since 2005 ("A Conscious Heart" 17), House published the final novel in the trilogy in 2004. Combining the climactic scene of three women banding together to save a cherished mountain with all three works' emphasis on the spiritual qualities of nature, readers can recognize House's path from his Rough South upbringing to his struggle to preserve that influential culture—a culture that depends on the many roles of the natural world.

Note

1. A broad form deed is a legal document by which landowners convey to coal companies mineral rights to a parcel of land, but retain surface rights to the land above the coal seam. According to *The Strip Mining Handbook*, "broad form deeds included language that waived mining companies' liability for surface impacts that were 'convenient or necessary' to the mining operation" (Squillace).

Works Cited

Blumhofer, Edith L. "Pentecostalism." *The New Encyclopedia of Southern Culture*. Ed. Samuel S. Hill. Vol. 1. Chapel Hill: U of North Carolina P, 2006. Print.

Burns, Shirley Stewart, Mari-Lynn Evans, and Silas House, eds. *Coal Country: Rising Up Against Mountaintop Removal Mining*. San Francisco: Sierra Club Books, 2009. Print.

Carpenter, Brian. "Introduction: Blood and Bone." *Grit Lit: A Rough South Reader*. Ed. Carpenter and Tom Franklin. Columbia: U of South Carolina P, 2012. xiii–xxxii. Print.

Emerson, Ralph Waldo. "Nature." *Essays and Lectures*. New York: Literary Classics of the United States, 1983. 5–49. Print.

House, Silas. *Clay's Quilt*. 2001. New York: Ballantine, 2002. Print.

———. *The Coal Tattoo*. 2004. New York: Ballantine, 2005. Print.

———. "A Conscious Heart." *Journal of Appalachian Studies* 14.1 & 2 (2008): 7–19. Print.

———. "A Conversation." *Clay's Quilt*. n.p. Print.

———. "A Conversation." *The Coal Tattoo*. 328–37. Print.

———. "A Conversation." *A Parchment of Leaves*. 281–89. Print.

———. *A Parchment of Leaves*. 2002. New York: Ballantine, 2003. Print.

Scanlan, Christopher. "Silas House." *clatl.com*. Creative Loafing Atlanta, 17 June 2004. Web. 26 Feb. 2013.

Squillace, Mark. *The Strip Mining Handbook*. sites.google.com. Google Sites, 13 Aug. 2009. Web. 27 May 2013.

Steve Yarbrough:
Transplanted Mississippian

Thomas E. Dasher

STEVE Yarbrough was born in Indianola, Mississippi, on August 29, 1956, the son of John and Earlene Yarbrough. After earning a BA in 1979 and an MA in 1981—both in English, both from the University of Mississippi—he earned an MFA in creative writing from the University of Arkansas in 1984. He taught at Virginia Tech from 1984 to 1988, then became the James and Coke Hallowell Professor of Creative Writing at California State University in Fresno, where he also directed the MFA. program. In 1999 he returned to Oxford to serve an academic year as the John and Renee Grisham Writer in Residence at the University of Mississippi. In 2009 he became a professor and graduate program director for creative writing at Boston's Emerson College, appointments he continues to hold.

No matter where he's lived, though, Steve Yarbrough has set most of his fiction in Mississippi, often in Indianola, where he grew up, or in the fictional town of Loring, its fictional near twin. In 2008, while living in California, he told an interviewer that he writes about his birthplace because

Mississippi has a storytelling culture. People talk endlessly about things that happened fifty years ago. I've lived in California for 17 years, but I find the culture to be shallow and everyone seems to live in the moment, or even more, in the future. I do it too when I'm here. In Mississippi, history is a part of the present. It is common to know stories about your great-great grandparents. Stories are passed down from generation to generation. You don't find that tradition just anywhere. I think if you grew up in a place like Mississippi, you wouldn't want to write about any place else. ("Interview with Steve Yarbrough")

Yarbrough fills his fiction with people who, if they ever leave home, must return to it. They don't necessarily return to the Eden they may think has been waiting for them, but they do return. In many ways they have never left, of course, for their home creates the context for the rest of their lives.

In Yarbrough's first novel, *The Oxygen Man* (1999) (which Matthew Guinn, in "Writing in the South Now," called "one of the best works of Southern fiction produced at the close of the twentieth century" [584]), no one travels far—no farther than Oxford or Greenville. Indianola, Mississippi, defines them. The situation doesn't have to be suffocating, but both Ned and Daze, the siblings at the center of the novel, find it so. At the same time, when they both finally find a way out of their isolation, they do so within the community itself. Denny Gautreaux, the doomed scion of local aristocrats, is attracted to Daze because of her difference from other local women. Denny dreams of the two of them escaping to a world different from the one in which they've been reared, but that dream ends when a boat accident shatters his skull. Even so, there is no reason to believe that what he dreamed had ever been possible. Could he have escaped his family and rescued Daze from the world that she believes she despises? Later, Beer Smith reaches out to her. Fifteen years her senior, he once drove the school bus with her sitting on the seat behind him. What he offers her is not in any way the kind of exotic life Denny had imagined, for they will surely stay in Indianola. But they will support one another, and their shared community will support them as well. Yarbrough suggests that Beer and Daze will manage to find and live out a meaningful life together in Indianola.

Luke May, the narrator of *Safe from the Neighbors* (2010), Yarbrough's fifth novel, is another son of Indianola, his life largely prescribed by the world in which he grew up and in which he still lives. Luke's parents are poor farmers, and even though he spends a few years at Ole Miss, he soon returns to his hometown to teach high school history. Like his wife, who teaches at Delta State University, he wants his students to understand the world around them and the local community still struggling to emerge from its dark past. Luke's personal past is caught up with his father's, particularly his father's actions in 1962, when James Meredith enrolled at Ole Miss. However, that past belongs not only Luke's father, for during the 1962 riots his father's close friend Arlan Calloway killed his adulterous wife Nadine with a shotgun. Calloway himself left town and was never punished for the murder, but he later returns through his daughter Maggie, with whom Luke begins an adulterous affair. Such betrayal and conflict creates an internal confrontation. Education doesn't change the situation. Socioeconomic conditions don't shift the consequences of individual actions caught in self-deception. Luke briefly believes that his affair with Maggie will end on his terms, with his wife and daughters none the wiser. Such is not to be, however. Like most betrayals, Luke's catch up with him. He is able to understand, finally, the actions of both his father and Arlan Calloway, but it is his own actions that will save or doom him. Earlier he described himself as "just a guy who'd never write a book or lead a boycott and take a stand against community mores or assault a beach or walk the streets of a bombed-out city. I was Mr. History. I read it and I talk about it, without ever once having done anything unusual enough to make it. Not even locally" (74). He is wrong, of course. His actions, his betrayals, his discoveries do indeed create history—his own and that of those closest to him.

Yet we also know that the past is always present. Yarbrough understands well the impact of history upon his native Mississippi and the South, and the fact that personal history can affect the present. In *The End of California* (2006), Yarborough's fourth novel and a finalist for the Mississippi Institute of Arts and Letters Award for fiction, Pete Barrington, another son of Loring—an outstanding student and star athlete who became sexually involved with a classmate's mother—returns home from California. He had run a successful medical practice there until his sexual involvement with a patient erupted into public scandal. There is no salvation awaiting him in Loring, however. Pete's best friend, Tim Kessler, begins an affair with Pete's wife, Angela. Then Angela is killed by Alan DePoyster, the childhood friend with whose mother Pete long ago had an affair. Even amid such melodrama, though, Yarbrough hints at peace and reconciliation at the end of the novel. At his daughter's insistence, Pete accompanies her on a visit to the DePoysters, where Pete recognizes the worn angel atop the Christmas tree as one he had owned as a teenager, a totem from the past that only he would recognize. Like some Damascus road experience, Pete and his daughter have their own epiphanies as to how the past is inextricably tied to the present that Loring connected to California, which connected back to Loring.

Regional history and the personal past can be intertwined, but in all of his novels from *The Oxygen Man* to *Safe from the Neighbors* Yarbrough compels us to understand that specific events continue to impact our daily interactions and goals. Yarbrough comments, "I guess what I'm really fascinated by—if I'm analyzing my own fiction . . . is that most of the characters are dogged by some sins from their past, some stain on their lives. And it's usually about twenty years back down the road, when it happened. I suppose I'm fascinated and horrified by the notion that there's a mistake you can make that you can't ever come back from" ("'Dogged by Some Sins from Their Past': An Interview with Steve Yarbrough" 118). In *The Oxygen Man*, both Ned and Daze had been fifteen in 1972, just sophomores in high school, one playing football, one painfully aware of how she does not fit in. Their parents had a terrible relationship and little money. The siblings recognize that their places in their peer group are precarious at best. But for teenagers these realities do not necessarily make one year more memorable than another. What marks a specific chapter from one's past is a specific action that remains a part of the ongoing struggle for identity and place. Ned smashes a bottle on a black storekeeper's head; Daze has a sexual relationship with Denny Gautreaux, who will die partially as a result of Ned's impulse, rage, and vulnerability. We measure the years by the changes that occur as we age, but one act, one impulse, one careless move can stay with us as a turning point after which we will never be the same. Daze allows herself to be swept up into Denny's dream of the future. Ned believes that he can make sense of his parents' relationship, and that being a successful athlete can at least momentarily erase the chaos into which he is continually thrust. But decisions are often not considered, consequences not anticipated, actions not planned, so both Daze and Ned remain haunted by particular episodes from the past that are still painfully part of the present.

Yarbrough's second novel, *Visible Spirits* (2001), is based loosely on a series of incidents that occurred in Indianola in 1902 and 1903. But, as Yarbrough admitted, "I'm not a historian, and sticking to what really happened would have rendered me incapable of writing about character the way I wanted to. So I felt perfectly free to alter and invent and have done so liberally" ("A Conversation with . . . Steve Yarbrough"). The novel tells of two brothers from Loring, Tandy and Leighton Payne, their intense antagonism toward each other, and the effects of racism upon them as individuals and as members of the community. Both brothers are finally destroyed by their actions—one noble, one despicable—and the community remains deeply racially divided. Sons of privilege, when they become men they become bitter antagonists who struggle against expectations that only Leighton can accept and disasters precipitated by Tandy's self-absorption and weaknesses.

Such distancing from reality is also true of the larger community. While local history and personal narratives dominate his novels, Yarbrough is always aware of the reality of race and how it has shaped the community's life, as well as the lives of inhabitants who try to coexist despite the color line. In *Safe from the Neighbors*, it is 1962, and Ole Miss is about to be integrated. As Yarbrough described the setting,

> The novel's set in the Mississippi Delta, in a town in which the racial mix is about 65-35 African-American to white. Race is on everybody's mind all the time. The town Loring is based on is still racially polarized. There's more public interaction among blacks and whites than there was when I was a kid—a lot more—but the gulf is still vast. In other words, it's almost impossible to write honestly about the place without writing about race. As far as research goes, well, I lived through the early '60s in the Delta, and I remember the days leading up to the central historical incident in the novel, the integration of Ole Miss. ("Steve Yarbrough")

In *Visible Spirits*, it is 1902, and the reality of slavery and reconstruction dictates the parameters of characters' choices and actions. In *The End of California*, Frank Henderson, Loring's black police chief, recognizes that he is no longer just a black man in a small town:

> The older scum that called the shots . . . used teenagers and even preteens to make deliveries and pick up change, so the kids who would've been cutting white folks' grass when Henderson was young would now bring them grass, and a lot worse, in plastic bags. Some of those kids would turn tail and run if they saw Frank driving by or walking down the street. Those he could tolerate. Others would plant their Air Jordans on the sidewalk and stick their chins up and their chests out, their eyes screaming *White Man's Nigger!*
> (253)

Like much of Yarbrough's fiction, the novel explores the past, the effect upon individuals when they betray one another, and the communities that try to balance personal stories with the history that ties one generation, one era, to another.

Yarbrough's third novel, *Prisoners of War* (2004), a finalist for the 2005 PEN/Faulkner Award, takes place in the 1940s. Yarbrough found the novel's epigraph in a letter that Czeslaw Milosz wrote to Jerzy Andrzejewski: "*Doubt is a noble thing.* I believe that if there were a recurrence of the Biblical experience of Sodom, it would be necessary to seek the righteous among those who profess doubt rather than among believers. And yet, as you know, doubt is traditionally bathed in a glow and accorded dignity solely because it serves the seekers of truth as a weapon. *Indeed, the most fervent people are doubters"* (italics mine). Set during World War II in and around a German prisoner of war camp outside Loring, *Prisoners of War* explores different types of prisons. There are certainly German POWs in the camp, but there is also Dan Timms, who desperately wants to join the army and escape from Loring. Marty Stark has already returned from the war and is psychologically imprisoned by what he experienced as a participant there. L. C., a young African American, knows that he is trapped by the color of his skin, and resists any suggestion that he, too, might fight for a country that has made his blackness a prison he can never escape. At one point L. C. tells Dan the following about parallel universes: "That's what the preacher say we living in, Dan. You got your universe, I got mine. I see you spinning by, you see me, time to time we both wave, say hey. But never the twain shall meet—and that last part come straight from the Bible" (4). Through the course of the novel, Dan must struggle with having lost both his father and his best friend. At the end, he must help L. C. escape Mississippi, where he will surely be punished for his refusal to remain subservient. Only then can Dan start the journey back home, return to a place he hopes will remember its champions the way a small town in Indiana does, inscribing names of its 1913 basketball champions on a large sign that Dan sees as he drives through.

What will it take to be remembered in a world so divided, so torn by ongoing conflicts between the races? Ned in *The Oxygen Man* has lived a life isolated from others. He believes he is a void, only a shadow of a man. Each year has left him more alone and more aware of what he lacks. Ned concludes that everyone is on a kind of road, one that ends only in death: "Death on the road was no disgrace, though dying was always a failure of sorts" (274). Ned's journey has been one into his empty self. What if, like Daze, his sister, he can rise, resurrected out of the emptiness of his life? Beer Smith is there to help Daze, but Ned has to take those final steps on his own. He will not survive, and few will truly understand why he shot Mack Bell, the man for whom he now works. But he knows. He had to shoot Mack because Mack had come to manifest all that Ned had failed to do. Mack did not force Ned to commit to any particular action, but he had been the catalyst for the worst of Ned's actions. Killing the storekeeper, pushing Denny out of the boat, throwing a black co-worker and his family out of their home—Ned had indeed been the void Mack filled. But Ned must finally take responsibility for being that nothingness. He cannot blame his parents; he cannot share his emptiness with Daze. And so he acts. In another moment, frozen in the narrative like the thud of the Coke bottle on the hull of the motorboat, he pulls the trigger and finds himself.

In Yarbrough's South, what one finally becomes has little to do with economic security, social standing, or educational background. There is no deep divide between those who come from privilege and those who struggle for every dollar. Pete Barrington attends medical school and establishes a successful medical practice in California. Dan Timms returns to Loring after helping his friend L. C. escape. Luke May is a well-known teacher whose students benefit from his knowledge and his concern for each of them. Of the three, however, only Dan returns home with a clear chance that the past will not compromise his future. For Pete and Luke, no matter what becomes of them, there will be no bright future. Their mistakes, like Ned's in *The Oxygen Man*, cannot be erased. Their infidelities, the impact of their betrayals upon those they love, will haunt them forever. Yarbrough does not reveal how they finally live out their lives, but we know that even though each may live a long time, neither will escape his past.

Yarbrough suggests the same is true of his beloved Mississippi. The people of the state are no better and, finally, no worse than those in California or New England. History is both the facts of what happened and the uncertainties of how that history plays out in individual. In Yarbrough's short stories and novels, education doesn't really change much. Ned's lack of an education, Pete's medical degree, and Luke's success at Ole Miss don't alter the consequences of personal responsibility. Ned dies. Pete loses his wife. Luke is left alone. None of these characters is finally free of the choices they've made. The fact that they are all sons of Mississippi doesn't doom or save them; however, like the state in which they were reared, they must confront the complexity of a world that denies the individual any chance of true isolation from others and the rest of the country.

In the epigraph for *Safe from the Neighbors*, Milan Kundera points out that we forget those moments that don't merit our remembering. However, it isn't art alone that captures the moments we have to remember. It is in the individual in the guise of the man he becomes that those moments become embedded forever. Pete and Luke, and Dan and L. C. will live into an indefinite future. Their thoughts and actions will propel them forward even, as their pasts and memories tie them to a place and time. Indianola and Loring are rich communities, filled with diverse inhabitants, facts that belie their small-town identities. Their people are, like others, trying to live lives that mean something. Much of what becomes meaningful will directly result from what they do and what they do not do. But there are aspects of every life beyond the individual's control. It is that mixture of responsibility and reconciliation that finally defines the individual, who—like Ned and Pete and Luke and Dan—has to find a way to do more than merely breathe.

Works Cited and Consulted

Dasher, Thomas E. "Steve Yarbrough: *The Oxygen Man." Still in Print: The Southern Novel Today.* Ed. Jan Nordby Gretlund. Columbia: U of South Carolina P, 2010. 91–104. Print.

Esposito, Scott. "Steve Yarbrough—Family Men." *conversationalreading.com. Conversational Reading,* 10 June 2005. Web. 21 Sept. 2008.

Guinn, Matthew. "Writing in the South Now." *A Companion to the Literature and Culture of the American South.* Ed. Richard Gray and Owen Robinson. Malden: Blackwell, 2004. 571–87. Print.

Yarbrough, Steve. "Author Interview: Steve Yarbrough." Interview by Jessica Anya Blau. *thenervousbreakdown.com. The Nervous Breakdown,* 25 March 2010. Web. 11 June 2013.

———. "A Conversation with . . . Steve Yarbrough." *randomhouse.com.* Random House, n.d. Web. 21 Sept. 2008.

———. "'Dogged by Some Sins from Their Past': An Interview with Steve Yarbrough." Interview by Tom Williams. *Arkansas Review: A Journal of Delta Studies* 33 (August 2002): 114–20. Print.

———. *The End of California.* New York: Knopf, 2006. Print.

———. *Family Men.* Baton Rouge: Louisiana State UP, 1990. Print.

———. "Interview: Steve Yarbrough." Interview by Juan Guzman. *mfafresno.wordpress.com.* California State University—Fresno MFA Program in Creative Writing, 19 Oct. 2009. Web. 11 June 2013.

———. "Interview with Steve Yarbrough." Interview by J. C. Robertson. *southernlitreview.com. Southern Literary Review,* 12 May 2009. Web. 21 Sept. 2008.

———. *Mississippi History.* Columbia: U of Missouri P, 1994. Print.

———. *The Oxygen Man.* Denver: MacMurray & Beck, 1999. Print.

———. *Prisoners of War.* New York: Knopf, 2004. Print.

———. *Safe from the Neighbors.* New York: Knopf. 2010. Print.

———. "Steve Yarbrough." Interview by Marie Lazaro. *superstitionreview.asu.edu.* Arizona State University, Fall 2011. Web. 11 June 2013.

———. *Veneer.* Columbia: U of Missouri P, 1998. Print.

———. *Visible Spirits.* New York: Knopf, 2001. Print.

Once a Paradise:
Brad Watson's Southern Afterlife

Wade Newhouse

IT'S recently become standard at conferences and in journals devoted to southern literature to ask whether southern literature itself is still a distinct category. The concept of the "postsouthern"—a multi-faceted recognition that such supposedly southern tropes as sense of place are constructed rather than organic—lets revisionist-minded readers find southernness in just barely southern texts, and chart the legacy of southern history and ideologies in historical moments with little direct connection to the geographical South.[1] For scholars in new southern studies, "southern" literature includes work produced as far from the old Confederacy as Caribbean and Central American nations, while critics have declared that novels as canonically New England as Hawthorne's *The House of the Seven Gables* (1851) unconsciously depend upon an antebellum southern agrarian ideal.[2] With the contemporary southern landscape increasingly marked by national rather than regional, economic, and cultural movements, literature produced *in* the South today by writers *from* the South might have little to do with subject matter unique to the South.

Brad Watson's novel *The Heaven of Mercury* (2002) lies squarely amid this matrix of evolving and competing Souths. A native of Mississippi who spent time in Florida, Watson is by rights a true southerner, without such common qualifiers as "adopted" or "expatriate" to dilute his pedigree. He did teach at Harvard after the publication of his short story collection *Last Days of the Dog-Men* (2001), but that experience only ties him more closely to William Faulkner, whose Quentin Compson commits suicide while studying at Harvard in *The Sound and the Fury* (1929). Watson sets his work largely in the contemporary South and writes with an eye for poetic embellishment of the tiny details of small-town life, consistently earning comparisons to Faulkner, Flannery O'Connor, and Barry Hannah.

The twentieth-century rise of the economically new South, and not only national but transnational patterns of development throughout many former Confederate states, suggest that such writers as Watson—"southern" first and foremost because they're from the South—may write about a "southern" experience fundamentally similar to, rather than distinct from, a larger American experience. For all Watson's reviewers' enthusiasm for his inheritance of the Faulkner-O'Connor tradition, the South as a sociohistorical entity is not particularly present in *The Heaven of Mercury*. While the scenery covers a wide range of expected southern tropes—fishing trips in the swamps, black settlements on the edge of town, hurricanes sweeping the Gulf Coast—the novel's main narrative is so intimate that its southerners almost seem to live outside the historical South.[3]

The Heaven of Mercury begins and ends with old Finus Bates, the octogenarian sage of Mercury, Mississippi, ruminating upon the death of Birdie Wells Urquhart, whom he has secretly loved from the sidelines of their unhappily parallel lives. The bulk of the narrative takes the form of vignettes, memories, and episodic revelations detailing their interwoven lives: Birdie's marriage to local magnate Earl Urquhart; her black housekeeper Creasie and her mysterious Aunt Vish; and a lifetime of rumors surrounding Earl's sudden and suspicious death. There is plenty here for fans of the modern southern gothic, including a necrophiliac mortician and a spooky wooden dummy that haunts Creasie throughout her life. But these colorful and inventive images, delivered in Watson's consistently poetic and velvety prose, seem more like baroque set pieces—bits of post-Faulknerian window-dressing—than organic elements of a particular conception of the contemporary South. In other words, attempts to evaluate what aspects of almost a century of southern life and culture *The Heaven of Mercury* depicts inevitably lead the reader to images—dialects, stock characters, scenery—rather than to a broad consideration of Mercury, Mississippi, as a nexus of the historical and economic factors that distinguish the South.

This is not, however, a criticism of Watson's novel. On the contrary, Watson's instinctive turn to expected "southern" imagery and tone and simultaneous lack of consistent interest in the South as a cultural idea may well represent a particular next phase in the evolution of southern literature—if we intend the genre to live on in the next century. In the "Reading Group Guide" included in the Norton paperback edition of his novel, Watson suggests that every southern writer's social landscape has changed in recent decades, implying that southern literature as a genre cannot help but be about that change. Small southern towns, he says, have "changed a lot, even though in appearance many small Southern cities and towns seem not to have changed much. Demographics, economics, social cauldrons, these have all been modified by changes from the civil rights movements to increasing urbanization and the death of small farms, and the move away from cheap-labor manufacturing (it's moved on to more fertile fields in developing countries)."[4]

Perhaps the most noticeable quality of *The Heaven of Mercury* as a novel set amid some eighty years of transformation is how little evidence there is of such change. Though the story's earliest episode—when young Finus Bates accidentally spies a naked Birdie Wells performing a cartwheel—takes place in 1917, and the novel's immediate present coincides with Birdie's death more than seventy years later, the great upheavals, transformations, and migrations Watson described are nowhere to be found. Perhaps Meridian, Mississippi, the model for Mercury, has resisted the most dramatic effects of those changes—at least in Watson's eyes. "In Meridian," he notes, "many of the family cleaning businesses, paint stores, clothing stores, barber shops, lumber yards, scrap yards, bakeries, and specialty shops survive." With this comforting local stability as his backdrop—with the reassurance that, comparatively, his small town has managed to resist the large-scale displacement from familial to impersonal and from local to corporate that has shaped the late twentieth-century South—Watson can turn inward to articulate his characters' dreams, passions, and frustrations with little concern for cultural forces beyond their immediate experience.

Only at the beginning and end of his novel does Watson pull back the camera far enough to see Mercury—and old Finus Bates as the panopticon within it—as part of a more comprehensive southern narrative. The novel's first chapter, which depicts Finus's daily life as an aging radio announcer, provides a bird's-eye view of the community as a stubborn survivor: the "once-plantation" system that has only recently allowed its black citizens to be "real human beings in the real world" (16); the great tornado of 1906; the "static death in a growing region" that is the downtown's legacy amid the "migratory growth flowing around it" (15). The chapter presents one of many scenes in

The Heaven of Mercury that lean heavily—consciously or not— on Faulkner's legacy. Watson's survey of Mercury's slow decline, for instance, recalls the dark unease evoked by the modernization of the local laundry service in the opening paragraphs of "That Evening Sun" (1931), and the migration and near extinction of wild animals on the town's periphery will certainly remind some readers of the vanishing wilderness of "The Bear" (1942) and "Delta Autumn" (1942).

When the flashbacks begin in the second chapter, however, such nods to the economic and material condition of the evolving South recede into the background. Watson's subject matter becomes almost exclusively interior, free-roaming processes of thinking and feeling unbounded by cultural or historical process. Characters change over the decades, their understanding of themselves and one another shifting and evolving, but Watson's sense of place, his depiction of the town as a system whose rules and boundaries allow these characters to be what they are, doesn't so much as flicker on the periphery. For most of the novel, then, *The Heaven of Mercury* not only might not be set in the South, but might not be set anywhere or in any time in particular. It's as if Watson, having summarized the fading century's worth of economic ebb and flow in the opening chapter, set his novel roughly in the immediate present and decided that such summary was enough to sustain the specific qualities of southern background that his narrative requires.

Watson appears to embrace the sort of postsouthern ethos that scholars have found in more and more southern fiction of the last few decades, which refuses to assert that characters and dramas set in southern states have a uniquely dramatic identity that stands out, for good or ill, from either a larger national or specifically personal identity. Thus *The Heaven of Mercury* features poor black characters who suffer while working for wealthier whites, but Watson does not investigate race. Characters engage in strange behaviors on the periphery of normally acceptable rules and standards (perhaps the only character weirder than necrophiliac mortician Parnell is his wife Selena, who derives sexual pleasure from pretending to be dead for him, but these oddities have no tie to social customs or Confederate ancestry or excessive humidity. For most of the novel, Watson's characters simply live out their interpersonal dreams and travails with no particular sense of regional affiliation. There's simply no southern cause for the particular effects of living in the South, and characters don't seem to think about the structure of their society or how the fault lines in it might bend or break. Creasie hates Earl Urquhart's father for raping her, but Watson never links that scene to any larger interrogations of southern patriarchy or racism. Both Birdie and Finus suffer through unhappy marriages for decades, but the novel never considers the network of gender and class assumptions upon which those marriages were based, which keep both characters from considering alternatives.

This is not to suggest that Watson's novel would somehow be better if it were more critical of its southern setting. I don't wish for an alternative version that attaches characters to a point of view more antagonistic toward the hints of racism and sexism that occasionally bubble to the surface. I simply suggest that this is how *The Heaven of Mercury* works: It briefly acknowledges that the twentieth century was a time of industrial and cultural change that made Mercury what it is, then goes about its storytelling business without looking back and detailing those conditions.

In a strange way, however, the conclusion of the novel directly and conscientiously considers what it means to set a story in the American South. In a dramatic turn to the kind of magical realism that fans of Gabriel Garcia Marquez will appreciate, the novel's final episodes follow Birdie Wells Urquhart's consciousness as it leaves her dead body and roams Mercury and the Gulf Coast, visiting deceased friends and relatives, reliving scenes from her earliest memories, and ultimately becoming part of an undead historical tapestry that intimately unites past and present. Here, as voices of the long dead mingle with the longings and regrets of the recently deceased, Watson's Mercury finally becomes connected to and part of a more comprehensively southern story—albeit one shaped largely by idealization of the traditional tropes that most of the novel avoids. Only death, it seems, allows one access to a version of the South large enough to evade the daily struggles of those who live there.

For both readers and characters, time is a flexible tool for measuring progress in *The Heaven of Mercury*. Watson seems more interested in narrating tiny moments than broad movements, so the story ends by fits and starts, suggesting an event and then backtracking for several chapters to fill in peripheral information from outside perspectives.[5] Thus Birdie's death takes place in the space between chapters, her final release from life into the new world "just the other side of the mockingbird" (252) is discussed and pondered and even remembered by Finus Bates and Creasie—with a detour into the strange sexual history of Parnell and Selena—for some forty pages before we join her postmortem travels. Once her spirit is on the move, we see Birdie confronting symbols of a dynamic southern history that the rest of the novel has not said much about.

Her first stop is the ravine in which Mercury's black folk have traditionally lived, "a place she'd never seen except from the lip of it, and far back from that, from the car. It'd been like a hades the edge of which she was too scared to approach" (252). Now, freed in death from the white upper-middle-class perspective that allowed black servants into her home but refused consideration of their lives outside her kitchen, Bertie moves easily into Creasie's shack. What follows is a fever dream in which she confronts Creasie one last time to ask forgiveness, while in real-time Creasie stands in Birdie's pantry, waiting for the ambulance that is too late to save her employer.

When Creasie questions what she is being asked to forgive Birdie for, the spirit-Birdie says only, "Well, I don't know. I done the best for you I could. I guess for being white, and you black." Creasie replies, "Nobody couldn't help that." Then, offering the forgiveness she was asked for, Creasie turns the request back on her white employer:

> You can forgive me, too.
> What for?
> I don't know, Creasie said. I can't say.
> Well, Birdie said, seeming distracted. All right then,   I forgive you.
> And at that moment she diffused so thoroughly into the air her presence in
> this space was but a mote that Creasie could no longer see.

Once the shade of Birdie leaves her consciousness, however, Creasie finds that she can say what she wants forgiveness for: "For hatin' you, she whispered" (253).

After this scene, Birdie forces a final conversation with her long dead husband, Earl, still moldering in his grave. From there, she pays visits to other dead souls, whom we will consider in a moment. For now, however, it is important to note how Watson's first depiction of death—and the connection between the living and the dead—allows a particular perspective on his southern community. First, death allows recognition of Mercury's racial caste system—something never attempted in the land of the living. Both black and white speak their need to be forgiven not for their own prejudices, but for the larger condition into which they were born. Creasie suggests that the condition is no one's fault—"nobody couldn't help that"—but the Birdie who has left that racial system behind apparently views it in a new light, as unfinished business she must tend to before she can move on.

Second, death—like so much scenery in Watson's prose—does not resolve anything. Being dead has not given Birdie new understanding of southern racism, and she cannot articulate just what kind of forgiveness she seeks. Creasie, moreover, is so grounded in submission that even talking to a ghost does not keep her from admitting hate is the driving emotion on her end of the relationship. What Watson's view of death allows is not an escape from the racial animosity that has so shaped his homeland's history, but only the beginning of an ability to speak more forthrightly about it.

Birdie has a similar conversation with Earl and other dead relatives, all of whom seem trapped in particular visions of their own afterlife, unable to rest even as Birdie glides and zooms from one place to the next. As with her visit to Creasie, her visit to Earl offers both a chance to acknowledge the unspoken discord that shaped their lives together. "You were the prettiest thing," notes Earl. "[I]t's just a shame. We weren't suited, were we." Birdie's response repeats the essential logic of her confrontation with Creasie: "It wasn't your fault" (255).

Earl is held in his grave by guilt over his life of adultery and bitterness about his own mysterious death, but Birdie's spirit wants to move past such earthly concerns. Seeking forgiveness and closure, she becomes attached to no particular time or place, "once again all in the present air" (255). In this condition, "[t]ime and space had no purchase on her" (261), and she joins her long-dead grandfather to meet the shades of Earl's family, in life "her tormentors." But now they sit bitterly around the parlor of a house preserved as it had been many decades before (261), their forms not quite those they had occupied in life, but warped now by "a thickening and coursing so that it became more like the fur of animals than human hair, and their features swollen like with some long night of debauchery, a permanent hangover of sorts, it seemed. And no solace" (261–62). They are not quite ghosts; Birdie sees them as "just dust gathering into the bygone shapes," but they cohere long enough for her to understand her difference from them. Weighed down by bitterness and pointless neo-aristocratic rage, the Urquharts found no pleasure in life, and now find no rest in death. Seen through Birdie's eyes, they remain stunted and angry and incapable of growth, even on the other side, where, as her Pappy explains, "All time is in a moment" (262), and the dead can apparently choose what form they want to take.

Once again, however, Birdie's visit is supposed to repair and restore earthly bonds, to assert in the afterlife what could not be conceived of in life. Pappy says to the unhappy Urquhart shades, "I think you all owe Birdie an apology. . . . All she ever wanted was peace on this earth, and to get along, and all you ever did was set upon her with lies, and jealousy, and thievery, and attacks upon her good name and character. . . . Apologize and let's all go, now." The demand is met by an "undercurrent of groans and something near quiet weeping" (263), and the forms disintegrate into unapologetic dust that swirls away into nothingness before Birdie leaves them behind.

Seen through the prism of the personalities around which Watson spins his novel, these episodes on the near side of eternity teach quiet and vivid lessons about tolerance and forgiveness and the penalties of dwelling on injustice. Restored to a southern context, however—not a story of individuals, but of representatives of a particular millennial view of the South—Birdie's passage from life into death allows for rituals of confession and attempted atonement that suggest an awareness of a more substantive historical reality. In particular, these images gesture toward acknowledgement of at least two great inequities upon which the modern South was founded—racism and patriarchy—and Birdie's willingness to concede and then simply move beyond them embodies engagement with this history rather than avoidance of it.

The final image of Birdie's afterlife depicts a return to the site of her earliest living memories, and also connects her finally to an image of southern history writ large. We see her bound up in an evocation of a larger South, whose meaning threatens to cross boundaries and collapse distinctions between epochs. Here, "sort of moving just ahead of some awareness of the body or of moving itself" (313), Birdie dives down to the Gulf Coast and visits the town of Fairhope, whose streets "were like none of the streets when she was a child and they would visit—all these homes had sprung up since then, and none of the old waterfront homes survived" (313–14). She dips below the Gulf waters and visits the watery graves of a sunken ferry and a World War II submarine whose entombed crewmembers bless her and the kiss she bestows upon them. She then moves on to the ruins of a Confederate fort and, further back, to a vision of pirates "hanging a man from the hanging tree" (315), and then even further to hear the sounds of the wild beasts who roamed the forests before the coast was settled. All these times and souls are one to her until a pair of voices attracts her attention: "[T]he spirits of two young girls who drowned in the storm of '06, huddled in the corner of a room in the house built by their father" (315).

On a basic narrative level, this extraordinary scene, redeems much of the novel's earlier wandering, sometimes tediously episodic structure by getting us out of the characters' heads—or more precisely by opening those characters' heads to an awareness of a world larger than themselves. For almost the first time in *The Heaven of Mercury*, we move beyond the somewhat myopic viewpoints of Watson's characters to fleeting glimpses of history itself, really moving—drowning, decaying, ultimately remaining to be touched and felt again. Birdie's sense of liberation as she effortlessly tunes in voices from the wide spectrum of historical moments stands in stark contrast to the dour, motionless eternity represented by Earl and his family, and even the unfortunate submariners weeping in their watery graves. More profoundly, however, the grand final images of Birdie and, now again, her grandfather caressing the movement of time, suggest that to narrate a southern history is merely to adopt a particular frame of mind. "This was a paradise, once," notes the shade of her grandfather. "It's all gone now" (316).

In the space of this single line, Birdie's Pappy reinstates *The Heaven of Mercury* in the great modernist myth of the decaying South. Pushing Birdie's memory gently into the past before the great hurricane, when she was barely a child herself, Pappy recreates for her and for readers an evocation of a time before the natural and manmade upheavals of the century: "There was life everywhere, it was full and teeming with life, and with joy. There was no locks on any of our doors, which people say but it was true, here, there was simply no one and nothing to fear here" (317). Pappy spins for Birdie a great tapestry of words in which the legendary hurricane of her childhood marked a transitional moment, a line that both cleaves the shimmering past from the material present, and stands testament to still more human fallibility that must be forgiven:

> It was like being made to leave paradise and the only life we knew, when it was destroyed. But we couldn't go back for the very land itself was washed away, nothing left. Wiped off the face of the earth. . . . It almost seemed like it was a punishment. Like we had grown proud and inward. You can have a little world of your own but you cannot be so proud that you shut out the rest of the world entirely. . . . A vague corruption, child. And then come the flood. It seemed like something from the good book, to me. (318)

Here Watson returns to one of the great tropes in the southern literary tradition, almost daring readers to have doubted him: the South as unsullied paradise, taken away by a heavenly vengeance that punishes the haughty, driving them away to a new world where nature and isolation give way to modernity and subsistence. Adding his voice to the great catalog of southern characters who stand, mystified, on the brink of some unknowable, lost past—Faulkner's Miss Rosa and Warren's Jack Burden, Percy's Binx Bolling and O'Connor's doomed grandmother—Birdie's Pappy ends the novel by putting Mercury at the small end of history. "This place was gone," he says, "disappeared, wiped off the face of the earth, and we couldn't help but see it as a sign that a time and place had ended and we should move on. That's when the Bateses helped us move up to Mercury. And so it's been, so it was" (320).

Like the family leaving paradise and relocating to Mercury, Birdie and Pappy, too, must recognize that, in death, "a time and place had ended" and they "should move on" into the unknown. Death, then—and the inscrutable transition from this world into something invisible—becomes for Watson a kind of metaphor for southernness itself, for the condition of thinking about history the way southern literature has taught so many of us to think about the South of the last century. It's impossible to know whether Pappy's memory of Birdie's childhood home as "once a paradise" is accurate or simply another nostalgic distortion, but by letting Birdie and Pappy dissipate into the evocation of this lost southern ideal, Watson reinforces the mythos from which his own literary ancestry grew. He recognizes as real the pre-modern paradise so little in evidence throughout the plot of the novel as simply too far in the past to be part of the material facts of the narrative. Separate and distinct from the story Watson tells, the fantasy nevertheless remains, to be recovered and treasured as often as the contemporary dead need it.

Watson's final image of the South, however, does not belong to the dead. After Birdie disappears into the shifting absence of history that's the ultimate "heaven of Mercury," the still-living Finus Bates returns for a few chapters to wrap up the truth of Earl's death (he accidentally drank the poison Creasie intended for his villainous father). Surviving his own brush with death after being trapped underwater by a golf cart, Finus visits the same Gulf Coast, and we get a parallel memory of a young child, a wise grandfather, and the need to preserve the fragile past:

> —That's the ivorybill, his grandfather said then. —Almost gone from this world. You should not ever forget it, Finus. You may not ever see them again. He wouldn't. The big storm would wash the hotel away, his grandfather would die just two years later, and for some time his family did not go to the beach. (332)

The novel ends with Finus on the beach, indulging in the great serenity that he has always shared with Birdie, alive and dead: acceptance of the world as it's found and in the unceasing conversation between past and present. On the final page, Finus rests on the ever-changing beach and dreams of the same idyllic past that Birdie has faded into; he even becomes a physical manifestation of the cyclical nature of that ideal, gathering and eating right from the Gulf the same oysters that Pappy described to Birdie as a sign of their antediluvian innocence. The past, it seems, need be neither lost forever nor clung to with stubborn disregard for progress. Once a paradise—if only in the imaginations of those left with the fruits of its evolution—Brad Watson's South is, like the literary tradition it spawned, forever available to be sampled, but kept in its place.

Notes

1. For analysis of the relationship between the "postsouthern" and the traditional southern emphasis on sense of place, see Bone.

2. John T. Matthews offered this reading at the 2010 conference of the Society for the Study of Southern Literature.

3. Matthew Guinn published *After Southern Modernism* before Watson's novel appeared, but his reading of such contemporary southern writers as Harry Crews, Larry Brown, Dorothy Allison, and Richard Ford is based upon a similar consideration of how this generation of writers simultaneously rejects and depends upon what Noel Polk called "the southern literary pieties" of the Renascence (xi). See in particular his "Introduction."

4. The "Reading Group Guide" lacks page numbers.

5. Much of the novel, in fact, feels more like a collection of short stories whose characters and conflicts eventually merge than like a single narrative. Watson's first and third books are both short story collections, and occasionally the figures in *The Heaven of Mercury* seem trapped in a form that does not quite know what to do with them.

Works Cited

Bone, Martyn. *The Postsouthern Sense of Place in Contemporary Fiction*. Baton Rouge: Louisiana State UP, 2005. Print.

Guinn, Matthew. *After Southern Modernism: Fiction of the Contemporary South*. Jackson: UP of Mississippi, 2000. Print.

Watson, Brad. *The Heaven of Mercury*. New York: Norton, 2002. Print.

Twenty-First-Century Writers:
The Rural Southern Tradition Continues

Jean W. Cash

Since 2000, several young southerners, nearly all born after 1975 and from middle-class rural and lower-class backgrounds, have begun to publish fiction. Both portraying the areas where they were born and grew up and transcending those settings to address more universal themes, they have produced a significant body of praiseworthy work. Most were born into rural families but received the benefits of post-secondary education. Most—John Brandon, Wiley Cash, Skip Horack, Barb Johnson, Michael Farris Smith, and Jesmyn Ward—now teach at universities themselves. All, however, seem committed to presenting the working-class South with realism and empathy.

Two contributors to this collection, Joe Samuel Starnes and Peter Farris, are among these new novelists. Starnes, who has published two novels—*Calling* (2005) and *Fall Line* (2012)—now lives and works in New Jersey. Born in Alabama, he grew up in Georgia and has the same connection with the state, its inhabitants, and its native spirituality that Flannery O'Connor did, and he identifies so closely with Larry Brown that he dedicated his first novel to him. In *Calling*, two men from the South, both damaged by heredity and experience, meet on a bus traveling from Las Vegas to Salt Lake City. The journey motif provides an apt setting for this novel of personal disclosure, tragedy, and redemption.

Starnes's second novel, *Fall Line*, like the work of Tim Gautreaux and Ron Rash, laments the destruction of the agrarian South during the first half of the twentieth century. All three writers see personal greed and capi-

Joe Samuel Starnes

talistic industrialism as the principal destructive forces. Starnes has said that he wrote the novel after hearing of a minor earthquake that occurred in Lake Sinclair, a man-made lake near Milledgeville, Georgia. In both novels, Starnes has produced work worthy of attention, providing real insight into how misguided ambition and the power of money and government contribute to the loss of the agrarian South both physically and spiritually. Both works transcend their immediate settings through Starnes's characterization of men incapable of adapting to daily life. Starnes knows his home region and its people and how to write about them with admirable authority and poetic understanding.

Peter Farris, who wrote the essay on Chris Offutt for this collection, was born in Memphis, but grew up in Atlanta and earned a sociology degree from Yale. His father, John Farris, writes noir and horror fiction, but Peter himself never considered writing until after college. He says,

Peter Farris

> After graduating from college, I found myself working a day job at a bank and touring/recording with an extreme metal band (I was the vocalist). I really enjoyed writing lyrics, and because the vocals were screamed and not sung, it allowed me a little more room to experiment with phrasing, [with the] lyrics [being] more abstract prose as opposed to a sing-song verse/chorus type of structure. Those pieces started to get longer, and I found my writing inching toward short fiction without really knowing it. (personal e-mail, "Re: your background")

When he asked his father about what to read, John Farris recommended Cormac McCarthy's *Blood Meridian* (1985), Don Delillo's *White Noise* (1985), and Barry Hannah's *Yonder Stands Your Orphan* (2001). He had already begun to read fiction by Larry Brown. Of his connection with Rough South writers, Farris says, "I learned from those authors that I could write about 'home' using simple language, and even if I was a college grad from the suburbs, there was plenty to intuit about my surroundings. For example, I can recall moments from working at the bank, subtle encounters that set off my imagination" (personal e-mail, "Re: your background").

Farris published a novel, *Last Call for the Living*, in 2012. Set in present-day rural Georgia, it's the intermingled tale of two men who come together because of a bank robbery gone wrong. Charlie Colquitt is a college student and part-time bank teller. Hobe Hicklin, recently released from jail, is a career criminal. The interaction between the two reveals Farris's ability to create believable characters who, in spite of their inherent weaknesses, appeal to readers. His attitude toward them is never patronizing. Farris also writes in a style characterized by both realism and lyricism. His next novel will be called "Ghosts in the Fields." According to Farris, "It's set in south Georgia, and about a teenage prostitute who finds sanctuary with an eccentric bootlegger" (personal e-mail, "Re: *Last Call*").

At least two women have joined the ranks of Rough South writers in the current century. One of them, Barb Johnson, probably most resembles writers like Larry Brown, William Gay, and Dorothy Allison, who grew up in impoverished families and worked various trades before becoming writers. Johnson was born in Lake Charles, Louisiana, but has lived more than thirty years in New Orleans. Of her background and the focus of her writing, she has said,

Barb Johnson

Here's a thing about the roughness of the Rough South: there are lots of poor and uneducated people in America, though we mostly associate them with the South. I often hear them described as "working class." That's a sweet euphemism meant, I suppose, to spare poor folks' feelings. It's like no one in America wants to say there's a lower class, but there is one. Same thing with "working poor"—those are the noble poor people; you can tell because there's "work" in their label. Screw that. Being poor and working isn't more noble than being poor and not knowing how to get or keep a job because you've never known anyone who worked for any amount of real time or because the schools you went to let you think you were an honor roll student when it turns out you can barely read and write and you don't even know it, but you do understand that the way to be on the honor roll is to be well-behaved and not cause any trouble. (personal e-mail, "Re: Interview")

After Johnson earned a bachelor's degree in English at the University of New Orleans in the early 1980s, she taught five years in an inner-city high school, then turned to carpentry. "I did what all English majors do," she joked. "I became a carpenter" ("Barb Johnson"). In 2004, at the age of forty-seven, Johnson entered the MFA program at UNO and was studying there when Hurricanes Katrina and Rita wiped out her carpentry shop. "I was a carpenter right up until [the] storm . . . trashed my shop. It was somewhat fortuitous. It's not like it was fun right away, don't get me wrong. It forced me to choose" ("Barb Johnson"). Johnson says that the loss of her shop and the physical injuries she suffered as a carpenter helped her decide to return to school and become a full-time writer.

Like Larry Brown, when he audited a creative writing course at the University of Mississippi in 1983, Johnson was immediately identified at UNO as a writer of considerable talent. She won several awards at UNO and published a collection of short stories, *More of This World or Maybe Another*, in 2009. Most significant for her financially was winning the $50,000 Gift of Freedom Award from the Room of Her Own Foundation in 2009. Johnson now directs UNO's Creative Writing Workshop—Low Residency program and is working on more short stories, essays, and a novel ("Barb Johnson").

The interconnected stories in *More of This World or Maybe Another* concern young people who live in New Orleans, and Johnson's treatment of them makes her unique among Rough South writers. Clearly, Johnson knows people like them. Through the nine stories in the collection, she deals with both their often unruly lives and their desire to rise above what they were born into. The need for connection and love is important to all of them. Central to several stories is Delia, who ultimately realizes her sexual attraction to women. Johnson is able to humanize Delia and her long-time partner Maggie in a way that helps us understand that love is love, regardless of the partnering. She is also sympathetic to her male characters, whose hideous lives as children impede their progress toward becoming viable adults. Though all of Johnson's characters are imperfect, her use of clear, direct, and often poetic language draws from us sympathy for them and recognition of our own shortcomings.

Of young southern writers who began their careers after 2000, Jesmyn Ward has received the most attention. She started her writing career in 2008 with the publication of *Where the Line Bleeds*. Though the novel, set in her native Mississippi, received little attention in the press, it won the 2009 Black Caucus of the American Library Association Honor Award. It was also an *Essence* book club selection and a finalist for two other awards, the Virginia Commonwealth University Cabell First Novelist Award and the Hurston/Wright Legacy Award.

Salvage the Bones (2011), Ward's second novel, won international acclaim, particularly after it won the National Book Award. On the basis of her success with this novel, Ward became the John and Renee Grisham Writer in Residence at the University of Mississippi for the 2010–2011 academic year. Currently Stokes Fellow of Creative Writing at the University of South Alabama, Ward specializes in creative nonfiction and literary fiction. Her most recent book, *Men We Reaped*, a memoir based on the plight of young black men in the rural South, appeared in September 2013.

Jesmyn Ward

Ward's background is distinctly Rough South. She was born and grew up in DeLisle, Mississippi, a rural community roughly thirty miles west of Biloxi. Her mother worked as a maid for a white family that paid Jesmyn's tuition at a private school. Black students had bullied her in her former public school, but her treatment at the white school was not much better. Her parents, however, wanted her to have advantages denied them. Gladly leaving rural Mississippi behind her, Ward went to Stanford, where she earned a BA in English and an MA in communication.

Ward has said that, in spite of her parents encouraging her to enter a profession, she committed herself to becoming a writer when her younger brother died in a hit-and-run car accident: "It changed everything for me; I wish I could express it without using profanity. Losing someone that close in that way, I realized, 'F——— it. What can I do to give my life meaning?' And I thought, 'Writing'" (Brockes). Of the focus for her writing, Ward has said, "The stories I write are particular to my community and my people, which means the details are particular to our circumstances, but the larger story of the survivor, the *savage*, is essentially a universal human one" ("Jesmyn Ward on 'Salvage the Bones'").

Ward earned an MFA in creative writing at the University of Michigan in 2005. Unable to find a job after graduation but still committed to writing, she held low-paying jobs while she tried to publish her first book. She was at home with her family in DeLisle when Hurricane Katrina hit in 2005. Her family barely managed to survive. Returning to Michigan after the storm, Ward felt stymied as a writer until one of her professors told her that she should write about the hurricane, as that was her story ("Hurricane Katrina"). Ward says, "Maybe it was time and distance that allowed me enough space so that I could access my creativity and funnel something of my experience of living through a category five hurricane into fiction" ("Hurricane Katrina"). Ward has also said that she needed to write about Katrina because she was "angry at the people who blamed survivors for staying and for choosing to return to the Mississippi Gulf Coast after the storm. Finally, I wrote about the storm because I was dissatisfied with the way it had receded from the public consciousness" ("Jesmyn Ward on 'Salvage the Bones'").

The Batiste family in *Salvage the Bones* prepares for and lives through the onslaught of the hurricane, but their experience during Katrina actually serves as only a backdrop for the family's poignant story. *Salvage the Bones* is a story of life in the Rough South. The family lives in impoverished circumstances in a south Mississippi community similar to the one in which Ward and her family lived. The family is African American, but Ward's book is in no way a novel about race. Her characters are human beings living with loss, lack of money, and the desire to move ahead. In this respect, Ward's treatment of them is like that of Larry Brown, who always asserts the simple humanity of his lower-class characters; he makes clear that they share problems common to all.

Skip Horack, whose background places him among the educated writers of the rural South, was born and grew up in Louisiana and spent five years as a young man in Florida, earning both undergraduate and law degrees at Florida State University. Horack has published two books, both set in the Deep South: *The Southern Cross* (2009), a collection of short stories, and *The Eden Hunter* (2010), a novel.

Skip Horack

Horack explains, "I grew up in Louisiana and spent about five years in North Florida as well, and so the Gulf Coast forests are very special to me both as a writer and a person" ("An Interview with Skip Horack"). Horack describes his younger self as "a dreamer [who] liked to wander around in the woods" ("The Southern Cross"). Of his rural background he has said, "I like to hunt and fish, and growing up in Covington, we lived on a good-sized piece of land out in the country where we had cattle, sheep, chickens" ("A Chat with Skip").

Horack has much in common with another southern writer, one of huge popular fame, Mississippian John Grisham. Like Grisham, Horack first studied law and spent several years as "a bottom-of-the-ladder attorney" in Baton Rouge ("The Southern Cross"). He began to write and submit stories for publication during those years, stories that grew out of his travel as a specialist in healthcare law: "I spent a lot of time on the road, visiting small towns in every part of the state and speaking with all sorts of interesting people. . . . [W]hat was helpful and inspiring was simply getting to meet so many folks and hear so many voices" ("The Southern Cross").

Horack left the law firm in Baton Rouge when he became a Wallace Stegner Fellow at Stanford, where he was also Jones Lecturer in Creative Writing. He took part in workshops with Tobias Wolff, John L'Heureux, Elizabeth Tallent, and Colm Toibin. He also studied in the Creative Writing Workshop—Low Residency program at the University of New Orleans and is now assistant professor in the Department of English at Auburn University. Horack is currently working on a novel "about a guy who gets injured while working on an oil rig in the Gulf of Mexico, then heads for California to meet a relative he never knew he had" ("An Interview with Skip Horack").

Stories in *The Southern Cross*, which received the Bread Loaf Writers' Conference 2008 Bakeless Fiction Prize and was nominated for a number of other awards, feature a wide variety of southern characters of varying classes, ages, and races. Horack employs a seasonal structure in the collection, beginning with spring and ending with winter. The year is 2005, and Hurricanes Katrina and Rita are vital to several stories. Horack says, "I was living in Baton Rouge at the time, and after that hurricane season, it was impossible to accurately write about the region without acknowledging that these disasters had occurred" ("The Southern Cross"). Several stories are flash fiction. "The Rapture" features a young pole dancer who solicits a ride home with a fundamentalist preacher who rants against the evils of the flesh, even as the girl arouses him sexually. Dropping her off at her home, he asks her whether "there [is] anything at all that you would like to pray for." She replies, "I'll finish you off for fifty bucks. Amen" (117), sending him into a frenzy.

Horack's *The Eden Hunter* presents a much earlier Rough South. In this work of historical fiction, set in Florida in the early eighteenth century, Horack bravely creates Kau, a pygmy from Africa, brought to Florida and sold into slavery. He presents a South inhabited by Native Americans, runaway slaves, and corrupt whites. The novel shows the violence of the then-frontier in a style somewhat reminiscent of Cormac McCarthy's *Blood Meridian*. Horack's stories and this novel show him to be a writer of great promise.

John Brandon is another new Rough South writer. Brandon was born in Bradenton, Florida, and moved to New Port Richey before he was five. His background is middle-class; his father worked at a power plant in New Port Richey. Brandon attended public schools there, graduating from River Ridge High School, where he became a serious reader from the eleventh grade forward. He especially liked Jack Kerouac and Ernest Hemingway: "I was very vulnerable to them because I had this feeling that I wanted something else. To see other things." He says he "had very good memories of my childhood and growing up in New Port Richey" (Napper). He has described similarities between Pasco County and the fictionalized counterpart he created in his second novel, *Citrus County* (2011):

> The similarities are the physical setting, all the sinkholes and strip malls, and maybe that it was hard to know what to do as an adolescent. You could play sports or else go to church or else roam about vandalizing things. There were old people everywhere. And the place had no identity. It was a suburb because it was way too far from Tampa for that. It wasn't rural because that implies some kind of farming or ranching. It certainly wasn't urban. No beach or amusement park or university. Nobody had much money but nobody was going to starve. Maybe that's the similarity, the feeling of being in a lost pocket of the country at a time when you're personally lost. ("Meet John Brandon")

After high school, Brandon earned at BA in English from the University of Florida and an MA in fiction writing from Washington University in St. Louis. He married a traveling nurse and moved with her throughout the South and as far afield as Oregon and New Mexico. He has said that he "tagged" along with her and took temporary jobs that left him the freedom he needed to write. He wrote and published a few stories and wrote a first novel that met only rejection. His first published novel, *Arkansas* (2008), caught the attention of Barry Hannah at the University of Mississippi, who invited him to Ole Miss as the John and Renee Grisham Writer-in-Residence for the 2009–2010 academic year. Brandon stayed another year as a stand-in for Hannah, who died in the spring of 2010. He published *Citrus County* the following year and a third novel, *A Million Heavens*, set in New Mexico, in 2012. He is currently assistant professor of creative writing at Hamline University in Saint Paul, Minnesota.

In several pivotal ways, Brandon is different from the other writers in this collection. The first difference obviously evolves from where he grew up: in north central Florida, which, as Brandon describes it above, is not really either

John Brandon

particularly southern or rural. Because he grew up in Florida, Brandon does not have that deep sense of the South as a distinct entity that characterizes the work of so many other southern writers. His fiction also seems more interior than exterior—physical location is far less important than the psychology of the characters he creates.

Another difference between Brandon and other rural South writers is that he writes mainly about adolescent characters struggling to find their way in a disturbing universe. Toby, in *Citrus County*, is a kind of rural, modern-day Holden Caulfield—a victim of modern family disintegration and of his own uncontrollable urges. One might even suggest that Brandon writes young adult fiction, for certainly his young characters would be easy for high school students to identify with.

His first novel, *Arkansas*, features three young characters, all highly intelligent—which Brandon suggests may be part of the problem. As his title reveals, the setting of the novel is Arkansas, both rural and urban, where the male characters drift into a career as drug runners for a notorious dealer and his henchman. The setting matters less than the action-filled plot, but Brandon's empathy and expertise with language elevate the novel almost to the level of tragedy.

Toby, the central character of *Citrus County*, is also a highly intelligent middle-school student. His home life is horrific. He lives with a befuddled uncle who spends most of his time smoking exotic concoctions (one made from hemlock), and either ignores Toby or regales him with rants about the meaninglessness of life. Having discovered an underground bunker that becomes a kind of negative haven for him, Toby kidnaps Kaley, the four-year-old sister of a female classmate. He has little awareness of why he has taken the child, but no intention of harming her. The plot unfolds with considerable complication and a somewhat contrived conclusion, but like *Arkansas*, the book shows promise.

Brandon's third novel, *A Million Heavens*, lies outside the parameters of this study, but reviewer Charles Bock applauds Brandon's success in combining themes similar to those of his earlier novels with elements of magical realism: "The book's gamble is that its panoply of fractured lives, mundane problems and simmering hopes will, when sprinkled with fairy dust, give rise to intersecting moments of transcendence."

North Carolina native Wiley Cash (no relation), contrasts sharply with John Brandon. If Brandon is more interested in internal than external spaces, Cash is a holdover, the likes of McCarthy, Brown, Rash, and Gautreaux, who have deep allegiance to their home regions. Cash, who was born and grew up in Gastonia, North Carolina, in the novel *A Land More Kind Than*

Home (2012) portrays the culture of that area with both resonance and reverence. Even the title of the novel has North Carolina roots: Thomas Wolfe's *You Can't Go Home Again* (1940). Cash has said, "I deeply love my native state of North Carolina, especially its mountains. I hope my love for this region is evident in *A Land More Kind Than Home*'s portrayal of western North Carolina's people, culture and religious faith" ("An interview with Wiley Cash").

Wiley Cash

After high school in Gastonia, Cash earned a BA in literature from the University of North Carolina-Asheville and an MA from the University of North Carolina-Greensboro. He earned a PhD in English from the University of Louisiana-Lafayette, where he studied under Ernest J. Gaines and Reggie Scott Young. Cash has published short stories and earned several grants and fellowships. He wrote the story that ultimately became *A Land More Kind Than Home* while at ULL. He says the idea for Christopher's death in the novel came from Young, who "brought in a news story about a young African American boy with autism who was smothered during a church healing in a storefront church on Chicago's South Side" ("Many Souths").

In 2008, Cash joined the English faculty at Bethany College in Bethany, West Virginia, but the success of his novel enabled him to leave teaching there. He still lives in West Virginia and is now on the faculty of the Low-Residency MFA Program in Fiction and Nonfiction Writing at Southern New Hampshire University. In early 2014, Cash published a second novel, *This Dark Road to Mercy*, which he says "is set in my hometown of Gastonia, North Carolina, and it's about a washed-up minor league baseball player who kidnaps his two daughters from a foster home and goes on the run" ("An interview with Wiley Cash").

A Land More Kind Than Home attracted several reviews, including that of Steve Yarbrough in the *Washington Post*, where Yarbrough praised Cash's command of the "rhythms of Appalachian speech." One of the novel's greatest strengths is Cash's effective use of point of view. Three characters serve as centers of consciousness in the novel. Cash has said that he used multiple narrators because of the many storytellers among his family and friends, and because he admires novels like William Faulkner's *As I Lay Dying* (1930),

Gaines's *A Gathering of Old Men* (1983), and Wolfe's *The Lost Boy* (1937) ("Many Souths").

The novel also has strong characterization. Jess Hall, an updated Scout from *To Kill a Mockingbird* (1960), is a good bit less stereotypical than Harper Lee's young girl. Miss Adelaide is reminiscent of Granny Rowe in Lee Smith's *Fair and Tender Ladies* (1988), but less mythical than her literary ancestor. The sheriff shares qualities with Cormac McCarthy's Ed Tom Bell in *No Country for Old Men* (2005), but in some ways is more resilient. Carson Chambliss shares the evil of other contemporary literary avatars, including Anton Chigurh from *No Country for Old Men* and Wade Jones from Larry Brown's *Joe* (1991), but Chambliss is worse because he's supposed to be a man of God. As Yarbrough writes, "Cash is ultimately interested in how unscrupulous individuals can bend decent people to their own dark ends, often by invoking the name of God." Cash's study of high melodrama, human good, and inhuman evil holds out the promise of other fine fiction from him.

The most recent entry into this group of Deep South writers is Michael Farris Smith, an associate professor of English at the Mississippi University for Women. His dystopian novel *Rivers* (2013), set on the Gulf Coast of Mississippi, presents a dramatic vision of what happens when that area, post-Katrina, becomes totally hurricane-ridden. Smith has previously published short stories and twice been nominated for the Pushcart Prize. He won the 2003 *Transatlantic Review* Award (for his early stories), a 2007 Alabama Arts Council Fellowship Award (for the first chapter of his highly-praised 2011 novella, *The Hands of Strangers*), and the 2010 Mississippi Arts Commission Literary Arts (for the first thirty pages of what would become *Rivers*).

A native of south Mississippi, Smith knows the landscape well. He was born in McComb, Mississippi, but moved often because his father was a Southern Baptist preacher. The family settled in Magnolia when Smith was ten and stayed there until he graduated from high school. He has said of those years:

> Life in Magnolia was almost perfect for a kid. We had six or eight kids in
> our neighborhood. A ballpark three blocks away. Basketball courts across
> the street from my backyard. Clumps of woods and hidden little streams
> scattered around. We always had a ballgame going on. We always had a gang
> of bicycles. And we were fortunate to be set free to roam. Our parents never
> worried about us being out and about and many summer evenings, my dad
> would come outside at twilight and if he didn't see us he would whistle and
> there we came. I was never where I couldn't hear that whistle. (personal e-
> mail, "Re: Your life")

Smith graduated from Mississippi State University and after college spent several years in France and Switzerland before returning to Mississippi and the University of Southern Mississippi, where he earned a PhD.

Smith was living in Alabama when Katrina hit the Gulf Coast, but members of his extended family in southern Mississippi lived through the storm. During a radio interview in March 2013, Smith spoke of his desire to write about Katrina: "For a couple of years, I wanted to write a post-Katrina novel, but I kept starting and stopping and it wasn't work-

Michael Farris Smith

ing. . . . I didn't like fabricating . . . that heartbreak. . . . I kept thinking about it and I don't know why I thought of it this way, but one day I just imagined, 'What if we just jacked Katrina up about fifty times over and what if for a couple or even five or even six or seven or eight years the Gulf Coast was just one Katrina after another?'" ("Dialogue").

Rivers is certainly an apocalyptic novel, one in some ways superior to McCarthy's *The Road* (2006). Smith makes clear the cause of Gulf Coast ruin: post-Katrina changes in weather and climate patterns. Smith's characterization is also superior to McCarthy's. His characters, rather than allegorical representations, are real and suffer as they face the kind of natural horror that most of us can only imagine. His central character, Cohen, is the sort of strong, individualistic American most of us admire. After the government establishes the Line, an arbitrary barrier beyond which nobody can legally live, Cohen realizes that staying will be futile. But he refuses to leave his home, where his family has lived for generations and where he had planned to follow that tradition with his own wife and child.

Smith's novel, of necessity, features high melodrama; however, *Rivers* is both gripping and believable. The people who remain in the area are simple victims with no means of escape, stubborn individualists like Cohen, or power-hungry and evil like the maniacal Aggie, a would-be despot who seeks to create his own oligarchy. In FEMA trailers left over from Katrina, he sets up a miniature community with female survivors of the deluge. He and his sidekick set out to impregnate the women, seeking to build a private community of enslaved survivors.

Smith also introduces greed as a theme in his novel. Characters like Charlie look to make a killing by selling black-market goods to the hapless souls who remain below the Line. Charlie and some of these people—as well as others who have deliberately sneaked into the area—seek buried treasure, money stashed, they think, by the owners of ruined Gulf Coast casinos. The most compelling part of the novel, however, involves Cohen's rescue of three young people who have unwittingly become part of Aggie's tribe: two brothers, Evan and Brisco, and a young woman, Mariposa, from New Orleans. Overall, Smith has created in *Rivers* a novel both dramatic and touching, one that deals with human disaster and degradation, the human need for connection, and the possibility for rejuvenation, even under the most horrific circumstances.

Clearly, novels that address southern characters in southern scenes will continue to be written, whether of the Rough South variety from writers like Barb Johnson or from writers like Ward, Horack, Brandon, Cash, and Smith, who grew up in and continue to celebrate other Souths and their many and varied inhabitants.

Works Cited and Consulted

Bock, Charles. "Desert Vigil / 'A Million Heavens,' by John Brandon." Rev. of *A Million Heavens*, by John Brandon. *Nytimes.com*. *New York Times*, 3 Aug. 2012. Web. 17 June 2013.

Brandon, John. *Arkansas*. San Francisco: McSweeney's, 2009. Print.

———. *Citrus County*. San Francisco: McSweeney's, 2010. Print.

———. "Meet John Brandon, Author of Citrus County." Interview by Sean Ennis. *southernlitreview.com*. *Southern Literary Review*, 3 Nov. 2010. Web. 15 July 2013.

Brockes, Emma. "A Real-Life Experience of Hurricane Katrina Inspired a Savagely Written Novel About Racism in the US South." *smh.com.au*. *Sydney Morning Herald*, 21 Apr. 2012. Web. 6 June 2013.

Cash, Jean W. "*Fall Line*, by Joe Samuel Starnes." Rev. of *Fall Line*, by Joe Samuel Starnes. *Studies in American Culture* 35.1 (2012): 172–75. Print.

Cash, Wiley. "An interview with Wiley Cash." Interview by Lisa Guidarini. *bookbrowse.com*. Book Browse, Apr. 2012. Web. 15 July 2013.

———. *A Land More Kind Than Home*. New York: Morrow, 2012. Print.

———. "Many Souths: An Interview with Wiley Cash." Interview by Brad Wetherell. *fictionwritersreview.com*. *Fiction Writers Review*, 17 Apr. 2012. Web. 15 July 2013.

———. "Why I Write About Home." *wileycash.com*. Wiley Cash, n.d. Web. 18 June 2013.

Childers, Doug. "Fiction Review: *A Land More Kind Than Home*." Rev. of *A Land More Kind Than Home*, by Wiley Cash. *timesdispatch.com*. *Richmond Times-Dispatch*, 15 Apr. 2012. Web. 15 July 2013.

Farris, Peter. *Last Call for the Living*. New York: Forge, 2013. Print.

———. "Re: *Last Call for the Living*." Message to the author. 10 May 2013. E-mail.

———. "Re: Your Background as a Writer." Message to the author. 13 May 2013. E-mail.

Horack, Skip. "A Chat with Skip." *turnrowbooks.typepad.com*. Rhythm and Books, 4 Dec. 2009. Web. 30 Apr. 2013.

———. *The Eden Hunter*. Berkeley: Counterpoint, 2010. Print.

———. "An Interview with Skip Horack." Interview by Paul Toutonghi. *bookslut.com*. Bookslut, Oct. 2010. Web. 10 Apr. 2013.

———. *The Southern Cross*. New York: Mariner, 2009. Print.

———. "The Southern Cross: Skip Horack on his Award-Winning, Debut Collection." Interview by Jessica Pitchford. *southeastreview.org*. Southeast Review, 18 Sept. 2009. Web. 30 Apr. 2013.

Johnson, Barb. "Barb Johnson: 'I did what all English majors do: I became a carpenter.'" Interview by Noah Bonaparte Pais. *bestofneworleans.com*. Gambit, 21 Oct. 2009. Web. 7 May 2013.

———. *More of This World or Maybe Another*. New York: Harper, 2009. Print.

———. "Re: Interview." Message to the author. 1 July 2013. E-mail.

———. "Re: *More of This World or Maybe Another*." Message to the author. 6 June 2013. E-mail.

———. "Re: Your Career as a Writer." Message to the author. 30 June 2013. E-mail.

"Last Call for the Living by Peter Farris—Review." Rev. of *Last Call for the Living*, by Peter Farris. *spinetinglermag.com*. Spinetingler Magazine, 12 June 2012. Web. 7 July 2013.

Napper, Robert. "Acclaimed Author John Brandon Got His Start in New Port Richey." *tampabay .com*. Tampa Bay Times, 21 May 2011. Web. 18 June 2013.

"The Rumpus Book Club Interviews John Brandon." *therumpus.net*. Rumpus, 19 June 2010. Web. 18 June 2013.

Smith, Michael Farris. "Dialogue." *thisisrealmedia.com*. Real Media, 28 Mar. 2013. Web. 24 June 2013.

———. "Re: Your Life and Career." Message to the author. 20 June 2013. E-mail.

———. *Rivers*. New York: Simon & Schuster, 2013. Print.

Starnes, Joe Samuel. *Calling*. Lookout Mountain: Jefferson, 2005. Print.

———. *Fall Line*. Montgomery: NewSouth, 2011. Print.

Ward, Jesmyn. "Hurricane Katrina Troubles and Inspires National Book Award-winning Author Jesmyn Ward." Interview by Tarra Gaines. *houston.culturemap.com*. CultureMap Houston, 24 Mar. 2013. Web. 6 June 2013.

———. "Jesmyn Ward on 'Salvage the Bones.'" Interview by Elizabeth Hoover. *theparisreview.org .Paris Review*, 30 Aug. 2011. Web. 6 June 2013.

———. *Salvage the Bones*. New York: Bloomsburg, 2011. Print.

Yarbrough, Steve. "Wiley Cash's 'A Land More Kind Than Home.'" Rev. of *A Land More Kind Than Home* by Wiley Cash. *washingtonpost.com*. Washington Post, 8 May 2012. Web. 2 July 2013.

Trash or Treasure?
Images of the Hardscrabble South
in Twenty-First-Century Film
Richard Gaughran

> [T]he camera seems to me, next to unassisted and weaponless conscious-
> ness, the central instrument of our time; and [that] is why . . . I feel such rage
> at its misuse.
> —James Agee, *Let Us Now Praise Famous Men*

Divisive images of the American South have appeared throughout the history of film. D. W. Griffith's *The Birth of a Nation* (1915)—controversial for
its racism, but important for its narrative innovations within an epic context—presented a decidedly partisan view of life in the South. The film might
have been "like history written with lightning," in Woodrow Wilson's famous
phrase, but the lightning was far from impartial. The film's rabid fear of mis-
cegenation and its segregation of characters by skin color and culture established a pattern of argument. Griffith, drawing on Thomas Dixon's novel *The
Clansman* (1914), sternly divided not only black from white, but also "good"
blacks from "bad," those who stayed loyal to their white "superiors" from "uppity" ones who supposedly lacked the cultural refinement and strength of
character required to advance civilization.

Film has been arguing with itself ever since, notably about how to portray the southerner—particularly the poor southerner. Twenty-four years
after Griffith's film came another iconic American movie, Victor Fleming's *Gone with the Wind* (1939). A nostalgic melodrama, its images are less
overtly provocative and revolting than those in Griffith's film, but they are
no less divisive. The slaves (after the war, the servants) at the O'Hara plantation seem eager to maintain the very system that subjugates them. These
are the "good" blacks, but there are others: the "ungrateful" ones who don't

know "their place." Furthermore, besides the noble whites—the O'Haras, the Wilkeses, others of their class—poor whites linger in the background, filling empty spaces on the screen and, during the war, mostly serving as cannon fodder. There are also the "white trash" Slatterys and the bands that Rhett Butler (Clark Gable) calls "scavengers," who loot Atlanta after Sherman burns it. Outside the plantation is a shantytown where the "riff-raff" (Rhett's term again) live. Mostly, however, *Gone with the Wind* is a Technicolor pageant in which the poor, whether black or white, are little more than extras in thrall to well-heeled whites and melodramatic spectacle.

Film's one-sided or indifferent depiction of the poor southerner finds its corollary—in many cases its source—in literature of or about the South. Pat Conroy has famously quoted his mother as saying, "All Southern literature can be summed up in these words: 'On the night the hogs ate Willie, Mama died when she heard what Daddy did to Sister.'" Whether Mrs. Conroy was humorously dismissing southern literature or celebrating its grotesque heritage, the images the remark conjures do indeed appear in literature of the South. As Erik Bledsoe's "The Rise of Southern Redneck and White Trash Writers" demonstrates, poor southerners, whether pathetic or villainous, have long been stock characters in fiction, and many of the works that feature them became sources for films like *The Birth of a Nation* and *Gone with the Wind*.

So as not to overgeneralize, it's also necessary to point out that there have been benign, even sympathetic films on the subject. Jean Renoir's *The Southerner* (1945) pays tribute to the endurance and perseverance of the struggling poor, showing more or less what *The Grapes of Wrath* (1940) would have been if the Joads had not ridden off to pick peaches in California. And once the cracks widened in the monolithic Hollywood studio system, making more room for independent productions, fresh depictions appeared, among them Joseph Anthony's *Tomorrow* (1972), based on the William Faulkner story of the same name (1940). Robert Duvall's Jackson Fentry, possibly an inspiration for Billy Bob Thornton's character in *Sling Blade* (1996), is uneducated and barely articulate, but his inner strength and selfless love come to the fore in this return to the Byron Bunch-Lena Grove story from *Light in August* (1932). Horton Foote, *Tomorrow*'s screenwriter, said in an interview that he wanted to counter the stereotype of the South as a venue for rape and lynching.[1]

And yet, stereotypes stubbornly hold. John Boorman's *Deliverance* (1972), based on the James Dickey novel (1970), took root in the popular consciousness for its depiction of lawless grotesques who inhabit the backcountry and threaten visitors from the suburbs. To be sure, the film does include startling violence perpetrated against a canoeing foursome by denizens of the back-woods. But those weekend survivalists surface as the real villains, first for their condescension—Bobby (Ned Beatty) says when he first sees the idiot Lonnie (Billy Redden), "Genetic deficiency; ain't that pitiful?"—and later for their ignorance and weakness of character. Yet, the image of forced sodomy is more graphic and hard to forget than the pusillanimity of the relatively affluent weekenders, the ones who should be seared into our memories as the true natural-born killers. Likewise, the idiot-savant banjo-picker arguably stays with us longer than his music, sustaining the stereotype of the inbred redneck.

In 2010, however, when director Debra Granik adapted Daniel Woodrell's *Winter's Bone* (2006), she consciously returned to and revised that stereo-typical image. Granik's film, along with others that have arisen in the new century, suggests that a new reading of the hardscrabble South is emerging. As writers like Dorothy Allison have done in print, filmmakers are attempting to humanize characters without smoothing out their rough surfaces. Allison has said of her work, particularly *Bastard out of Carolina* (1992), that she has consciously attempted to combat the stereotype:

> I show you my aunts in their drunken rages, my uncles in their meanness. And that's exactly who we are said to be. That's what white trash is all about. We're all supposed to be drunks standing in our yards with our broken-down cars and our dirty babies. Some of that stuff is true. But to write about it I had to find a way to pull the reader in and show you those people as larger than that contemptible myth. And show you why those men drink, why those women hate themselves and get old and can't protect themselves or their children. Show you human beings instead of fold-up, mean, cardboard figures. (qtd. in Bledsoe 87)

The new century's filmmakers attempt much the same in key films portraying the Rough South. Many of these productions originate from young, independent filmmakers often operating on small budgets: the aforementioned Granik; David Gordon Green, director of *George Washington* (2000) and *Joe* (2013), adapted from the Larry Brown novel (1991); Green's fellow Arkansan Jeff Nichols, director of *Shotgun Stories* (2007), *Take Shelter* (2011), and *Mud* (2012); and Scott Teems, director of *That Evening Sun* (2009), based on the William Gay short story (2000). Even some outsiders—among them Granik, an alumna of New York University's film school—have contributed to this new wave of films about the South: *Searching for the Wrong-Eyed Jesus* (2003) is the work of British documentarian Andrew Douglas; *The Wild and*

Wonderful Whites of West Virginia (2009) is the work of New York native Julien Nitzberg; *Beasts of the Southern Wild* (2012) is that of another New Yorker, Benh Zeitlin.

The trend outlined by these and other filmmakers suggests that a conscious revision is underway: an attempt to bring the rough characters to the fore, to rescue them from their fates as cinematic extras and give them their own voices; to reexamine the conditions that give rise to "redneck," "hillbilly," and "white trash" stereotypes; and not to condescend to but reclaim dignity and humanity for southern characters not likely to enter Tara or Twelve Oaks through anything but the back door. The films in this group, in a move toward verisimilitude, are shot on location and often employ local amateur actors or even non-actors in key roles. The fact that young filmmakers are spearheading this reassessment in itself represents a break from the past. Curiously, the films also often feature children or adolescents as main characters, again suggesting a future promise instead of a backward glance. A closer look at two of the films in this category—one from the beginning of the new century, one from the end of its first decade—reveals some of the forms this revisionist project has taken.

David Gordon Green was just twenty-five when he directed *George Washington*, set in small-town North Carolina. The film is contemplative and lyrical, both modest in its scope and ambitious in its way of letting the particular speak for the universal. Its camera movement and tone show the influence of Terence Malick, and the first sounds we hear are from young Nasia's (Candace Evanofski) voiceover, evoking Linda (Linda Manz) from *Days of Heaven* (1978), or Holly (Sissy Spacek) from *Badlands* (1973). Nasia's words, like the images that accompany them, strike viewers at first as mysterious and disjointed, but careful attention shows that she quietly provides both context and contrast. She begins, "They used to get around, walkin' around, lookin' at stuff. They used to try to find clues to all the mysteries and mistakes God had made." "They" are Nasia's friends George Richardson (Donald Holden), Vernon (Damien Jewan Lee), Buddy (Curtis Cotton III), and Sonya (Rachael Handy). The adolescents trek through a broken neighborhood as Nasia narrates. Buildings are in ruins; roofs have collapsed, and graffiti-splashed walls demarcate abandoned buildings where only broken, rotting furniture remains. The four curious children investigate. One picks up a book—seemingly an abandoned diary—from a floor. Sonya lifts a ragged doll from a nail on a wall. Mysteries and mistakes.

Nasia's next words should be hopeful, but her tone is mournful, suggesting loss: "My friend George said that he was gonna live to be a hundred years old. He said that he was gonna be the president of the United States. I wanted to see him lead a parade and wave a flag on the Fourth of July. He just wanted greatness." We hear a clue to the film's strange title. Soon, we will learn about the title character's medical condition: His skull has never properly fused together, leaving him vulnerable to injury. He therefore wears protective headgear, often an old football helmet.

The adolescents' youth and hopefulness contrast with the negative outlooks of the film's struggling adults, whose world Nasia's voiceover next introduces. As she speaks, we watch as George's uncle Damascus (Eddie Rouse) works at a railway yard. Stripped to the waist and sweating, he struggles to de-couple two cars as Nasia says, "The grown-ups in my town, they were never kids like me and my friends. They had worked in wars and built machines. It was hard for them to find their peace. Don't you know how that feels?" She pauses as Damascus struggles at his job, then returns to her more immediate world: "I like to go to beautiful places . . . where there's waterfalls and empty fields. Just places that are nice and calm and quiet." The low-angle camera frames the branches and leaves of young trees as Nasia speaks of beautiful places; it then cuts to the railroad tracks, a reminder of the ominous machine in the garden. Next we see the children at play in this despoiled natural setting. There's a ripped-up couch in "the beautiful place," as well as other rubbish. But the children have their animals. George plays with a frog, while Nasia arrives with her cousin's cat. We'll soon hear about George's dog, a flea-bitten mutt he found sitting in feces. "It didn't have anywhere to go, no one to love it," Nasia says, speaking of the same dog that Damascus will later kill when it reminds him of a childhood trauma.

These and other references to animals figure prominently in the film and, coupled with those from other films, represent a trend in this southern new wave, suggesting that reconnection to the natural world can provide a modicum of redemption and the inner peace that Nasia says is so hard for some to find. It's a major theme in both *Winter's Bone* and *Beasts of the Southern Wild*, a film whose title refers to both humans and animals and in which the child narrator and protagonist, Hushpuppy (Quvenzhané Wallis), holds crabs and the like to her ear, eager, it seems, to know what they have to say. Jim White also expresses this connection in the idiosyncratic documentary *Searching for the Wrong-Eyed Jesus* when he says—while driving through a Southern landscape he views with new eyes—"See that swamp there? I couldn't see the beauty in it." In *George Washington*, the camera later shows us George and Buddy in the pew of a church to which they have inexplicably and without comment brought a live ferret—as though a ferret in church is the most natural thing in the world.

The adolescent protagonists of *George Washington* carry within them the potential for redemption. Such is the suggestion of the film's lyricism: the way the camera lingers on certain images: the churchly organ of the score that flavors certain sequences; the open professions of love uttered by these naïfs amid their awareness of brokenness and loss. To be sure, the young characters exhibit confusion, sometimes in humorous ways. Nasia's diction and delivery, for instance, comically mimic those of someone far older, especially when she explains that she broke up with Buddy because he acts like a "little kid," and that she is now seeking someone more mature. The humor extends to George's ridiculous superhero outfit, his directing traffic, his pronouncements about heroism: "I think a hero should be wise, strong, and very talented. They should also have a list of dangerous and poisonous things."

This adolescent confusion also manifests itself in alarming ways, most notably in the central scene of the film: the accidental death of Buddy after he cracks his skull on a bathroom floor, the result of the friends' roughhousing. The fearful children attempt to conceal the body, and Sonya and Vernon's subsequent struggle with guilt is so fierce that they steal a car, presumably to run away. They soon flip it and are lucky to get out alive. The film avoids the temptation to sentimentalize these children, in other words. The seeds of redemption they carry within themselves may never sprout. In fact, Nasia's voiceover comes from some point in the future, and she sounds wistful and sad. She also narrates in the past tense, as when she speaks near the end of the film about George: "He said he would fight great wars, lead nations and build back up from a broken land. Everyone thought he was crazy but me." But what finally happened to him—or Vernon or Sonya? In the end, we don't know. As Nasia says, "We all want families who love us, because friends go separate ways. Some of us know our place, our home, our comfort. But for some, it's not that simple." What we do know is that these poor young southerners, though they may play among and pick through trash, are not trash themselves, but embodiments of the potential for love and redemption.

It hardly needs repeating that race and race relations have been defining issues for southern culture. Viewers of *George Washington* will marvel, then, that it depicts race mixing without comment. George, Nasia, Buddy, and Vernon are black. Sonya comes from a poor white family, a troubled one. Damascus is black, but other workers around the rail yard are white. Rico Rice (Paul Schneider) is one of these, and he has an easygoing relationship with the black kids who cross his path. He also is romantically involved with Whitney (Derricka Rolle), a black woman. The only comment about this state of affairs comes from Tim Orr's roving camera, and it says that's just the way things are. We've come a long way, in other words, from *The Birth of a Nation*.

George Washington, appearing at the start of a new century, signals a new emphasis for films depicting the American South. Green has not always continued in this vein or focused his camera on the same region, but his Malick-tinged lyricism appears in other films—notably Nichols's *Shotgun Stories*, which he produced and which features small-town Arkansans struggling to shake off the legacy of the past. A family splits into two factions, and a violent feud ensues—until, finally, one young person refuses to play the game any longer and breaks the deadly pattern. Poor southern characters, as in *George Washington*, no longer have to play by the rules of the past, and neither does film itself.

Granik's *Winter's Bone* does not employ the lyrical tone or languorous pacing of *George Washington*. It depicts a rough, violent, overtly damaged Ozark community that has turned to methamphetamine production as a way of life. Its central character, Ree Dolly (Jennifer Lawrence), must find either her father Jessup or his corpse, so that she can keep a roof over her head and those of her two young siblings and their mother, who is sinking into dementia. Her father had pledged the family home and land as bond, but then failed to appear at a court hearing. The seventeen-year-old is persistent and practical, but her quest is essentially spiritual, a mostly tacit attempt to preserve what connection to the natural world remains, or to reintegrate elements that seem lost.

As *Winter's Bone* dramatizes, the making of quick profit through meth production severs the connection to the earth and ultimately to humanity. Folklorist W. K. McNeil, in *Ozark Country*, speaks of the Ozarker's traditional connection to the land: "Traditionalists believe that only those born in the Ozarks are capable of making a living from the rugged, often low-quality soil. They also regard the land as a refuge and a source of important values" (20). Granik's film repeatedly illustrates the loss of these values and this connectedness. The living arrangements of those in this rural crank culture are typically shoddy, neglected, broken down. As Ree makes her rounds, asking questions, the camera registers the junked items littering yards and roadsides—old furniture, old cars, buildings in dire need of attention, if not beyond repair.[2]

This disfigurement of living spaces and the environment also mirrors the mutilation of certain characters. Ree's Uncle Teardrop (John Hawkes), a crank chef, eventually reveals a hidden heart, but he has obviously suffered damage. The early scenes in which he appears show a violent, abusive man, but viewers eventually understand that he has become one of hardship's victims. In Woodrell's novel, Teardrop suffers physical damage when a batch of meth he was cooking severely burns his face. The film doesn't depict or explain this mutilation, but the actor convincingly conveys the psychic damage with his craggy face, his wiry body, and his overall rugged bearing.

The film shows Ree stubbornly searching for her father, and her mostly silent or violent reception. But when she isn't actively searching, she's often teaching her siblings how to survive in their rugged setting: how to shoot and handle guns, how to hunt and skin squirrels, how to cook deer stew. Ree also demonstrates an intimate knowledge of the natural environment. When Blond Milton (William White) takes her to a burned-out house in which he claims Jessup was killed when a batch went wrong, she knows he's lying because the weeds growing inside the burned structure are too tall for the fire to have been recent. Ree also periodically retreats to secluded natural spaces, seemingly to gather her wits.

If Ree cannot find her father or his corpse, one of her few options will be to sell the family timberland before authorities claim it and the house. Theirs is a much-coveted patch of old-growth forest. Although Uncle Teardrop at one point advises her to sell, she never seriously considers such an exploitative alternative. As Ree drifts off to sleep—aided by painkillers given her to mitigate the effects of a severe beating—the film briefly shifts to a black-and-white sequence, presumably her dream. It shows a panicky squirrel and the threatening sounds of a chainsaw, then tall, tottering trees, vultures tearing at roadkill, smoke rising from a downed forest. Surely, Ree has a profound understanding that to sell the timberland would be an act of betrayal that would leave an additional hole in the natural environment.

In the lessons Ree provides her siblings, she demonstrates the importance of family connectedness. She's passing on skills she presumably learned from her father in his better days. The duty of family members and neighbors toward each other has long been a kind of code in this environment, but the culture of exploitation has eroded this value, among others. When Ree's siblings see meat curing on their relatives' trees, one of them inquires about the possibility that they might be given some: "Don't kin ought to?" Ree answers, "That's what is always said."

Pleading with others for help in her search, Ree often reminds them of the sanctity of such connections. When Teardrop warns her not to ask questions of certain people, she responds, "But we're all related, ain't we?" She's even more forceful and incredulous when she approaches the house of Thump Milton, an intimidating character with the bearing of a mob boss. When a threatening woman named Merab (Dale Dickey) tells her to leave, Ree responds, "Some of our blood at least is the same. Ain't that s'posed to mean somethin'—isn't that what is always said?" The woman doesn't answer, her silence suggesting that a new order—or disorder—is rapidly supplanting the old.

In *The Unsettling of America: Culture & Agriculture*, Wendell Berry, long a forceful advocate for the restoration of human connections to the natural environment, puts this loss of cooperative spirit in the context of the division between specialist exploiters and non-specialist nurturers: "Because by definition they lack any such sense of mutuality or wholeness, our specializations subsist on conflict with one another. The rule is never to cooperate, but rather to follow one's own interest as far as possible" (22). The loss of wholeness, of connectedness, explains the doors shut in Ree's face; the refusal to speak or in any way provide information; the severe beating Ree receives at the hands of the sisters at Thump Milton's. Even the seeming cooperation that resolves the plot—the women finally take Ree to Jessup's body—stems not from a spirit of kinship, but from the need to quash rumors that might jeopardize the meth business and the power structures built upon it.

Music—which film can incorporate and draw upon in ways print cannot—expresses this lost or fading sense of wholeness. Both Woodrell's novel and Granik's film end with a visit from a bondsman who hands Ree money an anonymous person provided so Jessup could be released, evidently to be killed. The film, unlike the novel, ends by de-emphasizing the money in order to highlight the importance of music to this culture. After Teardrop comes by with a gift of two chicks for the children to raise, they hand him their father's banjo, signaling for him to play. "It's been a long time," Teardrop says, but he strums the instrument well enough to indicate that he was once an accomplished player. The scene suggests the possibility of redemption for Teardrop and bodes well for the future when Ree's sister, Ashlee (Ashlee Thompson), picks up and plucks at the banjo. The scene quietly says that this culture has lost vitality, but that the loss is not necessarily permanent. The sense of wholeness can be restored. Granik consciously alludes to *Deliverance* here. Knowing, as she says, that "a banjo can still be a loaded symbol," she risked inserting this one. In the end, though, "the banjo found its way into the film, offering notes of hope and perseverance. I came to think of it as a fresh start for that image."

Southern music has entered southern film as a way of exemplifying the vital spirit of poor folk. Scarlett O'Hara might have had her lavish dances, where she and Rhett Butler could pair up for the Virginia reel, but the disparaged folk of the hill cabins and trailer parks have their pickin' sessions, where talent is on display and music expresses both joy and sorrow. The "Dueling Banjos" theme from *Deliverance* tries to get at this point, but as noted above, the point might be lost. But films of the new century keep turning to the vitality of music, as in *Winter's Bone*. Other examples include *Searching for the Wrong-Eyed Jesus*, in which the central character, Jim White, is a musician who visits various venues. The theme appears prominently in another quirky documentary, *The Wild and Wonderful Whites of West Virginia*, especially in scenes featuring "the Dancing Outlaw" Jesco White and Hank Williams III. And whatever Joel and Ethan Coen's *O Brother, Where Art Thou?* (2001) might be—a parody of Homer, a character study of a dandy, a pastiche of legends about the South—it is certainly a celebration of music from the South, the region, after all, where most American musical styles were born. Even Craig Brewer's pulpy, borderline-pornographic *Black Snake Moan* (2006) celebrates music throughout, especially in the archival footage of Delta bluesman Son House.

Woodrell once hosted Granik and her film crew in the Ozarks, and when the group stopped at a local pickin' session there, they encountered singer Marideth Sisco. Granik eventually worked Sisco into the film, featuring her in a scene in which such a session is underway. The first song we hear from Sisco is Ola Belle Reed's "High on a Mountain." The lyrics speak of loss, but they also celebrate the vitality and beauty of the natural world:

As I look at the valleys down below
They are green just as far as I can see
As my memories return, oh how my heart did yearn
For you and the days that used to be
High on a mountain top, standing all alone
Wondering where the years of my life have flown
High on a mountaintop, wind blowing free
Thinking about the days that used to be (lines 1–8).

Granik's film implicitly argues for restoration of the values suggested in the song, as well as for a strong sense of family and an intimate knowledge of the natural world—above all, the standard of nurture. As Berry says, "A healthy culture is a communal order of memory, insight, value, work, conviviality, reverence, aspiration. It reveals the human necessities and the human limits. It clarifies the inescapable bonds to the earth and to each other" (43). In *Winter's Bone* Ree seeks not only her father's remains, but also—and more importantly—a reaffirmation of the values that support a healthy culture, one vitally connected to the natural world.

In the case of film images of the American South, the new does not necessarily cancel the old. What reviewer Steve Rose has called "hicksploitation" films, in which every poor southerner is "branded as a murderous, ignorant, inbred rural deviant whose idea of fun is dismembering urban teens with farm equipment,"[3] will no doubt continue. *Black Snake Moan*'s image of a scantily clad white nymphomaniac chained in a black man's house will likely supersede whatever else the film attempts to convey. And John Hillcoat's *Lawless* (2012), though it honors family solidarity and rugged individualism, ultimately celebrates . . . well, lawlessness. But evidence shows that new visions have appeared, that in the twenty-first century filmmakers are actively bringing more complexity to portrayals of the hardscrabble South, combatting what one reviewer has called "one of the mustiest cultural traps—the proposition advanced by scores of movies, that the South is little more than a barbecue pit of frail eccentrics, secluded matriarchs, white-linen Lucifers, and outright steaming maniacs" (Lane 80).

Rose makes these remarks in his deceptively light review of a decidedly simple film, Eli Craig's *Tucker and Dale vs. Evil* (2010). The film succinctly makes the point of this essay. Affluent college kids venture into the rural South for a weekend of frivolity, blinded by prejudices imbibed from cultural artifacts that demean poor southerners. The title characters are not the visitors, but rather the guiltless and ultimately nurturing rural southerners who withstand the murderously paranoid assaults of the intruders, the "Evil."

Notes

1. Obviously, a comprehensive review of how the South has appeared in twentieth-century film would be impossible here. I am merely choosing a few examples I subjectively deem iconic in the American imagination. A more thorough list, with brief summaries and evaluations, can be found in Larry Langman and David Ebner's *Hollywood's Image of the South: A Century of Southern Films* (Westport: Greenwood P, 2001). Other helpful resources include Edward D. C. Campbell Jr.'s *The Celluloid South: Hollywood and the Southern Myth* (Knoxville: U of Tennessee P, 1981); Allison Graham's *Framing the South: Hollywood, Television, and Race during the Civil Rights Struggle* (Baltimore: Johns Hopkins UP, 2001); Deborah E. Barker and Kathryn McKee's *American Cinema and the Southern Imaginary* (Athens, GA: U of Georgia P, 2011); and Andrew B. Leiter's anthology of criticism, *Southerners on Film: Essays on Hollywood Portrayals Since the 1970s* (Jefferson, NC: McFarland, 2011).

2. In interviews, both Debra Granik and David Gordon Green have expressed something besides disgust or revulsion at the debris littering the living spaces in their films. They both find beauty in these images as well, including, in Green's case, the sequences at a garbage dump, and, Granik says, "Abandoned debris and trucks with plant life growing out of their windows, those things are inherently photogenic because they're both disturbing and beautiful." To be sure, the images express something profound about human presence on the earth, the

struggles and losses. That these filmmakers find beauty in such images further illustrates their commitment to a revisionist project, as they transform all aspects of "trash" into art.

3. Rose makes these remarks in his deceptively light review of a decidedly simple film, Eli Craig's *Tucker and Dale vs. Evil* (2010). The film succinctly makes the point of this essay: Affluent college kids venture into the rural South for a weekend of frivolity, blinded by prejudices imbibed from cultural artifacts demeaning poor southerners. The title characters are not the visitors to the area, but rather guiltless and ultimately nurturing rural southerners who withstand the murderously paranoid assaults of the intruders, the "Evil" of the title.

Works Cited

Berry, Wendell. *The Unsettling of America: Culture & Agriculture*. New York: Avon, 1977. Print.

Bledsoe, Erik. "The Rise of Southern Redneck and White Trash Writers." *Southern Cultures*. 6.1 (2000): 68–90. Print.

Conroy, Pat. "Pat Conroy talks about the South, his mother, and *The Prince of Tides*." *patconroy. com*. Marly Rusoff Literary Agency, n.d. Web. 9 May 2013.

George Washington. Dir. David Gordon Green. Criterion, 2000. DVD.

Granik, Debra. "Winter's Bone." *landmarktheatres.com*. Landmark Theatres, n.d. Web. 9 May 2013.

Lane, Anthony. "Mad About You." Rev. of *Stoker*, dir. Park Chan-wook. *New Yorker* 11 Mar. 2013: 80. Print.

McNeil, W. K. *Ozark Country*. Jackson: UP of Mississippi, 1995. Print.

Rose, Steve. "Tucker & Dale Sticks Three Fingers up at Movie Redneck Clichés." Rev. of *Tucker & Dale vs. Evil*, dir. Eli Craig. *guardian.co.uk*. *Guardian*, 16 Sept. 2011. Web. 20 Jan. 2013.

Winter's Bone. Dir. Debra Granik. Lionsgate, 2010. DVD.

CONTRIBUTORS

Barbara Bennett is associate professor of English at North Carolina State University. Her primary interests are contemporary literature, American literature, southern literature, women's literature, and environmental literature. The author of *Understanding Jill McCorkle* (University of South Carolina Press, 2000), she has devoted considerable time to wildlife preservation in Namibia and in 2010 published *Soul of a Lion: One Woman's Quest to Rescue Africa's Wildlife Refugees* (National Geographic Society).

Thomas Ærvold Bjerre is associate professor of American studies at the University of Southern Denmark, where his research focuses on American popular culture—particularly southern literature, the western, and representations of war in film and fiction. He is coauthor of *Cowboynationen: Westernfilmen og det moderne Amerika* (University Press of Southern Denmark, 2009), the first Danish book about the American western, and a contributor to *Perspectives on Barry Hannah* (University Press of Mississippi, 2006), *Larry Brown and the Blue-Collar South: A Collection of Critical Essays* (University Press of Mississippi, 2008), and *Still in Print: The Southern Novel Today* (University of South Carolina Press, 2010).

Erik Bledsoe is the author of the seminal article "The Rise of Southern Redneck and White Trash Writers," first published in *Southern Cultures* in 2000. He taught English at the University of Tennessee–Knoxville for eight years and is the editor of *Getting Naked with Harry Crews* (University Press of Florida, 1999) and a co-editor of *Perspectives on Harry Crews* (University Press of Mississippi, 2001). He is currently webmaster for the College of Communication and Information and for the Center for International Education at UTK.

Jean W. Cash is professor of English emerita at James Madison University, where she continues to teach a course in southern literature every semester. She is the author of *Flannery O'Connor: A Life* (University of Tennessee Press, 2002); co-editor, with Keith Perry, of *Larry Brown and the Blue-Collar*

South: A Collection of Critical Essays (University Press of Mississippi, 2008); and the author of *Larry Brown: A Writer's Life* (University Press of Mississippi, 2011).

Thomas E. Dasher is professor of English at Berry College, where he served as provost from 2000 to 2007. Previously, he taught at Valdosta State University, where he was head of the English Department and dean of the College of Arts and Sciences. He is the author of *William Faulkner's Characters: An Index to the Published and Unpublished Fiction* (Garland, 1981) and various articles on southern literature, among them an essay on Steve Yarbrough in *Still in Print: The Southern Novel Today* (University of South Carolina Press, 2010).

Robert Donahoo is professor of English at Sam Houston State University. His primary teaching interests are southern literature, literary theory and criticism, and drama. He has published on subjects ranging from Tolstoy's novel *Resurrection* (1899) to American cyberpunk fiction, but most of his research and writing addresses the fiction of Flannery O'Connor. A former president of the O'Connor society and co-editor of *Flannery O'Connor in the Age of Terrorism* (University of Tennessee Press, 2010), he served in the summer of 2014 as co-director of the NEH-sponsored conference "Reconsidering Flannery O'Connor."

Peter Farris is the author of the novels *Last Call for the Living* (Forge, 2013) and *Ghost in the Fields*, forthcoming in France from Editions Gallmeister.

Richard Gaughran teaches American literature, world literature, and film studies at James Madison University. A former Fulbright lecturer in Skopje, Macedonia, he translates literary works from Macedonian into English, most recently he has translated the novel *Bayazid and Olivera* (2009), by Dragi Mihajlovski. His recent scholarly work includes articles on Larry Brown's *The Rabbit Factory*, the Coen brothers, David Lynch, and Sam Peckinpah.

William Giraldi, author of the novels *Busy Monsters* (Norton, 2010) and *Hold the Dark* (Liveright, 2014), is fiction editor for the journal *AGNI* at Boston University.

Rebecca Godwin is professor of English at Barton College, where she directs the Sam and Marjorie Ragan Writing Center. She is particularly interested in southern literature and has a special interest in North Carolina writers. She is the author of *Gender Dynamics in the Fiction of Lee Smith* (International Scholars Publications, 1997) and has published articles on Smith, Josephine Humphreys, Fred Chappell, Tim McLaurin, Robert Morgan, and Thomas Wolfe.

Joan Wylie Hall, a lecturer in the Department of English at the University of Mississippi, has published more than fifty book chapters and journal articles on, among others, Eudora Welty, Tennessee Williams, Ann Patchett, William Faulkner, Anna Deavere Smith, and Natasha Trethewey. She has written more than one hundred book reviews, is the author of *Shirley Jackson: A Study of the Short Fiction* (Twayne, 1993), and the editor of *Conversations with Audre Lorde* (University Press of Mississippi, 2004) and *Conversations with Natasha Trethewey* (University Press of Mississippi, 2013).

Marcus Hamilton earned his BA (2009) and MA (2011) degrees from James Madison University and is currently an instructor in the Department of English, Rhetoric, and Humanistic Studies at Virginia Military Institute. He presented "Rethinking Sexuality in 18th-century New England" at the North Carolina State University Association of English Graduate Students Manifest Identity Conference in 2011, and "Mythorealism, Lower-class Revenge, and the Ambivalence of Slumming: Recovering the Poor White Southerner in Cormac McCarthy's Southern Fiction" at the Southwest Popular/American Culture Association Conference in 2014.

Gary Hawkins is an independent filmmaker from Thomasville, North Carolina. He has written and directed six films, including *The Rough South of Harry Crews* (1991), which won a Regional Emmy Award, and *The Rough South of Larry Brown* (2002), which *Oxford American* named an Essential Southern Documentary. He teaches screenwriting, acting for the camera, and nonfiction filmmaking at Duke University and wrote the screenplay for the film adaptation of Larry Brown's *Joe* (1991), directed by David Gordon Green, starring Nicolas Cage and Tye Sheridan, and released by Lionsgate in 2014.

David K. Jeffrey is dean of the College of Arts and Letters at James Madison University, has been editor or contributing editor of three books, and has presented more than thirty papers at conferences. He was co-editor of *Southern Humanities Review* for five years, associate editor for seven, and is the author of *A Grit's Triumph: Essays on the Works of Harry Crews* (Associated Faculty Press, 1983), one of the earliest academic treatments of Crews and his fiction.

Emily Langhorne graduated from James Madison University in 2009 and earned an MPhil from Trinity College, Dublin, in 2012, writing a dissertation entitled "Exiles from the Old South: Diaspora Theory and the Work of William Faulkner." She has taught English to native speakers in Chile and currently lives in Washington, DC, where she completed the MEd program at George Washington University in 2015.

Shawn E. Miller, associate professor of English at Francis Marion University, specializes in modern and contemporary American literature, with a particular emphasis on the literature of the American South. He has written and spoken on a range of southern writers, including William Faulkner, Andrew Nelson Lytle, Zora Neale Hurston, Cormac McCarthy, Dorothy Allison, and Natasha Trethewey.

Wade Newhouse is assistant professor of English at Peace College, where he teaches American drama and southern literature. He has appeared in productions of *Desire Under the Elms, Assassins,* and *Rosencrantz & Guildenstern Are Dead* and has directed productions of several Shakespeare plays. He helped found the Raleigh-based improv troupe Village Idiot in 1997 and has performed with them frequently during the past seven years, also appearing in Peace College productions of *A Midsummer Night's Dream* and *Cabaret.*

L. Lamar Nisly is associate dean of Academic Affairs and professor of English at Bluffton University. He has published articles in a number of academic journals, is the author of *Wingless Chickens, Bayou Catholics, and Pilgrim Wayfarers: Constructions of Audience and Tone in O'Connor, Gautreaux, and Percy* (Mercer University Press, 2011) and *Impossible to Say: Representing Religious Mystery in Fiction by Malamud, Percy, Ozick, and O'Connor* (Praeger, 2002), and is the editor of *Conversations with Tim Gautreaux* (University Press of Mississippi, 2012).

Keith Perry is a professor of English at Dalton State College, where he teaches American literature, southern literature, and film. He is the author of *The Kingfish in Fiction: Huey P. Long and the Modern American Novel* (Louisiana State University Press, 2004); co-editor, with Jean W. Cash, of *Larry Brown and the Blue-Collar South: A Collection of Critical Essays* (University Press of Mississippi, 2008); and guest editor of the winter/spring 2008 issue of the journal *Post Script: Essays in Film and the Humanities,* which focuses on the films of Joel and Ethan Coen.

bes Stark Spangler is professor of English emerita from William Peace University, where she taught for twenty-six years and was distinguished alumnae professor from 2000 to 2003. She has published essays and delivered papers on various southern writers, among them Caroline Gordon, Eudora Welty, Robert Penn Warren, Larry Brown, Heather Ross Miller, Martha McFerren, and Marly Youmans. She currently teaches online courses in English as an adjunct professor at Excelsior College.

Joe Samuel Starnes has published two novels, *Calling* (Jefferson Press, 2005; re-issued as an ebook by MysteriousPress.com/Open Road in 2014) and *Fall Line* (NewSouth Books, 2011). His third novel, *Red Dirt*, was published in 2015. He has published articles in the *New York Times*, *Washington Post*, and several magazines and has taught creative writing at Widener University, Rowan University, and Saint Joseph's University.

Scott Hamilton Suter is associate professor of English and department chair at Bridgewater College. He has lectured widely and served as a consultant to a number of museums, including the Historical Society of Western Pennsylvania, the Museum of the Shenandoah Valley, and the Blue Ridge Institute. His publications include *Tradition & Fashion: Cabinetmaking in the Shenandoah Valley, 1850–1900* (Shenandoah Valley Folk Art & Heritage Center, 1996), *Shenandoah Valley Folklife* (University Press of Mississippi, 1999) and *Harrisonburg* (Arcadia Publishing, 2003).

Linda (Byrd Cook) Webster is professor of English at Sam Houston State University and the author of *Dancing in the Flames: Spiritual Journey in the Novels of Lee Smith* (McFarland, 2009). She has also published a number of articles on Smith and other women writers, including Kate Chopin.

PHOTOGRAPH CREDITS

Harry Crews, courtesy of Harry Crews Estate

Cormac McCarthy, courtesy of Derek Shapton

Tim McLaurin, courtesy of Erica Berger and Carol McLaurin

Larry Brown, courtesy of Tom Rankin

Dorothy Allison, courtesy of John Foley (with permission from David March on behalf of Dorothy Allison)

William Gay, courtesy of Julie Gillen

Tom Franklin, courtesy of Maude Schuyler Clay and Tom Franklin

Ron Rash, courtesy of Ron Rash

Tim Gautreaux, courtesy of Winborne and Tim Gautreaux

Chris Offutt, courtesy of Sandra Dyas and Chris Offutt

Daniel Woodrell, copyright © 2010 by Daniel Woodrell. Reprinted by permission of Daniel Woodrell.

Kaye Gibbons, courtesy of Judy Griesedieck

Lee Smith, courtesy of Roger Haile and Lee Smith

Clyde Edgerton, courtesy of Brent Clark and Clyde Edgerton

Jill McCorkle, courtesy of Tom Rankin and Jill McCorkle

Silas House, courtesy of Cyndi Williams (www.cwilliamsphotography.net) and Silas House

Steve Yarbrough, courtesy of Antonina Parris-Yarbrough and Steve Yarbrough

Brad Watson, courtesy of Nell Hanley and Brad Watson

Joe Samuel Starnes, courtesy of Joe Samuel Starnes

Peter Farris, courtesy of Peter Farris

Barb Johnson, courtesy of Barb Johnson

Jesmyn Ward, courtesy of Tulane University

Skip Horack, courtesy of Skip Horack

John Brandon, courtesy of John Brandon

Wiley Cash, courtesy of Tiffany B. Davis and Wiley Cash

Michael Farris Smith, courtesy of Chris Jenkins and Michael Farris Smith

INDEX

CPSIA information can be obtained at www.ICGtesting.com
Printed in the USA
BVOW08*1728220116

433800BV00004B/6/P